In Perpetuity

New Brunswick Military Heritage Series, Volume 30

In Perpetuity

The First World War Soldiers of the Fredericton War Memorial

edited by **JAMES ROWINSKI**
with a foreword by **ALAN SEARS**

Goose Lane Editions and the Gregg Centre for the Study of War and Society

Edited by Brent Wilson and Barry Norris.
Cover and page design by Julie Scriver.
Cover illustrations: Fredericton War Memorial, 2011, by Bill Jarvis (flickr.com). Canadian stretcher bearers evacuating the wounded during the Battle of Passchendaele (William Rider-Rider/LAC/PA-002140). "Ypres: 1915" by Alden Nowlan from Alden Nowlan Selected Poems © 1996 House of Anansi Press. Reproduced with permission. www.houseofanansi.com
Printed in Canada by Marquis.
10 9 8 7 6 5 4 3 2 1

Goose Lane Editions acknowledges the generous support of the Government of Canada, the Canada Council for the Arts, and the Government of New Brunswick.

Goose Lane Editions and the Gregg Centre for the Study of War and Society at the University of New Brunswick are located located on the unceded territory of the Wəlastəkwiyik whose ancestors along with the Mi'kmaq and Peskotomuhkati Nations signed Peace and Friendship Treaties with the British Crown in the 1700s.

Goose Lane Editions
500 Beaverbrook Court, Suite 330
Fredericton, New Brunswick
CANADA E3B 5X4
gooselane.com

Library and Archives Canada Cataloguing in Publication

Title: In perpetuity : the First World War soldiers of the Fredericton war memorial / edited by James Rowinski ; with a foreword by Alan Sears.
Names: Rowinski, James, editor.
Series: New Brunswick military heritage s eries ; v. 30.
Description: Series statement: New Brunswick military heritage series ; v. 30 | Includes bibliographical references and index.
Identifiers: Canadiana 20230207014 | ISBN 9781773103167 (softcover)
Subjects: LCSH: Soldiers—New Brunswick—Fredericton—Biography. | LCSH: World War, 1914-1918—Personal narratives, Canadian. | LCSH: World War, 1914-1918—Monuments—New Brunswick—Fredericton. | LCSH: World War, 1914-1918—Registers of dead—New Brunswick—Fredericton. | LCSH: War memorials—New Brunswick—Fredericton. | LCGFT: Biographies.
Classification: LCC D640.A2 I46 2023 | DDC 940.4/8171—dc23

New Brunswick Military History Project
The Brigadier Milton F. Gregg, VC,
Centre for the Study of War and Society
University of New Brunswick
PO Box 4400
Fredericton, New Brunswick
CANADA E3B 5A3
unb.ca/nbmhp

For those whose stories have yet to be heard.

He died the noblest death a man can die
fighting for God and right and liberty
and such a death is immortality.

—John Oxenham, quoted on the Fredericton
War Memorial

Oh, I know they were mercenaries
in a war that hardly concerned us.
I know all that
Sometimes I'm not even sure that I have a country.

But I know that they stood there at Ypres
the first time the Germans used gas,
that they were almost the only troops
in that section of the front
who did not break and run,
who held the line.

Perhaps they were too scared to run.
Perhaps they didn't know any better.
That is possible, they were so innocent,
those farm boys and mechanics, you have to only look
at old pictures and see how they smiled
perhaps they were too shy
to walk out on anybody, even Death.
Perhaps their only motivation
was a stubborn disinclination.

And that's ridiculous, too, and nothing
on which to found a country.
Still it makes me feel good, knowing
that in some obscure, conclusive way,
they were connected with me
and me with them.

—Alden Nowlan, "Ypres, 1915"

Contents

(opposite) The Fredericton War Memorial at the
Remembrance Day Ceremony, November 11, 1932. PANB/P32-318

Rededication service for Lieutenant Charles Blair at Sunny Bank Cemetery, Fredericton North, November 2019. James Rowinski

Foreword

On a cold, snowy November morning in 2019, my wife and I gathered at Sunny Bank Cemetery in Fredericton, New Brunswick, with a small number of community members along with the senior commanders and an honour guard from The Royal New Brunswick Regiment. We were there to honour the life and service of Lieutenant Charles Edward Blair of the 236th Battalion and to reflect on the important social changes that had occurred in both military and civilian culture since his death in 1920. Lieutenant Blair was a forgotten casualty of the Great War. He was one of the first Canadians to enlist when war began in 1914, and he was on the ground in Belgium by the time of the first Canadian engagements in the spring of 1915. Early in the war he was recognized as a military leader and in 1916 received a commission as a lieutenant. Despite his obvious successes as a soldier, four years of war broke the physical and mental health of Lieutenant Blair. Records reveal that he returned home to Fredericton in 1919 suffering from war injuries and severe post-war trauma. A year later he took his own life.

After his funeral Blair was buried in the family plot in Sunny Bank Cemetery, located in the former town of Devon, on the northside of present-day Fredericton. At the time, his name was not added to the family memorial, perhaps because of how he died, and a Commonwealth

War Graves Commission headstone, typically reserved for soldiers from the British Commonwealth who died because of war service, was never erected. Additionally, his name was not included on the list submitted to the Fredericton War Memorial Committee for inclusion on the Fredericton War Memorial in 1923, presumably because his death might not have been considered war related. Apart from being named on St. Paul's United Church's First World War Memorial, he was a forgotten man and was never properly commemorated alongside other soldiers from the area who died from war service.

This was the case until students working with the *Fredericton Soldier Biography History Initiative* became perplexed by the discrepancy raised by his name being on a church memorial for veterans but not on the War Memorial. Their subsequent investigation of military and civilian archival records uncovered Blair's story, and they were disturbed. For them it was obvious that Blair's psychological problems stemmed at least in part from his wartime service. They knew that, although "shell shock" was not considered a battle wound in the early part of the twentieth century, it is now. They began advocating for him to be commemorated appropriately, and that resulted in our gathering in Sunny Bank Cemetery around the new military service headstone installed and donated by the Last Post Fund to memorialize Blair. A military chaplain led the service, a young student read Blair's biography, which is included in this student collection, senior officers commended both Blair and the students who had uncovered his story, and there was a twenty-one-gun salute. After a hundred years, Blair finally received the recognition given to so many other Canadian soldiers who have died from war service. Despite this recognition, the Commonwealth War Graves Commission continues to disqualify him as an official war casualty.

All of this is to say that the work of these hundreds of middle school students involved in studying the history of the Great War period through the lens of soldiers with a connection to Fredericton matters. It was not simply a nice activity that engaged students in the commemoration of individuals; it was critical historical investigation that adds to what we know of the era of the Great War and post-war commemoration practices, and it has implications for our lives and society today. For those worried about young people's lack of appreciation for Canada's history generally and its wartime exploits in particular, the work in this collection should put those concerns to rest. It demonstrates students' ability to learn and understand both the events of the time and their social and political implications. The biographies collected here cover Canada's participation in the First World War from the initial arrival of Canadian troops on Salisbury Plain in late fall 1914 to the liberation of Mons, Belgium, in the last days of the war. It includes veterans of the army, navy, and Royal Flying Corps. Soldiers included here fought in all the big engagements, from the Second Battle of Ypres through the Somme, Vimy Ridge, Passchendaele, Amiens, and Cambrai. This book not only focuses on those who died in the heat of battle, but also includes soldiers such as Lance Corporal George H. McKee, who, at the age of thirty-seven, volunteered in September 1914 as soon as the war started but died of pneumonia before going overseas. It also includes Private Guy McBean, who made it to England but arrived ill and died shortly after from diphtheria.

The historical investigations recorded here engaged students not only with the heroics and tragedy of wartime conflict, but also with medical issues, the kinds of work individuals left in order to enlist, the toll on families left behind, and the myriad forms of remembrance and commemoration that followed the war, including iconic memorials to the missing, such as the Canadian monuments at Vimy Ridge and the Menin Gate in Ypres, battlefield cemeteries, and the cenotaphs, plaques, and other memorials that pepper the Canadian landscape. All of these are part of ongoing debates highlighting the relationship between the military and the civilian society they serve. This work involved students in locating, sifting through, and analysing various forms of evidence from military service files, period newspapers, census records, and family records to interviews with surviving descendants of those studied. Like all historical sources, these records are often incomplete, contradictory, and confusing. Students built their narratives carefully, often weighing several factors in deciding what was true or not and what to include or leave out. These are the same processes in which academic historians regularly engage. But this work extends far beyond history. The location, assessment, and weighing of evidence to make informed choices and decisions is a key aspect of the life of every human being and citizen. The students involved in this project demonstrated the ability to do all these things and more. Like those who dug into Lieutenant Blair's story, these students demonstrated how to apply what they learned about history and evidence to contemporary debates about public policy and the common good. In short, they illustrate the capacity for good citizenship.

I have been a history educator for more than forty years. Over that time, the kind of work in which James Rowinski engaged these students to produce this collection has been advocated as best practice in the field. It is often resisted by teachers and others who claim, among other things, that students will not be interested or do not have the capacities to do it at a serious level, or that it focuses on disciplinary skills and inhibits the learning of important historical content. This substantial collection adds to a significant body of research evidence from around the world that demonstrates conclusively that those objections are without merit. It is an important record not only of the history of Canada and the Great War, but also of the potential of students to produce scholarship well beyond our expectations.

ALAN SEARS
Professor Emeritus, University of New Brunswick

Introduction

The idea for this book was initially developed in 2015, one year after returning from an intensive two-week tour of Canadian battlefields in France and Belgium with the University of New Brunswick's Gregg Centre for the Study of War and Society, alongside academics, educators, students, and civilians. Focused on Canada's role in the First and Second World Wars, the opportunity was led by a passionate group of respected scholars and educators committed to cutting-edge history research and best-practice approaches to the teaching of history. I was profoundly transformed personally and professionally by the experience. A spark had been lit. I have been consumed ever since by all things tied to the complexities of history teaching and learning—most especially how best to approach teaching history ethically to young people in school contexts.

Understanding how Canadians experienced the First World War forms the broad scope of this book. It does so, however, through the lens of those whose fate we already know in advance: individuals whose names first appeared on the Fredericton War Memorial in 1923 and some who have never been added. This book is a testament to what young people can achieve when given the appropriate time, resources, teaching supports, and opportunities to take part in meaningful historical research—a process that certainly has its own aches and pains for the seasoned historian.

The Gregg Centre's battlefield tour, 2014. Gregg Centre

Our hope is that, in learning more about these individuals, readers will also gain a deeper appreciation of the complexities of commemoration processes in Fredericton during and immediately following the war. By revealing relevant omissions and mistakes, we encourage a broader dialogue on the civic obligation, if any, we might have today to sites of commemoration such as the Fredericton War Memorial, including what they promote, what they neglect, and who gets to decide.

In *Death So Noble: Memory, Meaning, and the First World War*, Jonathan F. Vance notes that, following the First World War, Canadians often chose to remember the conflict in ways that bore little resemblance to its realities. (For details on the sources cited in the Introduction, see the Selected Bibliography.) However, for many Canadians still looking for ways to find meaning in something that demanded answers, he argues that thinking which strayed from truths about the war operated to serve a far deeper purpose, explained something of what had happened, or promised a better future that actualities could never console. Refusing to succumb to the potential spiritual desolation that critics of the war offered, half-truths and myths about what it all meant were an important antidote to the profound sadness that came "from the grief, the hope, and the search for meaning of a thousand Canadian communities" (p. 267).

Although one hundred years has passed since the Fredericton War Memorial was unveiled as a space of consolation to grieving families and friends left grappling with what happened to loved ones overseas and to those who succumbed to injuries and illness at home, it is important to ask how deeply this grief still lingers today. What purpose do sites of commemoration continue to mediate for families and communities? Why should we care? The enormous gratitude we have received over the years from across Canada, the United States, and Europe from people tied to soldiers in this collection and others simply grateful for the work hints at something beyond explanation. This is not solely a practice of nostalgia; it is an attempt to comprehend the incomprehensible — a context completely foreign to our own. It is a quintessential human quality.

During the height of the conflict, finding ways to make sense of what was unfolding certainly mattered to many people in Fredericton and the wider New Brunswick community. This was especially true for those who were feeling most acutely the sting of loss. In 1916 University of New Brunswick (UNB) students and their families were among the first to begin organizing a plan, with the support of the university's senate, alumni, and alumni associations for a memorial to all UNB students who enlisted for the war. One year later, the *Daily Gleaner* reported that the triangle and juncture at Parliament Square and Church Street was gradually "being built up and there is some talk of a memorial to the Fredericton boys who have fallen in the field of battle." According to the *Daily Gleaner*, by July 1918 discussions led by the Fredericton Branch of the Great War Veterans' Association (GWVA) in consultation with local leaders and the public had expanded to include talk of a memorial building, to be "a fitting memorial to the brave boys who have made the supreme sacrifice, but also as a home for returned men."

As the war ended in late 1918, the community turned to the work of finding a more potent way to make meaning of it all; however, it was not a straightforward process. While commemorating the dead appeared to be of utmost importance to many, how to do this was greatly debated, and some even questioned if there was a better way to honour soldiers and the principles for which they had died than through "a beautiful but worthless piece of architecture," as the *Daily Gleaner* reported. Because the work of the Imperial War Graves Commission (IWGC) restricted the repatriation of bodies from war zones, except for Canadians who died in the United Kingdom, the commemoration process took on a new kind of complexity for grieving families. It was not until February 20, 1920, that a public meeting was held at Fredericton's City Hall "for the purpose of considering the desirability of erecting some form of memorial to our brave countrymen who fell in the great war." According to the *Daily Gleaner*, a large and widely representative crowd was expected, anxious to have a memorial for those who had perished.

It would take three more years of public discussions before the building of the Fredericton War Memorial was completed and then unveiled on a Sunday coinciding with the fifth anniversary of Armistice Day. However, plans and processes that led to the public unveiling—including determining the list of names to be included for consideration on the plaque, what was reported regarding names that ultimately appeared on the plaque, and even details about the ceremony—highlighted the likelihood of inconsistencies and mistakes, gaps that students uncovered through their research. Apart from weeks of reported confusion in newspapers over the ceremony itself, on Saturday, November 10, 1923, the *Daily Gleaner* published a list of 106 names that were to appear on the plaque during the ceremony the following day. Three days later, they published the list again for readers, this time including 109 names. We leave readers to make up their own minds over whether it is likely mistakes were made. As you read the stories that fill these pages, we encourage you to consider what it means for us today.

It is commonplace to find local public histories on the war memorial and what led to its creation that portray the process as a neat and straightforward narrative in which "a group of public-spirited citizens decided that some form of lasting memorial should be erected in Fredericton to honour those members of the community who had laid down their lives for their country." While we certainly appreciate that these individuals might have

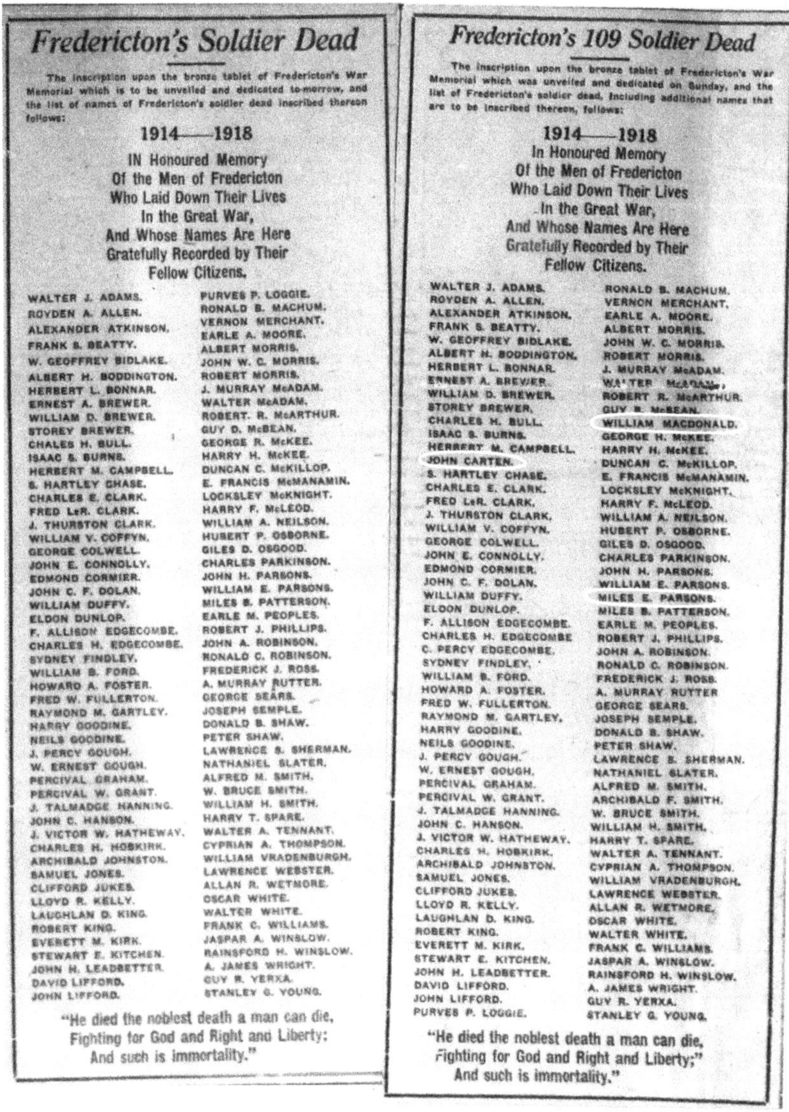

Fredericton's Soldier Dead		Fredericton's 109 Soldier Dead	

The inscription upon the bronze tablet of Fredericton's War Memorial which is to be unveiled and dedicated to-morrow, and the list of names of Fredericton's soldier dead inscribed thereon follows:

The inscription upon the bronze tablet of Fredericton's War Memorial which was unveiled and dedicated on Sunday, and the list of Fredericton's soldier dead, including additional names that are to be inscribed thereon, follows:

1914——1918

IN Honoured Memory
Of the Men of Fredericton
Who Laid Down Their Lives
In the Great War,
And Whose Names Are Here
Gratefully Recorded by Their
Fellow Citizens.

1914——1918

In Honoured Memory
Of the Men of Fredericton
Who Laid Down Their Lives
In the Great War,
And Whose Names Are Here
Gratefully Recorded by Their
Fellow Citizens.

Left column (clipping 1)		Right column (clipping 2)	
WALTER J. ADAMS.	PURVES P. LOGGIE.	WALTER J. ADAMS.	RONALD B. MACHUM.
ROYDEN A. ALLEN.	RONALD B. MACHUM.	ROYDEN A. ALLEN.	VERNON MERCHANT.
ALEXANDER ATKINSON.	VERNON MERCHANT.	ALEXANDER ATKINSON.	EARLE A. MOORE.
FRANK S. BEATTY.	EARLE A. MOORE.	FRANK S. BEATTY.	ALBERT MORRIS.
W. GEOFFREY BIDLAKE.	ALBERT MORRIS.	W. GEOFFREY BIDLAKE.	JOHN W. C. MORRIS.
ALBERT H. BODDINGTON.	JOHN W. C. MORRIS.	ALBERT H. BODDINGTON.	ROBERT MORRIS.
HERBERT L. BONNAR.	ROBERT MORRIS.	HERBERT L. BONNAR.	J. MURRAY McADAM.
ERNEST A. BREWER.	J. MURRAY McADAM.	ERNEST A. BREWER.	WALTER McADAM.
WILLIAM D. BREWER.	WALTER McADAM.	WILLIAM D. BREWER.	ROBERT R. McARTHUR.
STOREY BREWER.	ROBERT. R. McARTHUR.	STOREY BREWER.	GUY D. McBEAN.
CHALES H. BULL.	GUY D. McBEAN.	CHARLES H. BULL.	WILLIAM MACDONALD.
ISAAC S. BURNS.	GEORGE R. McKEE.	ISAAC S. BURNS.	GEORGE H. McKEE.
HERBERT M. CAMPBELL.	HARRY H. McKEE.	HERBERT M. CAMPBELL.	HARRY H. McKEE.
S. HARTLEY CHASE.	DUNCAN C. McKILLOP.	JOHN CARTEN.	DUNCAN C. McKILLOP.
CHARLES E. CLARK.	E. FRANCIS McMANAMIN.	S. HARTLEY CHASE.	E. FRANCIS McMANAMIN.
FRED LeR. CLARK.	LOCKSLEY McKNIGHT.	CHARLES E. CLARK.	LOCKSLEY McKNIGHT.
J. THURSTON CLARK.	HARRY F. McLEOD.	FRED LeR. CLARK.	HARRY F. McLEOD.
WILLIAM V. COFFYN.	WILLIAM A. NEILSON.	J. THURSTON CLARK.	WILLIAM A. NEILSON.
GEORGE COLWELL.	HUBERT P. OSBORNE.	WILLIAM V. COFFYN.	HUBERT P. OSBORNE.
JOHN E. CONNOLLY.	GILES D. OSGOOD.	GEORGE COLWELL.	GILES D. OSGOOD.
EDMOND CORMIER.	CHARLES PARKINSON.	JOHN E. CONNOLLY.	CHARLES PARKINSON.
JOHN C. F. DOLAN.	JOHN H. PARSONS.	EDMOND CORMIER.	JOHN H. PARSONS.
WILLIAM DUFFY.	WILLIAM E. PARSONS.	JOHN C. F. DOLAN.	WILLIAM E. PARSONS.
ELDON DUNLOP.	MILES S. PATTERSON.	WILLIAM DUFFY.	MILES E. PARSONS.
F. ALLISON EDGECOMBE.	EARLE M. PEOPLES.	ELDON DUNLOP.	MILES S. PATTERSON.
CHARLES H. EDGECOMBE.	ROBERT J. PHILLIPS.	F. ALLISON EDGECOMBE.	EARLE M. PEOPLES.
SYDNEY FINDLEY.	JOHN A. ROBINSON.	CHARLES H. EDGECOMBE	ROBERT J. PHILLIPS.
WILLIAM B. FORD.	RONALD C. ROBINSON.	C. PERCY EDGECOMBE.	JOHN A. ROBINSON.
HOWARD A. FOSTER.	FREDERICK J. ROSS.	SYDNEY FINDLEY.	RONALD C. ROBINSON.
FRED W. FULLERTON.	A. MURRAY RUTTER.	WILLIAM B. FORD.	FREDERICK J. ROSS.
RAYMOND M. GARTLEY.	GEORGE SEARS.	HOWARD A. FOSTER.	A. MURRAY RUTTER.
HARRY GOODINE.	JOSEPH SEMPLE.	FRED W. FULLERTON.	GEORGE SEARS.
NEILS GOODINE.	DONALD B. SHAW.	RAYMOND M. GARTLEY.	JOSEPH SEMPLE.
J. PERCY GOUGH.	PETER SHAW.	HARRY GOODINE.	DONALD B. SHAW.
W. ERNEST GOUGH.	LAWRENCE S. SHERMAN.	NEILS GOODINE.	PETER SHAW.
PERCIVAL GRAHAM.	NATHANIEL SLATER.	J. PERCY GOUGH.	LAWRENCE S. SHERMAN.
PERCIVAL W. GRANT.	ALFRED M. SMITH.	W. ERNEST GOUGH.	NATHANIEL SLATER.
J. TALMADGE HANNING.	W. BRUCE SMITH.	PERCIVAL GRAHAM.	ALFRED M. SMITH.
JOHN C. HANSON.	WILLIAM H. SMITH.	PERCIVAL W. GRANT.	ARCHIBALD F. SMITH.
J. VICTOR W. HATHEWAY.	HARRY T. SPARE.	J. TALMADGE HANNING.	W. BRUCE SMITH.
CHARLES H. HOSKIRK.	WALTER A. TENNANT.	JOHN C. HANSON.	WILLIAM H. SMITH.
ARCHIBALD JOHNSTON.	CYPRIAN A. THOMPSON.	J. VICTOR W. HATHEWAY.	HARRY T. SPARE.
SAMUEL JONES.	WILLIAM VRADENBURGH.	CHARLES H. HOSKIRK.	WALTER A. TENNANT.
CLIFFORD JUKES.	LAWRENCE WEBSTER.	ARCHIBALD JOHNSTON.	CYPRIAN A. THOMPSON.
LLOYD R. KELLY.	ALLAN R. WETMORE.	SAMUEL JONES.	WILLIAM VRADENBURGH.
LAUGHLAN D. KING.	OSCAR WHITE.	CLIFFORD JUKES.	LAWRENCE WEBSTER.
ROBERT KING.	WALTER WHITE.	LLOYD R. KELLY.	ALLAN R. WETMORE.
EVERETT M. KIRK.	FRANK C. WILLIAMS.	LAUGHLAN D. KING.	OSCAR WHITE.
STEWART E. KITCHEN.	JASPAR A. WINSLOW.	ROBERT KING.	WALTER WHITE.
JOHN H. LEADBETTER.	RAINSFORD H. WINSLOW.	EVERETT M. KIRK.	FRANK C. WILLIAMS.
DAVID LIFFORD.	A. JAMES WRIGHT.	STEWART E. KITCHEN.	JASPAR A. WINSLOW.
JOHN LIFFORD.	GUY R. YERXA.	JOHN H. LEADBETTER.	RAINSFORD H. WINSLOW.
	STANLEY G. YOUNG.	DAVID LIFFORD.	A. JAMES WRIGHT.
		JOHN LIFFORD.	GUY R. YERXA.
		PURVES P. LOGGIE.	STANLEY G. YOUNG.

"He died the noblest death a man can die,
Fighting for God and Right and Liberty:
And such is immortality."

"He died the noblest death a man can die,
Fighting for God and Right and Liberty;"
And such is immortality."

(left) The names of war dead listed in the *Daily Gleaner*, November 10, 1923. (right) Three extra names (circled) were listed on November 13. Miles Parson does not appear in the book as his addition is likely a clerical error combining the first and last names of the soldiers above and below his entry. PANB F2960

been "public-spirited" about creating a lasting memorial, to portray the community's history in this fashion oversimplified the complexity of what the evidence suggests. It also distorted what we have come to learn about those we feel we are honouring. I am sure they would appreciate a fuller understanding of who they were and the complexities around what the war meant to them and to their families and loved ones, even in death. We are still permitted to linger in grief, but we honour their memory more deeply when we share their stories within a wider context.

Inquiry-orientated and historical-thinking approaches to history education have been around for more than a century in Canada, and over that time they have taken on many forms. According to history educator and professor of education Ken Osborne (2012), however, during this time, translating what is known about effective history teaching in research to effective history teaching practice in public education has not been a smooth process. Some have suggested that what is known in scholarship has had less impact than we might have hoped by now on school or public history practices (Clark, Levesque, and Sandwell 2015); others believe there is reason to think things are beginning to change for the better (Clark and Sears 2020). This change in tone has much to do with increased collaboration among scholars across disciplines; more important, it has been precipitated by intense public debates over how history has operated both outside and inside the classroom, heightened by the work of the Truth and Reconciliation Commission (2015) and #BlackLivesMatter, which have drawn increased attention to the experiences and histories of Indigenous people, those who identify as part of the Black diaspora, and recent immigrants. Like debates that have unfolded before, the current moment has again brought greater immediacy to questions such as: Whose history matters? How should history be taught to students? Who and what gets left out? And who gets to decide?

The most popular history teaching model advocated in Canada is Peter Seixas's framework for historical thinking, popularized in his book with Tom Morton, *The Big Six Historical Thinking Concepts* (2013). It is the latest attempt at developing an effective approach for school history teaching generally, and one that appropriately supports students' conceptual development in historical thinking particularly. Through this approach, not only are students expected to engage critically with history and to learn what those in the discipline know about the field of history; they are also expected to learn how individuals connected to the field of history employ their craft. Teachers who successfully use the Big Six model in their classrooms anchor approaches to doing history for students that those in the discipline use themselves, including teaching students how to establish historical significance, use primary evidence, identify continuity and change, analyse cause and consequence, take historical perspectives, and understand the ethical dimension of historical interpretations. Although many teachers have begun integrating this approach, there is still much work to do.

Consensus has grown substantially over the inappropriateness of traditional approaches to teaching history that focus on rote memorization, facts, too much repetition, limited access to primary source materials, content inconsistencies, and ready-made pre-scripted texts. These approaches have led to the perception of history as one of the most disliked subjects by students and one of the most intimidating for teachers without a background in its subject matter or deep understanding of the discipline. As such, current trends in best-practice approaches to history teaching, coupled with public debates over the treatment of history both inside and outside the classroom, have led to greater urgency to ensure that teachers are effectively supported and resourced in their work with young people across the range of K–12 schooling. Despite the debates and trends affecting history teaching, however, research in Canada has revealed very little about what is happening with history teaching in our schools, nor do we understand what students are saying about how they experience it. In the small amount of research that does exist, far from being portrayed as disinterested in history, young people appear to have much to say about what they are taught and how it unfolds, and want in on the conversation.

Within this context, the *Fredericton Soldier Biography History Initiative* was born out of a desire to address growing expectations being placed on social studies teachers, often operating without the requisite time, appropriate access to resources, and professional development opportunities to be effective in their subject areas, and to do so at a time when increased attention was being given to the centenary of the First World War period in Canada (1914–19). As such, the project offered teachers and students alike, often for the first time, a chance to be actively involved in inquiry-orientated disciplinary historical learning, while also engaging critically in popular accounts of the First World War period and post-war commemoration practices.

In the winter of 2015, I met with a team of middle school teachers to outline the broad goals and parameters of the project and to determine an effective approach to best engage students in the history of the community within the context of the First World War. Because engaging with the community was a central purpose of the initiative, the decision to focus on the names listed on the Fredericton War Memorial, church memorials, cemeteries, and various other sites of commemoration (including names of buildings and streets) was our starting point because these offered the most potent public historical connections and representations of the period. By engaging directly with these spaces, students quickly learned that memorials were often limited in terms of what they conveyed about the individuals listed; in some cases, the information contained on memorials was incomplete and filled with inaccuracies. As many families with ties to those named on the Fredericton War Memorial either had limited knowledge and/or access to military documents of loved ones or were no longer living in the area, students found that their work was the first time anyone had carried out original research on these individuals. With this knowledge, students took seriously the historical-thinking aspects of their work, including how to engage ethically with history, how to consider historical perspectives, how to work with evidence, and how to deliberate significant events in an individual's life and military service.

Between 2015 and 2019, hundreds of middle school students spent eight months of the year working with primary source materials obtained from Library and Archives Canada, the Provincial Archives of New Brunswick, the Commonwealth War Graves Commission, and various other databases, to piece together meticulously the life and military experiences of individuals named on the Fredericton War Memorial. Additionally,

George Street Middle School students researching at the
Provincial Archives of New Brunswick. James Rowinski

during this time, students spent countless hours learning about the work of archivists and historians by working directly with them. It was commonplace for students to go to the archives on their own time once they had learned the methods used to search for documents and material to support their work. They arranged phone and in-person interviews, organized year-end events, published research in newspapers to ensure the accuracy of their work, and became involved in various centenary events and annual ceremonies outside of school. In short, by investing their time in the research process and drawing attention to debates and concerns that flowed from their work, students learned what it meant to do history actively by being the primary proponents of research that had never been completed. In 2017, students were recipients of a Fredericton Heritage Trust Award for their contributions to raising awareness of the history of local memorials. As such, their work has been recognized as providing a significant contribution to Fredericton's heritage that enhances historical understanding of the lives of those listed on the Fredericton War Memorial while drawing attention to a post-war commemoration process that left some forgotten altogether by the community.

The chapters in this book are structured to help readers follow the First World War chronologically, beginning in 1914 through to its completion in 1918, and the subsequent years leading up to the unveiling of the Fredericton War Memorial in 1923. For anyone interested in teaching about the First World War, the biographies highlight a vast array of personal and military experiences helpful for contextualizing the period and post-war commemoration practices for students. It may also be used as a model for how to do this kind of work in one's own personal family research. To counter some limitations of public memorials and public histories, the book moves from the first casualties of the war from Fredericton to the last. By organizing biographies this way, the intention is to draw attention to the common connections and experiences soldiers had in their lives at key points in the war and to highlight the final resting places of soldiers, who often died together during the more intense periods of fighting. As the Fredericton War Memorial was designed for a different purpose, those seeking detailed information on the structure might be disappointed, depending on what you are looking to learn. The memorial, however, is an important space of material history that, we have learned, tells us much about the community at the time. As a result of the level of detail provided in this book, readers will find greater clarity around the number of Fredericton soldiers commemorated on memorials such as the Menin Gate or the Vimy Memorial and which soldiers are buried alongside others from Fredericton in Commonwealth War Cemeteries and local community cemeteries.

Although these biographies have been carefully researched and written using source material from the late nineteenth and early twentieth centuries, they are the interpretations of thirteen- and fourteen-year-old students doing this kind of work for the first time and with limited information and material that is routinely conflicting. As a result, they are not designed to be the final word on what happened to these individuals, nor should they be read as definitive military histories, since those who produced them are not historians themselves. They have been edited to provide greater clarity around student thinking, and are a first step in helping to share what happened to these individuals. Consequently, these stories could change as more evidence emerges. They might also contain information inconsistent with family stories and/or public histories. This is the work of history.

It was often the case that students were faced with conflicting evidence and had to consider all information available to them before deciding on such things as birthdates, age of soldiers, dates of death, and determining the location of soldiers in the field. For this reason, we have included a QR code that will allow readers to access the military service record of each soldier who served with the Canadian Expeditionary Force (CEF), to get a limited sense of the kind of material with which students were working. At times, the service record spells a soldier's names differently to the memorial, or reveals that an individual was promoted during the war. This book identifies soldiers by the rank originally listed on the service record and follows the spelling of the names listed on the memorial. Of course, this was only one small part of the documentation students used during the research process; however, we hope it is only the beginning of more learning about these individuals and how the community responded to the loss.

Finally, I hope that this collection will help correct what has been a common mistake in writing we have found on the Fredericton War Memorial. Although some local authors indicate 109 names are present on the First World War plaque, there are only 106 names, as a quick count in person will confirm. This might also be a reminder that getting out in the field often yields important insights that authors might overlook in their archival and library research. Perhaps the work of these students will finally set the record straight. As this is the first substantial work done on all individuals named from the First World War listed on the Fredericton War Memorial, we hope that the work completed here by students will lead to the inclusion of more individuals who were left out in 1923. Perhaps the centenary of the Fredericton War Memorial will be an opportune moment to do just that.

First draft of soldiers from the 71st York Regiment parade behind the Soldiers' Barracks on Queen Sreet., Fredericton, August 1914, before leaving for Camp Valcartier, where they joined the 12th Battalion. PANB P5/884

Chapter One

1914–1915

Canada entered the First World War, or the Great War as it was called at the time, on August 4, 1914, as a member of the British Empire. The country quickly raised an infantry division that proceeded to England in late August, and then crossed to France in February 1915. First Canadian Division fought its first major battle at Ypres in Belgium in late April. Other battles followed at Festubert and Givenchy in May and June. At the same time, members of the Royal Canadian Navy served on active operations with Britain's Royal Navy.

1. Hatheway, John Victor W. (November 1, 1914)

Midshipman MO/406, Royal Canadian Navy

John Victor W. Hatheway was born on May 24, 1895, in Granville, Nova Scotia, to Frederick W. Hatheway and Christina Grace Bogart. According to records, Frederick and Christina were married on June 6, 1883, at the Church of Holy Trinity in Granville Ferry. The Hatheway and Bogart families had strong ties to the Digby and Annapolis Valley area through the shipbuilding industry. Granville Ferry was a small shipbuilding community on the Bay of Fundy. Spending his childhood between Granville Ferry and Saint John, Victor had six siblings named Samuel, Muriel, Harold, Beatrice, Leslie, and Charles. Charles passed away when he was only four months old while the family was living in Saint John. There are few details of Victor's early life in Nova Scotia, but records show that, on March 18, 1900, his mother, Christina, passed away, age just thirty-seven, leaving Frederick to raise the large family. Dealing with this tragedy, the family moved to Fredericton and settled on a farm in the Springhill area of Kingsclear Parish. All the children in the family attended the Kingsclear St. Peters Church as well as local community schools. His brothers moved away to other provinces for jobs in the banking industry, while Victor enrolled at Fredericton High School. Upon graduation in 1911 he went to the Halifax Royal Naval College, where he later graduated and received a commission as a midshipman. By this time, Frederick had moved to Regent Street in Fredericton and later to 36 Waterloo Row with his sister. Samuel continued working the family farm.

At age eighteen, prior to the outbreak of war, Victor was spending extended periods on the Atlantic Ocean aboard the British cruiser HMS *Berwick*, sailing off the coast of Ireland and then on to Mexico. Newspapers report that, while in Mexico on leave, he strayed too far inland and was shot in the arm by "rebel rifle fire." He returned home for a holiday in the early summer of 1914 and to celebrate his nineteenth birthday. His break was cut short, however, when war was declared in August. As Victor's

HMS *Good Hope*, the Royal Navy armoured cruiser Midshipman Victor Hatheway was serving aboard when he was killed on November 1, 1914.

Symonds & Co. Collection, Imperial War Museum (Q 21297)

service began so early on in the war and because he served with Britain's Royal Navy, there are few offical Canadian records of his military service. As a result, newspapers at the time provide the best available information on what happened to Victor, described as one of the most popular young men in Fredericton. His brothers Harold and Leslie also enlisted.

Victor left for Halifax immediately upon the outbreak of war after being recalled to the British cruiser *Suffolk*, described as the "flagship of the British Atlantic Squadron" by newspapers. Along with Victor, three other young men from Nova Scotia who had also recently graduated from the Royal Naval College also joined the British crew. According to the *Daily Gleaner*, "like every good sailor and soldier, he was glad when the call to arms came, and he responded heartily." During his time aboard *Suffolk*, Victor wrote home as much as he could to connect with family and loved ones. At some point, the group of Canadian midshipmen was transferred in mid-ocean to the cruiser HMS *Good Hope* when it became the flagship for Admiral Christopher Cradock's fleet, which was heading to South America. The ship was one of four Drake-class armoured cruisers built for the Royal Navy in 1900, and at the outbreak of war it was tasked with searching for German commerce raiders off Central and South America. Eventually, *Good Hope* made its way to the Southern Pacific Ocean, near the coast of Chile, where it encountered a German naval squadron. On the late afternoon of November 1, during the Battle of Coronel, *Good Hope* sustained repeated hits from German cruisers before it could return fire. All personnel on board perished in what was described at the time as one of the worst defeats of the Royal Navy in a century. Midshipman Victor Hatheway and Nova Scotian Midshipmen J.W. Cann, Arthur Silver, and W.A. Palmer were all lost at sea, the first official Canadian casualties of the First World War.

News of Victor's death reached Fredericton a few days later, and newspapers began reporting that he had been lost at sea. On Sunday, November 15, citizens from across the Fredericton community gathered at Christ Church Cathedral to pay their respects to family and friends. Described at the time as "not only one of the most impressive services of the kind ever held at the historic edifice, but one of the greatest tributes Fredericton has ever paid to one of her sons," the memorial service was praised for bringing the community together during a difficult period. In Halifax, the death of these young men prompted some of the earliest memorials for service personnel killed during the First World War, as plaques were placed in their honour in St. Mark's Church, CFB Halifax, and later at the Royal Naval College of Canada. At the time of his death, Victor was nineteen years old.

Lest We Forget

Midshipman J. Victor W. Hatheway is memorialized on the Halifax Memorial, located in Point Pleasant Park. According to the Commonwealth War Graves Commission, the memorial is dedicated to the 274 individuals from the First Word War and 2,847 from the Second World War who have no known grave after being lost at sea. The majority of those named on this memorial are sailors, merchant seamen, soldiers, and nursing sisters whose bodies were never recovered. (No digital record)

2. Chase, Silas Hartley (January 16, 1915)

Private 22559, 71st York Regiment, 12th Overseas Battalion

Silas Hartley Chase was born in Fredericton on October 1, 1889, to Edward and Melissa Chase. The 1901 census shows that Hartley had two sisters, Sadie and Alice, and a brother, Samuel. By 1911, three more children, Ora, Faria, and Flossie, had been born into the family. Few records reveal what Hartley's early life was like; however, in November 1909 the death of their father at the age of forty-one likely brought sadness and difficulties to the home. Edward's death certainly put added pressure on the boys of the home to help out and provide in his absence. Only a teenager at the time, Hartley began working as a labourer while still living at his mother's home. He also had been active volunteering with the local militia, spending eight years training with the 71st Regiment. By 1914, when war came to Fredericton, Hartley was one of the first to enlist and head off to Camp Valcartier in late summer, where he joined the Canadian Expeditionary Force's 12th Overseas Battalion. According to his attestation paper, signed on September 24, 1914, in Quebec, Hartley was young and well trained, having already spent a significant number of years with the 71st Regiment. He was twenty-two years of age, unmarried, and stood five feet six inches tall. He was described as having a dark complexion, grey eyes, and black and grey hair. As well, given that he was a labourer, he was likely the kind of soldier needed for the tough work ahead in Europe. Unfortunately, his family would never see him again.

Private Chase left with the 12th Battalion for England less than a week after formally enlisting. According to his service record, his unit sailed from Quebec City, October 3, aboard the SS *Scotian* and in mid-October arrived in England. Hartley trained with his unit at Salisbury Plain over the winter of 1914–15 in preparation for sending a Canadian division to the front in early 1915. However, on January 13, 1915, Hartley was admitted to No. 1 General Hospital and later transferred to Bulford Manor

Hospital. Doctors diagnosed him as seriously ill, suffering from spinal meningitis. After receiving some medical treatment for his illness, Hartley unfortunately passed away at 12:50 p.m. at Bulford Hospital, three days after being admitted.

News of Private Chase's death reached New Brunswick papers two days later and, according to reports, there was great sympathy in Fredericton for Hartley's family. At a memorial service held at St. Paul's Presbyterian Church and led by Reverend Dr. W.H. Smith, members of the Fredericton Brass Band played the entry and exit of local soldiers in attendance. In an editorial column printed in the Saint John *Standard* the day of Hartley's death notice, criticism was leveled at politicians for choosing the site of Salisbury Plain for Canadian troops, calling it "a death-trap...where good men have succumbed to meningitis, pneumonia and other diseases induced by the bad weather and insufficient shelter of the camp." Although Canadians would endure hardships much worse in early 1915 and over the course of the war, the illnesses and diseases that claimed thousands of Canadians is an often-forgotten result of the First World War. Private Silas Hartley Chase was twenty-two years old at the time of his death. According to Hartley's record of service, his mother received her son's medals and pension, and continued to live at 482 University Avenue until moving to Needham Street before her death in the winter of 1933.

Lest We Forget

Private Silas Hartley Chase is buried at the Bulford Church Cemetery located in Wiltshire, England. According to the Commonwealth War Graves Commission, seventy-one First World War burials took place for soldiers who trained at Bulford Camp on Salisbury Plan.

3. McKee, George H. (April 21, 1915)

Lance Corporal 69672, 26th New Brunswick Battalion

George Hamilton McKee was born on December 22, 1877, in Fredericton to Hamilton McKee and Myra George. According to records, George had four siblings named Mabel, Maude, Samuel Hanford, and Alexander Colton. The McKee family lived in downtown Fredericton and attended St. Paul's United Church. Although there are few details of his childhood, George eventually attended the University of New Brunswick and graduated in 1899. He went to work as a clerk for the local post office and eventually met a young woman named Davieda Patterson Manzer. George and Davieda married on October 4, 1904. Together, the McKees lived on King Street over the next few years and had their first child, Ralph Hamilton, on September 15, 1905, followed by George Burton on March 15,

1907. Newspapers reveal that for several years George was a physical instructor at the YMCA and prominent athlete. Just prior to the war, the McKees moved to Boston, Massachusetts, where George worked as a bottler and merchant.

Grave of Lance Corporal George H. McKee, the first member of the 26th Battalion to die on active service, Fredericton Rural Cemetery. Brent Wilson

When war broke out in the summer of 1914, he immediately came home to New Brunswick with his family, and enlisted in Saint John with the 26th Battalion on September 28, 1914. According to his attestation paper, he had light brown eyes, dark hair, a dark complexion, and stood approximately five feet four inches tall. Although George did not have any formal military experience, at age thirty-seven his desire to serve was likely hard to ignore. His two brothers, Hanford and Colton, also enlisted for duty overseas.

In the winter of 1914–15, Lance Corporal McKee left Saint John for Halifax for routine military training. According to his service record and newspaper accounts, he returned to Saint John a few months later in preparation for going overseas to England with the 26th Battalion. While his wife and children stayed with family in Saint John, George lived in a boarding house at 36 Horsfield Street. On April 16, 1915, George took part in an afternoon military parade but became ill that evening at the Saint John Armoury with a severe cold. The next day, newspaper accounts suggest that he was instructed to go to his barracks to rest; however, as his condition worsened, physicians diagnosed the illness as pneumonia, which affects one or both lungs, a painful condition usually caused by bacteria and other environmental factors. As was often the case in those years, living in close quarters with a large number of people made the spread of these viruses much worse. During the course of the war, pneumonia was often diagnosed as a result of the extreme conditions soldiers had to experience. It was believed at the time that his condition was not critical, but a few days later George's immune system weakened, and he passed away on the evening of April 21.

George's death was a complete shock to everyone who knew him and was devastating news for his wife and two young boys. According to the *Daily Gleaner*, the following day his remains were brought to Fredericton, and on April 23 a military funeral was held at his parent's home on King Street in his honour. A firing party from the Divisional Ammunition Column was present at his burial along with members of the 28th Field Artillery Battery, the 55th Battalion, and officers of the 71st Regiment.

At the time George succumbed to his illness, he was thirty-eight years old and had been on active duty for only six months. His death was a clear reminder of how short military service could be during the First World War, even when not active in the field overseas.

Lest We Forget

Lance Corporal George McKee is buried at the Fredericton Rural Cemetery in Fredericton. The cemetery is located along the St. John River just off the Woodstock Road. His name appears on the UNB Honour Roll in Memorial Hall.

4. Phillips, Robert James (May 1, 1915)

Private 38823, 12th Overseas Battalion,
1st Battalion, 3rd Dorset Regiment, British Army

Robert James Phillips was born on February 11, 1882, in Fredericton. Although there is limited information on Robert's birth parents, the 1891 census shows that he was raised primarily by his uncle Paul, a local police officer, and a woman named Jane Wilbur, as well as his aunts Elizabeth and Maggie. Newspapers suggest that Robert, or "Bob" as he was known to friends and family, was a well-known young man in the area and grew up attending the Brunswick Street Baptist Church. As a teenager, Robert was a successful baseball player. When the Boer War broke out in South Africa, the nineteen-year-old joined the Canadian Mounted Rifles (CMR) and left from Halifax in January 1902.

Upon his return from service in South Africa, he met a young woman from Doaktown named Margaret May Parker. Records reveal that Margaret had a child named Clyde Price from a previous relationship; there is no evidence, however, that she was ever previously married. Although accounts clearly show that Robert and Margaret were married

December 9, 1909, there are no marriage documents to confirm this. On May 25, 1910, their son, Frederick Henry Phillips, was born. At the time of their son's birth, Robert and Margaret were living at 648 King Street with their uncle and Robert was working as a painter and labourer in the area. Newspapers show that he likely had close ties with another Boer War veteran in the community, Francis McManamin. When war broke out in Europe, both Robert and Francis went overseas together with the 12th Battalion, but enlisted with British units once in England. Robert was described as standing five feet seven inches tall and was thirty-three years old at the time of his enlistment in Southampton, England.

On January 21, 1915, Private Phillips was posted to the 1st Battalion of the 3rd Dorset Regiment. On February 10, Phillips wrote home explaining that he was heading to the front as part of a draft of reinforcements and that "there's no fooling here and it don't take them very long to make a soldier out of a man ... we'll be in the fighting within two weeks. The boys in this regiment think a great deal of us because we are Canadians." A week later, Robert was in northern France. According to the war diaries of the 3rd Dorset Regiment, he was in Ypres, Belgium, by March 1. Over

Private Robert J. Phillips is commemorated on the Ypres (Menin Gate) Memorial in Ypres, Belgium. Marc Ryckaert, CC BY-SA 4.0

the next few months, he remained in the Ypres Salient with British units. While in the trenches in late April, Robert experienced for the first time the devastating impact chemical weapons could have on a battlefield. On April 22, at approximately five o'clock, the German army released more than 160 tons of chlorine gas into a north-east wind along the Salient against British, Canadian, and French forces. Many of those caught in the massive gas cloud died of asphyxiation, while others felt burning in their throat, eyes, and nose, and had scars that would never fully heal. Having escaped the first few uses of chlorine gas, Robert was with the Dorsets near Hill 60 when more gas was released on May 1. This time he would not survive and his body would never be recovered. In a letter written home to family, Colonel H.S. Scholes explained: "It is my painful duty to inform you that a report has this day been received from the war office notifying the death of Private R.J. Phillips, which occurred with the British Expeditionary Force in France on the 1st day of May 1915. I am to express to you the sympathy and regret of the Army Council at your loss. The cause of death was poison gas."

Newspapers reported Robert's death, noting that his four-year old son, Frederick, "was almost heart-broken this morning when he learned that his father had been killed." As news spread of his death, deep regret and sympathy was felt by many in the community who knew him. Many expressed sincere sorrow for his wife and son. Robert's wife passed away in 1963, while his son Frederick served during the Second World War and returned to New Brunswick, later to become the first photo archivist of the Provincial Archives of New Brunswick. Frederick passed away in 1988.

Lest We Forget

Private Robert James Phillips is honoured on the Ypres (Menin Gate) Memorial in Ypres, Belgium, designed by British architect Sir Reginald Blomfield. The memorial was unveiled by Lord Plumer on July 24, 1927. Between October 1914 and September 1918, hundreds of thousands of servicemen marched through Ypres on their way to frontline trenches. The memorial, one of the best-known of its kind in the world, now stands as a dedication and reminder of the approximately fifty-five thousand Commonwealth troops who died in the Salient, which stretched from Langemarck in the north to the northern edge in Ploegsteert Wood in the south, and whose bodies have never been found. (No digital record)

5. Jones, Samuel (May 8, 1915)

Private 22591, 12th Battalion, Princess Patricia's Canadian Light Infantry

Samuel Jones was born in Fredericton in 1870 to Stephen Jones and Levina Whitlock. By 1891, the Jones family had expanded to include three more sons, David, Ray, Arthur, and three daughters, Ida, Ellie, and Lucie. According to newspaper records, in the late 1800s and early 1900s, the Jones family had a home in the Devon area across the St. John River from Fredericton, and Stephen and his sons found work at the local Marysville mill as labourers and mill workers. Although there are few records detailing his early life as a child, as a teenager and young man Samuel was a member of the 71st Regiment and later enlisted in the 2nd Special Service Battalion, The Royal Canadian Regiment, on October 24, 1899, in Saint John, and served during the Boer War. The *Daily Gleaner* reports that, while in South Africa, Jones "distinguished himself by his unusual feats of valor" and earned for himself a reputation as a reliable soldier of fortune. After returning to Canada, Samuel divided his time over the next ten years working in Fredericton and Portland, Maine, all the while remaining single. Documents suggest that, although he was an older man before the First World War, he used his experiences with military service whenever possible. When the United States began raising an army to send to Mexico prior to the war, Samuel enlisted, before returning to Canada once he heard a force was being raised at home. His attestation paper reveals that he enlisted with the 12th Battalion on September 13, 1914, in Saint John. He was described as having black hair, brown eyes, and a fair complexion, although his attestation paper for the South African War described him as having a dark complexion. At age forty-five, not only was Private Jones much older than the usual age for service, but he was also taller than normal, standing five feet nine inches tall. After enlisting in Saint John, Samuel arrived at Valcartier with the first contingent of recruits from the 71st Regiment for overseas service with the Canadian Expeditionary Force.

On October 4, 1914, Private Jones left Canada from Quebec aboard the SS *Scotian* for Salisbury Plain. He spent the winter of 1914–15 with the 12th Battalion in England. According to his service record, he was often found resistant to military protocols, as he routinely was absent without leave, broke arrest and detention, and was repeatedly fined for "drunkenness." Despite these problems, because the first winter of the war was difficult for the Canadian contingent and Jones was a veteran of previous conflicts, he was likely an important figure for many young and less experienced soldiers trying to adapt to life during the war. By late April 1915, Private Jones was in northern France and Belgium as part of a group of reinforcements filling gaps in other battalions. According to newspapers, he joined the 14th Battalion (Royal Montreal Regiment) near St. Julien, Belgium. Jones arrived just as the use of chemical weapons on the Western Front was being introduced. On April 22, during the Second Battle of Ypres, the Germans launched an offensive that began with the usual artillery bombardment of enemy lines. When the shelling died

down, the Allies waited for the first wave of German attack troops, but instead encountered chlorine gas wafting across no-man's-land and down into their trenches. Arriving just a few days after this gas attack, on the night of May 8, Samuel was leading a night listening patrol of German trench lines when he encountered enemy barbed wire and machine-gun fire directed at his position. In total, the patrol had

The St. Julien Canadian Memorial commemorates 1st Canadian Division's actions during the Second Battle of Ypres; Private Samuel Jones was killed in action near St. Julien on May 8, 1915. Melicans Matkin CC BY-SA 3.0

eleven casualties, including Private Jones, injured or killed when they were unable to escape from the impossible situation. Shortly after the incident, newspapers in Fredericton reported Sam as missing and likely killed. At the time of his death, Samuel Jones was approximately forty-seven years old. His body has never been recovered.

Lest We Forget

Private Samuel Jones is remembered on the Ypres (Menin Gate) Memorial, in Ypres, Belgium.

6. Shaw, Peter Darius (May 24, 1915)

Private 69886, 26th Battalion

Peter Darius Shaw was born on September 9, 1890, in Fredericton to Claron H. Shaw and Mary Cronkite. His parents married on December 15, 1883, in Woodstock at the home of his mother's family. According to records, Claron worked as a mill labourer and engineer, and had previous experience with the British Army. In addition to Peter, Mary and Claron had an older daughter named Sarah, also known as "Sadie," and an adopted daughter named Dolly. The family lived at 100 Lansdowne Street. Although little is known of his early life, newspapers and records suggest that Peter was very popular in the community and lived in Fredericton for most of his life. He attended the Brunswick Street Baptist Church and worked as a salesman in a local furniture store prior to the war. Peter worked out west a short time, but when war broke out in 1914 he returned to New Brunswick and enlisted in Saint John with the 26th Battalion. Given his short record of service, there is limited information regarding his physical appearance or details about where he was living at the time of his enlistment. Accounts from a variety of sources suggest he was unmarried, had no previous military training, and that much of his life at the time was spent supporting his family through work. Peter was twenty-four when he enlisted.

Along with other young men from the Fredericton area, Private Shaw arrived in Saint John during the winter of 1914–15 ready for training, and was expecting to go overseas as soon as possible. After only a few months, in May 1915, Peter was hospitalized at the Saint John General Hospital with a severe cold that was diagnosed as pneumonia. According to the *Daily Gleaner*, Peter spent a full week in hospital, but his condition failed to improve. On May 24, 1915, doctors could offer him no more treatment, and Peter passed away that day.

News of his death spread quickly in Saint John and Fredericton newspapers, highlighting how popular young Shaw was with his friends and military comrades. The day after his death, his remains were returned to Fredericton, where a small funeral and reception was held at the family's home on Lansdowne Street. His body was taken from the home and carried on a gun carriage as friends and military personnel marched in procession down Woodstock Road toward the Fredericton Rural Cemetery. Peter was the only son to Claron and Mary. He was twenty-four at the time of his death.

Lest We Forget

Private Peter Darius Shaw is buried at the Fredericton Rural Cemetery in Fredericton. His grave is marked with a Commonwealth War Graves Commission headstone near his comrade-in-arms, Lance Corporal George McKee.

Chapter Two

1916

Throughout 1916, Canadian soldiers from the Canadian Expeditionary Force fought in several major battles, including the St. Eloi Craters and Mount Sorrel in late March–early April and June, respectively, as well as many smaller engagements. Then, between September and November, they were engaged in much heavy fighting during the later stages of the Somme campaign, including the Battle of Flers-Courcelette in mid-September. They suffered more than twenty-four thousand casualties at the Somme. At the end of the year, the Canadian Corps took up positions opposite Vimy Ridge. By then, the Corps numbered four divisions and other formations totalling about one hundred thousand troops. At home, the last of the overseas units assembled and headed across the Atlantic to act as reinforcements. Canadian servicemen also joined the Royal Flying Corps and Royal Naval Air Service and flew combat missions at the front during the second half of 1916.

Canadian soldiers "stand to" in frontline trenches; one is looking at
no-man's-land through a trench periscope.

Canada, Department of National Defence/Library and Archives Canada/C-006984

7. Dunlop, Eldon (April 26, 1916)

Private 116007, 2nd and 11th Canadian Mounted Rifles

Eldon Dunlop was born on July 26, 1886, in Upper Caverhill, New Brunswick, to Martha Agnes Morgan and John Dunlop. According to census records, Eldon grew up in a large family on a farm in the Caverhill community, located in the parish of Queensbury, just beyond Mactaquac. He had seven siblings: Burton, Joseph, Eva, Charles, Idella, Herman, and Nellie. Although there is limited information about his early upbringing, Eldon's childhood was likely similar to that of most rural farming families structured around farm labour and church. The family were Methodists. Prior to the First World War, Eldon had moved to various places for work, including Skowhegan, Maine, western Canada, and eventually the Yukon, where he found a job as a teamster. Given his upbringing on a farm in rural New Brunswick, teamster's work, which usually involved working closely with a team of draft horses, oxen, or mules, was likely appealing and easy for him. By 1913, however, Eldon's father had passed away, leaving Martha a widow to raise the remaining children, Herman and Nellie, in the family home. According to Eldon's attestation paper, he enlisted in Vancouver on March 20, 1915, with the 11th Canadian Mounted Rifles (CMR). He was described as having a fair complexion, blue eyes, brown hair, and standing five feet five inches tall. Twenty-eight years of age at the time, Eldon had never married and had no military training. He spent the next few months in Canada with the 11th CMR training in preparation for going overseas to England. During his absence, records suggest his mother moved to Marysville and lived with Mildred Hoyt for a time before relocating to Bathurst.

Private Dunlop left Canada with the 11th CMR during the summer of 1915. For some reason, the specific details of Eldon's early arrival in England and on the Western Front were never recorded in his service record, possibly because it was so early in the war. Documents do show, however, that he transferred from the 11th CMR to the 2nd CMR less than a month after he arrived. After being in England for a short time to receive additional training, Eldon arrived in France on September 22, 1915. He remained with the 2nd CMR over the winter of 1915–16 in northern France, but it was not until the spring of 1916 that he wrote home describing his experiences. Received by his eldest brother Burton, who had been living in Maine, the letter, which was published in the *Daily Gleaner*, reads as follows:

I have been in some tight corners the last seven months back. I was helping build a dugout one night back and a shell came over and killed four men alongside of me. One man was filling the same sandbag I was. Another man and myself had to carry a wounded man in. This is surely scientific warfare. One hardly sees a German and yet we are so close we can almost hear them breathe. We have been out of the trenches for sixteen days, but we had quite a casualty list the last time we were in. We are going in now for quite a period so if I come out alright, I may get a pass to England for ten days. The Canadians are holding an important part of the British front and the Germans are using all kinds of machinery of destruction. They have gassed us twice, but we are giving them as good as they sent. The weather now is very good, but we had a hard winter and there was some snow in March. The Germans are trying to break through, but the French can hold them even though they must sacrifice thousands of men. The Germans are doomed to defeat but it may take some time.

According to the *Daily Gleaner*, these would be the last words written home to family, as the letter was sent just before Eldon headed into the trenches in southern Belgium. The record of his circumstances of death notes that, during actions in the vicinity of Maple Copse, near Sanctuary Wood, on April 26, 1916, Private Dunlop "was wounded by the explosion of an enemy rifled grenade, and a few minutes later, whilst his wounds were being dressed, another grenade exploded in the trench killing him and the Medical Orderly, instantaneously." Newspapers suggest that news of Eldon's death was received by his brother Burton, as military officials found it difficult to locate his mother, Martha, who had moved away from Fredericton. Eldon was approximately twenty-nine years old.

Lest We Forget

Private Eldon Dunlop is buried in Maple Copse Cemetery, located in West-Vlaanderen, Belgium. According to the Commonwealth War Graves Commission, Eldon is one of approximately 258 burials. The cemetery memorial was designed by Sir Edwin Lutyens, and was created there because the area was close to the frontline trenches.

8. Kirk, Everett Meredith (April 26, 1916)

Private A6428, 6th Canadian Mounted Rifles, 12th Reserve Battalion, 1st Battalion (Western Ontario)

Everett Merideth Kirk was born on March 1, 1885, in St. Stephen, New Brunswick, to George William Kirk and Annie Young. According to records, George and Annie married in New Brunswick and they had four children. In addition to Everett, the other siblings were named James Arthur, Mary E., and Sarah. According to the 1901 New Brunswick census, Everett was the youngest child in the family. While George worked in a variety of jobs as a labourer, Annie raised the children and kept the home. Although few details exist of his early life, records show that Everett was employed in St. Stephen as a stonemason before going to Fredericton to work as a plumber. He met a young woman named Mina Lawton, who came from a large Richibucto family, and they eventually got married in Fredericton on October 3, 1909. The 1911 New Brunswick census reveals that, while Everett found work in the McAdam area, Mina worked in Fredericton as a domestic hand. In the summer of 1913, the Kirks had their first child, a baby girl named Thelma Alberta. A little over a year later, in the winter of 1914, their second daughter, Emma Everetta, was born. Although not revealed in birth records, additional documents suggest they had another daughter together prior to his military service. Everett's service record indicates that he had no prior military experience, but according to birth records he was already a soldier with the local regiment in 1913–14. At the time of his formal enlistment on March 30, 1915, in Amherst, Nova Scotia, Everett, Mina, and their young family were living in at 304 York Street in Fredericton. According to his attestation paper, Everett had blue eyes, black hair, and a dark complexion, and was approximately five feet seven inches tall. He also had close ties to the Presbyterian Church in the Fredericton area. As other Fredericton men from the area began enlisting, Everett joined the 6th Canadian Mounted Rifles and started his preparations for overseas service. Although he never left a will for his wife, a daughter named Estella Kirk was named as beneficiary to his pension and medals. At the time Everett left Canada for England, he was thirty years of age, leaving behind a young family he would never see again.

There are inconsistencies in his service record, but it appears that Private Kirk left Canada in the early summer of 1915. Upon arrival in England, Everett transferred to the 12th Reserve Battalion before going with a draft to France on August 28. Over the winter of 1915–16, Everett remained with the 1st Battalion, from western Ontario, in northern France and the Ypres Salient. By the spring of 1916, letters had been received at home, after nearly six months without hearing a word, indicating that Everett had seen Archie Smith and others from Fredericton in the trenches. He also expressed hope to Mina that he would be home by the following Easter. Three days after writing home to his family, he was with his unit in Belgium occupying trenches at Hill 60, near Zillebeke, when he was hit by shrapnel. According to his circumstances-of-death record, his wounds were untreatable. Everett died shortly after on April 26. A week and a half would go by before the *Daily Gleaner* reported his death, less than a year after he had left Canada to go overseas. According to reports, Mrs. Kirk was "overcome with shock" over the death of her husband. Approximately nine months later, Mina remarried a widower named

Sterling Saunders and together they eventually had a child of their own, a baby girl who is unnamed in provincial birth records. Over a year and half later, on October 18, 1918, Mina Kirk passed away from an unknown illness, leaving behind her children to the care of her sister Jennie. A tragic end to two lives. At the time of Everett's death in 1916, he was thirty-two years old.

Lest We Forget

Private Everett Meredith Kirk is buried at the Sanctuary Wood Cemetery, located in West-Vlaanderen, Belgium. According to the Commonwealth War Graves Commission, Everett is one of approximately 642 identified casualties there. Like so many other CWGC cemeteries, Sanctuary Wood was designed by Sir Edwin Lutyens.

9. Gough, James Percy (May 7, 1916)

Private 22569, 12th Battalion, 15th Battalion

James Percy Gough was born on March 26, 1893, in Fredericton, to James Wellington Gough and Isabel Amelia Sturgeon. James's father was from Fredericton and his mother from White Rapids in northern New Brunswick. The 1911 census shows that James, the eldest son, had six siblings, including four brothers, Walter Ernest, Norman, Kenneth, and Robin, and two sisters, Barbara, the eldest child, and Jean. Three of the Gough brothers — James, Norman, and Walter — would enlist for service during the First World War. The family lived at 63 Shore Street in Fredericton, close to the St. John River. Records show that, just prior to the war, James was working as a shoemaker at the Hartt Shoe Factory on York Street in Fredericton, as was his brother, Walter Ernest. According to his service record, James stood five feet six inches tall, had a dark complexion, dark hair, and brown eyes. Newspapers reveal that he, like his brother Walter, was a well-known amateur baseball player with the local Fredericton Imperials, who won the city championship in 1914. When war broke out in the late summer of 1914, James left right away for Camp Valcartier, Quebec, with the 71st York Regiment's contingent. At age twenty-one, he enlisted for service overseas on September 24, 1914, with the 12th Battalion. Although James often wrote letters home about his experiences in France and Belgium, he never returned to his family.

According to his service record, after spending late August and all of September at Camp Valcartier, he left for England on October 3 with the 12th Battalion aboard the SS *Scotian*. After training with the 12th Reserve Battalion in England during the fall and winter of 1914–15, Private Gough went to France on April 27, 1915, as a member of a draft joining the 15th Battalion (48th Highlanders of Canada). His service record confirms that he was with the 15th Battalion in the field on July 31 and remained with this unit over the next ten months. James received a week-long leave of absence at the beginning of 1916, but he was soon engaged in serious fighting in the Ypres Salient by April. According to the official war diary of the 15th Battalion, the spring found them just southwest of Ypres in the Poperinghe area. Letters home and reports in newspapers reveal that, during his time in the field, Gough had numerous "remarkable escapes" and shared with friends back home his "luck" while in the trenches. In late April, however, Gough's close calls caught up to him. On April 28, James was reported to have received gunshot wounds to his head while with his unit in the field. His medical history sheet shows that he was admitted to No. 17 Casualty Clearing Station for treatment of a depressed fracture of the parietal region of his skull. Doctors immediately operated to repair the skull fracture before recommending he be moved to England for further surgery, as Gough appeared to be in a "semi-stupor state all the time." He arrived at Epsom War Hospital in London on May 3, where his medical officer, Captain J.H. McGee, noted the development of a large hernia on his skull near the wound shortly after his arrival. Four days after being admitted, Private Gough was unable to recover from his wounds, and he died in the early hours of May 7. The eldest son of James and Isabel Gough, James was twenty-three. The news of his death came as a tremendous shock to the young soldier's family, relatives, and the community as a whole.

Lest We Forget

James Percy Gough is buried in the Epsom Cemetery, Surrey, England, where there are 182 Commonwealth burials from the First World War and 49 from the Second World War. According to the Commonwealth War Graves Commission, 149 of the 1914-18 war burials are located in Plot K, where James is buried. These war burials are commemorated at the north end of the plot on a screen wall, where bronze panels bear the names of those buried there.

10. Graham, William B. (May 20, 1916)

Private 69342, 26th Battalion

William B. Graham was born on June 20, 1872, in St. Stephen, New Brunswick, to John Graham and Adeline Jones. According to the 1901 census, William was the oldest of four children; the others were Frederick, Mary, and Edith. There are few details about his parents; however, according to the Saint John *Daily Telegraph*, William spent most of his childhood in St. Stephen. A woodsman by trade, William moved to Fredericton prior to 1895 and joined the 71st Regiment. While there he became a member of Wilmot Church and eventually met a young woman named Annie R. Hooper, although it is unclear where William and Annie met. On August 11, 1897, they married in St. Stephen surrounded by family. Given the nature of William's work in the woods and the fact that Annie was from Calais, Maine, the family shifted a lot between southern New Brunswick and Maine. While living in the United States prior to the war, Annie gave birth to two children: Harry born in 1898 and Irene born four years later in 1902. Their last child, Charles, was born in 1917. Newspapers suggest that for years William was eager to become involved in military engagements overseas. Twice he had attempted to enlist and both times he failed. When the Spanish-American War broke out, he was rejected because he was unable to meet physical requirements; the same occurred when he attempted to join a Canadian unit during the Boer War in South Africa. On his third attempt, however, he was successful. When war came in the summer of 1914, William immediately went to Saint John and joined the 26th Battalion. According to his attestation paper, he had grey eyes, brown hair, a mild complexion, and was approximately five feet nine inches tall. William was forty-two — much older than the average soldier at the time. Despite his age, he had a wealth of experience through his work that would make him valuable to the Canadian Expeditionary Force going to England. It is unclear if he had an opportunity to see his family again before going overseas. William spent the winter of 1914–15 in Canada training with the 26th Battalion, while Annie and the children remained in Maine during the war.

Soldiers of the 26th Battalion, including Sergeant William Graham, departing Saint John for England on June 13, 1915, on board the SS *Caledonia*. NBM/X-13284

Sergeant Graham left Canada with the 26th Battalion from Saint John on June 13, 1915, aboard the SS *Caledonia*. Arriving in England a week later, William spent the first few months of his service in England before going to France on September 15. His service record suggests that, prior to leaving England, he might have spent time enjoying his last few days before going to the front, as he was "severely reprimanded" for intoxication on September 3. Over the next three months little was reported on his whereabouts until it was noted that he was detailed to a grenade school in January 1916 and rejoined his unit January 29. By early spring, the 26th Battalion was near Ypres. A month before the Battle of Mount Sorrel was set to begin, William was in the trenches with his unit when, according to his circumstances-of-death record, he received a gunshot wound to the head. On May 20, he was evacuated quickly to No. 3 Casualty Clearing Station near Poperinghe, where he succumbed to his wounds. A week and a half after his death, the Saint John *Daily Telegraph* confirmed a story in Maine newspapers that he had been killed and that the family was notified. William was described as being "well known and highly esteemed on the border," and the news story added that his death was met with sincere regret by everyone. At the time of his death, William was forty-four, leaving behind his wife and three children. All his medals went to his wife and mother. The couple's third child, Charles, was born while William was overseas and would never meet his father. Charles later served in the United States Army during the Second World War and the Korean War. In 1952, at age thirty-five, he was killed in action in Korea.

Researching the life of William Graham was difficult because in 1923 his name was incorrectly inscribed on the war memorial plaque as "Percival Graham." Records obtained through the Provincial Archives of New Brunswick confirm that there is no "Percival Graham" on any church rolls and that no one by that name from the area had been killed during the war. William B. Graham, the young man who attended Wilmot Church and whose name is listed on the church honour roll, should have his name corrected on the war memorial.

Sergeant William B. Graham is buried at Lijssenthoek Military Cemetery, approximately twelve kilometres west of Ypres, Belgium, close to the French border. During the First World War, the village of Lijssenthoek was situated on the main communication line between the Allied military bases in the rear and the Ypres battlefields. Close to the front but out of the extreme range of most German artillery, it became a natural place to establish casualty clearing stations for Commonwealth forces beginning in June 1915. According to the Commonwealth War Graves Commission, there are 10,121 identified casualties, making it the second-largest Allied cemetery in Belgium.

11. Smith, Archibald Fleming (May 26, 1916)

Private 22647, 71st York Regiment, 12th Battalion, 5th Canadian Mounted Rifles

Archibald Fleming Smith was born on July 26, 1883, in Fredericton, to Robert William Smith and Emma Cochrane. Archie's family lived on the corner of Charlotte and Regent streets for most of their lives. He belonged to a large family, including three sisters: Grace, who married another soldier, John E. Connolly; Almira, who married Gordon Hazlett; and another unnamed sister who newspapers suggest was married to a Massachusetts man named Sewell. Archie also had three brothers: Alonzo, Allan, and Alfred. Although few records highlight his early life in New Brunswick, newspapers suggest he came from a strong military family. They also reveal that Alonzo enlisted and served overseas, as did his other brothers at different times. Census documents reveal that, just prior to the war, Alfred, Alonzo, and Allan were still living in the area. Before the outbreak of the war, Archie married Elenora A. Mason on September 9, 1909, and they lived at 104 St. John Street. Elenora later moved to 29 Harding Street in Saint John as a widow and married Frederick Brown. Few documents reveal the total number of children Archie and Elenora had together, but newspapers and census documents indicate they had two sons named Donald and Raymond, and they also might have had another child. According to his enlistment papers, Archie stood five feet nine inches tall, had blue eyes and light hair, and was a member of the Church of England. At the time of his enlistment in September 1914, Archie was thirty-one years old and had spent time at Camp Sussex before the war. He left for Valcartier, Quebec, in the autumn of 1914, not knowing at the time that he would never again return to his wife and children.

On October 4, 1914, Archibald left from Quebec City aboard the SS *Scotian* with the 12th Battalion, and remained in England for training before becoming one of the first to volunteer for drafts of reinforcements. According to newspapers, he went to France in the winter of 1914–15 and joined the 5th Canadian Mounted Rifles. In March, he wrote home to reassure his family that he was "not downhearted yet and was getting a few Germans all the time." In April the *Daily Gleaner* published an account of his experiences of life in the trenches:

> We are not having such an awful hard time after all, for there is a lot of fun "getting" those fellows, and I think we're getting our share. Of course, they get one of our men every now and then, but then that is nothing. In the trenches last night, they were calling over to us not to shoot. They said we would be out of this country in a few weeks. I think they are right for as soon as the weather gets satisfactory this promises to be a very busy place. We have to watch for spies and German sympathizers among the people and it makes it hard for us. I think we will be home by July anyway.

Later in April, he was seriously wounded, suffering from a gunshot wound in the face while fighting in the Ypres Salient. According to the *Daily Gleaner*, he was the first soldier from Fredericton to be wounded at the front. By July, he had recovered sufficiently to return to his unit, and fought again for more than ten months until he received shrapnel wounds to the head on May 26, 1916, just before the Battle of St. Eloi. Archie was taken to No. 10 Casualty Clearing Station, where he later died of his wounds. According to an article published in the *Daily Gleaner* a week after his death, the news of her husband's death came as a terrific shock to Mrs. Smith, who was alone with her young sons, Donald and Raymond, when she received the telegram. Later, however, she recovered somewhat and expressed pride in her husband and said that she would have to accept her loss as bravely as she could, the same as other brave wives and mothers all over the British Empire were doing. Archibald Fleming Smith was the fourth Fredericton man killed in action during the Great War. He was thirty-three when he died.

Lest We Forget

Private Archibald Smith is remembered at the Lijssenthoek Military Cemetery.

12. Dolan, John Frederick (June 2, 1916)

Private 111145, 6th and 4th Canadian Mounted Rifles

John Frederick Dolan was born in Fredericton on July 23, 1889, to James Dolan and Catherine Mulligan. According to marriage records, the Dolans lived at 333 Charlotte Street in Fredericton and James worked as a caretaker. James and Catherine had three children: in addition to John, there was an older sister, Mary, and a younger brother, Daniel Leo. The 1911 census shows that, just prior to the war, all three children, Mary, then twenty-six, John, twenty, and Daniel Leo, sixteen, were still living at the Dolan home and that John was attending the University of New Brunswick studying civil engineering. Mary eventually married Enoch Colby in January 1914. Records reveal that John was a well-respected New Brunswick athlete in professional baseball and, according to newspapers, was "one of the finest football and basketball players" while a student at UNB. The university's First World War Honour Roll also reveals that John was a member of the St. Dunstan's Catholic Church choir early in his life and that he enjoyed taking part in community and college plays as an actor. When war broke out in Europe, John was working as a surveyor with the Saint John Valley Railway. Although newspapers in November 1914 suggest that he was one of the local Fredericton recruits with the 26th Battalion stationed in Saint John, his service record reveals that he did not formally enlist until June 4, 1915, in Amherst, Nova Scotia, with the 6th Canadian Mounted Rifles (CMR). Young, educated, experienced, and well liked, at twenty-four years old and single, John was the ideal soldier. According to his attestation paper, he was five feet seven inches tall, had blue eyes, dark brown hair, and had a dark complexion. Dolan weighed 142 pounds, was in good shape for training, and soon left with his unit for Camp Valcartier in Quebec. While appearing to have everything the military wanted in a soldier, John's service record over the next year illustrates an uneasy relationship with military discipline. By July 8, shortly after arriving at Valcartier with his unit, John was reportedly absent without leave for three days and lost pay as a result. It is unclear if he ever saw his family again during his last month in Canada prior to going overseas.

On July 18, 1915, Private Dolan left Quebec City with the 6th CMR for England aboard the SS *Herschel*, arriving at Devonport on July 26. Days later, on July 31, John was again disciplined for being AWL from his unit; in October he lost pay once more for disciplinary infractions. Dolan left England for France with the 6th CMR on October 24. Just prior to leaving, John named his brother Daniel Leo in his will as beneficiary. Despite his run-ins with military discipline, John spoke well of his superiors, his friends from back home, and of his experiences in the trenches in letters written in late December:

> I have met nearly all the boys from home, including "Tit"
> McGibbon, Karl Walker, "Cort" Otty and others, and all the
> old officers of the old 12th are O.K., with Col. Harry McLeod
> as one of the best when it comes to meeting a friend from your
> own hometown. He is a prince. All I can say is, "This is the life,"
> as far as it has gone. It may be harder this winter, but we will

Private John Dolan is among the almost seven thousand missing Canadian
soldiers whose names appear on the Ypres (Menin Gate) Memorial.

never have the hardships endured by the fellows in the First
Contingent.

By January 1916 John had joined the 4th CMR in 3rd Canadian
Division, and realized that he would encounter equally difficult hardships
during his time in northern France and Belgium. That month, he was
admitted to hospital, where he stayed for about a week. By February he
was again being disciplined for his conduct while on duty. A military court
eventually found him guilty of "drunkenness while on active duty," and he
spent twenty-eight days undergoing "field punishment" in a confinement
camp: two hours over a three-day period cuffed to a "heavy stationary
object" such as a wagon wheel. By March Private Dolan and the 4th CMR
were in Belgium, near Sanctuary Wood and Zillebeke. On May 3, John

was again punished for three days for disobeying orders. It was during this period that John's whereabouts and activities became unclear and questions about what actually happened to him would persist. On June 2, the opening day of the Battle of Mount Sorrel, the 4th CMR were in trenches close to Armagh Wood when a four-hour "tornado of fire" came down on to their positions. According to G.W.L. Nicholson's *Canadian Expeditionary Force 1914-1919*, that morning their trenches vanished and those within them were completely blown away. The position that Private Dolan was in at the time received 89 percent casualties: only 72 of 702 officers and men came out unhurt. According to the 4th CMR war diaries, 258 prisoners were taken by the Germans, including Private Dolan. While John's circumstances of death suggest that he was "shot by a machine gun bullet from a German plane near Zillebeke," letters written home by Privates J. Edwin P. Tracy and Fred W. Boyd reveal that he was taken as a prisoner of war to Germany.

On June 29, 1916, the *Daily Gleaner* reported: "Official telegrams from Ottawa brought the word that five young men from Fredericton were members of the 4th Canadian mounted rifles were reported missing on the 2nd of June 1916. That very day the third battle of Ypres began. The five members were Corporal Alleyne Y. Clements of Claremont, Privates Fred W. Boyd, John F. Dolan, and John Carten, of Fredericton, and John Saunders of St. Marys. They were members of the D Company and the Machine gun section of the 4th Canadian mounted rifles. The unit was in the thick of fighting and suffering heavy losses."

A year would go by before any more news of John's whereabouts was shared in newspapers. On November 27, 1917, after reporting on local men involved in the battle of Passchendaele, special word was received that John had escaped with five other soldiers and was quarantined in Holland. The report suggested that, according to word received by John's father, James, he had attempted to escape three times but had been captured and taken back. Despite reports of his escape and safety, John never arrived home, and his official record presumed him to have died on June 2, 1916, during the Battle of Mount Sorrel in Belgium. Given all that is known of John, an educated and experienced young man who challenged discipline, yet spoke highly of his mates and superiors, it is a safe bet that Private Dolan would never have given up an opportunity to get home to family and friends after being taken prisoner by the Germans in Belgium. When his mother, Catherine, died in the winter of 1923, newspapers reported Dolan as having been killed during the Great War. His family and community were then finally able to come to terms with his loss. While we do not know for certain when Private Dolan died and how, we can find solace in the fact that he likely did so with a fight.

Lest We Forget

Private John F. Dolan is remembered on the Ypres (Menin Gate) Memorial in Ypres, Belgium.

13. Ford, William Dalgleish (June 2, 1916)

Lance Corporal McG166, 11th Battalion,
Princess Patricia's Canadian Light Infantry

William Dalgleish Ford was born on April 22, 1890, in Portneuf, Quebec, to Joseph Ford and Mary Jessica Dalgleish. According to census records, Joseph and Mary had five other children in addition to William: Joseph Jr., Eric, Thomas, Catherine, and Mary. The couple both came from Portneuf, a small community between Quebec City and Montreal, and likely knew each other growing up. They married in 1887 in Thorold, Ontario, when Joseph was thirty-two and Mary was twenty-one. At the time, Joseph was working in manufacturing and the paper industry. Despite being married in Ontario, the family lived and kept a residence in Portneuf. Although little is known of William's early life growing up in the small community, he eventually attended and graduated from Macdonald College, McGill University's agricultural campus near Montreal. New Brunswick's 1916

Agricultural Report suggests that he came to the province from Quebec prior to the war, and described him as "a young man just beginning his chosen life work." He was immediately seen as a valued member of the Department of Agriculture, working as an animal husbandman. Recognized as a very capable young man in his line of work, newspapers reveal that William was also a member of a Canadian livestock judging team that won a competition in Chicago in 1913. In early 1914, he was made Superintendent of the Provincial Livestock Division and was working as an agricultural instructor for the province. During this time, William attended St. Paul's United Church in Fredericton.

When war broke out in the summer of 1914, civilians working in private business as well as in public service chose to leave their positions for service overseas. According to departmental records, despite sensing deep

German dead at Mount Sorrel, June 1916.
Canada, Department of National Defence/Library and Archives Canada/PA-000186

admiration for those who chose service to country, the loss of public servants was felt "to a very considerable extent." William left New Brunswick for Montreal in 1915, and enlisted with the Princess Patricia's Canadian Light Infantry (PPCLI) on June 7. His brother Eric also enlisted in Montreal. According to his attestation paper, William had blue eyes, brown hair, a fair complexion, and was about five feet ten inches tall. While not having had overseas military experience, he had some militia training that would be useful once in England. Unmarried at the time and only twenty-five years old, William began training in Quebec in preparation for going overseas to join the Patricias, who were already in Belgium serving with the British Army. It is unclear if he ever saw family and friends again.

On June 29, just a few weeks after his enlistment, Lance Corporal Ford embarked for England aboard the SS *Olympic*, sister ship of the ill-fated *Titanic*. Arriving about a week later, William remained in England until August 24, when his draft left for Rouen, France, arriving just after the Battles of Festubert and Givenchy. According to his active service record, he remained with the PPCLI in northern France and Flanders over the fall and winter of 1915–16 at a time when both sides were busy preparing for engagements in 1916. On April 4, 1916, William was granted a nine-day leave-of-absence in France, a break that would be important in the lead-up to the Battle of Mount Sorrel and the start of the Battle of the Somme. By this time, the Patricias had joined the Canadian Corps' 3rd Division directly south of the Ypres Salient and could be used to support fronts in Flanders and France. On the morning of June 2, a German artillery barrage opened up all along forward Canadian positions near Mount Sorrel and on other important pieces of high ground. Lasting for almost two weeks, the fighting resulted in over eight thousand casualties. Ground that was at first lost to the Germans was retaken on June 13 by a well-organized Canadian counterattack. On the second day of this fighting, William was in forward trenches north of Mount Sorrel with the PPCLI near Sanctuary Wood when artillery fire came down close to his position. According to his circumstances-of-death record, William "was last seen with four other comrades in a bay that was afterwards completely destroyed by enemy shell fire." Lance Corporal Ford's body was never recovered.

News of his death spread quickly in local papers and information was passed along to the Department of Agriculture by family members. According to Secretary J.B. Daggett, "Mr. Ford was an efficient officer and did splendid work as a member of our staff. His death will be learned with general regret among the livestock men of the province and the host of friends he made while connected with this department. We were all looking forward to his return as a member of the staff." William was twenty-six at the time of his death.

Researching the life of William D. Ford was incredibly difficult because his name was very common at the time, inconsistencies in spelling were found in documents and records, and his name is spelled incorrectly on the war memorial in Fredericton as "William B. Ford." According to the St. Paul's Church Roll, service records, and other supporting evidence, William's name should be inscribed on the cenotaph as "William D. Ford."

Lest We Forget

Lance Corporal William D. Ford is honoured on the Ypres (Menin Gate) Memorial located in Ypres, Belgium.

14. Merchant, Vernon Keith (June 6, 1916)

Private 444652, 71st York Regiment, 55th Battalion, 58th Battalion

Vernon Keith Merchant was born on December 14, 1899, in Colchester, England, to William and Annie Maria Merchant; he was their only child. After moving to Canada, Vernon and his parents eventually occupied a residence on Queen Street in Fredericton. Although few records detail his early life growing up in England and Fredericton prior to the war, Vernon was working in Fredericton as a plumber and had begun camp training with the local militia. He and his family were also active members of the local Church of England. When he enlisted in Fredericton on April 5, 1915, with the 55th Battalion, his attestation paper indicates that he was approximately five feet four inches tall, both his hair and eyes were brown, and was nineteen years old. According to his birth certificate, however, obtained from the Provincial Archives of New Brunswick, the truth is that he had just celebrated his fifteenth birthday. Newspapers later confirmed that he was underage for military service. Although not legally old enough for military service, Vernon remained with the 55th Battalion in Canada for the next six months to train in preparation for going overseas. It is unclear if he ever saw his family again prior to leaving for England.

On October 30, Private Merchant sailed from Montreal on the SS *Corsican*, arriving in England, his place of birth, on November 9 after more than a week at sea. Vernon spent the next five months training in England with the 55th Battalion until being transferred on April 12, 1916, to a central Ontario unit, the 58th Battalion of 3rd Canadian Division. Two days later, Vernon wrote his final will, leaving everything to his mother. On April 15, he left for France to join the 58th, which had been at the front since late February. After being in the field for less than two months in southern Belgium, Vernon was killed along with four others on June 6 during the Battle of Mount Sorrel. Although there are few details of the specifics of his death, June 6 was, according to the war diary of the 58th Battalion, "a warm, clear, and windy day," and Major J.D. Mackay stated that there had been significant "heavy enemy shelling all day." Vernon was just a few months short of his seventeenth birthday when he died. A few weeks later, New Brunswick newspapers reported his and another young man's death, indicating "much sympathy from friends in the city." In hindsight, what is most noteworthy of the report of his death in the papers is how little attention was given to his young age and that he should not have been allowed to enlist in the first place. As with most "boy soldiers," one wonders if his parents gave their permission for him to enlist or tried to have him sent home once he had joined up. As the couple's only child, Vernon's death at such a young age was a tremendous loss to the family.

Lest We Forget

Private Vernon Merchant is buried in the Railway Dugouts Burial Ground (Transport Farm), located southeast of Ypres, Belgium. According to the Commonwealth War Graves Commission, Vernon Keith is one of 2,459 burials honoured here.

15. Lifford, John (June 9, 1916)

Private 444230, 55th Battalion, 12th Reserve Battalion, 4th Battalion, 1st Canadian Trench Mortar Battery

John Lifford was born on June 25, 1881, in Fredericton to David Lifford and Ellen Hurley. According to documents obtained from the Provincial Archives of New Brunswick, David and Ellen married on January 8, 1869, in Fredericton. They had four sons named John, Harry, David, and Joseph, as well as two daughters, Nellie and Elizabeth. The family had a residence in downtown Fredericton on Regent Street. Newspapers point out that John's father, David, was a member of the British Army with the 22nd Regiment, which was stationed in Fredericton in the late 1860s, and was active with the local militia, while his mother, Ellen, worked in the home raising their six children. While few records exist to highlight John's early life in Fredericton, some details in newspapers reveal that he was working as a labourer and clerk in the area when he met Jennie Roberts. It is unclear how long John and Jennie knew each other prior to their marriage, but they eventually had two children before the war named Thomas Elwood and Francis Ernest. Another child was born sometime during the war, as newspapers suggest that John and Jennie had three children, although birth records confirm only two children prior to 1914. The family lived at 274 King Street.

When war broke out, all four sons enlisted for service, with John joining up on March 31, 1915, in Saint John with the 55th Battalion. According to his attestation paper, he had blue eyes, dark brown hair, a medium complexion, and was approximately five feet eight inches tall. David joined a British unit, while his other brothers, Harry and Joseph, served with Canadian units while overseas. John was approximately thirty-seven years old. Given the limited amount of time between enlisting and leaving to go overseas, he might not have seen his family again before departing.

On June 19, Private Lifford embarked from Lévis, Quebec, aboard the SS *Corsican* for England, arriving at Shorncliffe Barracks in Kent ten days later. Upon arrival, John transferred to the 12th Reserve Battalion for training in England, and then five months later was drafted to go to France as a reinforcement with the 4th Battalion from central Ontario—like so many other New Brunswickers, ending up serving in a unit from another part of Canada. In the period leading up to his heading to the front, however, John's record illustrates some difficulties with military discipline. Although it was not an uncommon punishment, he was admonished on two occasions: the first time he was given forty-two days' detention, the second time while in France, where he received twenty-eight days' detention for being improperly dressed and intoxicated. It appears that being away from his family may have taken a toll on him, as were the experiences he was likely having while preparing to go to the front. Also worth noting is that he was in the same unit as his brother, Joseph, who had been invalided home as a result of injuries sustained in the winter of 1915–16. Despite these few difficulties he had early in the war, John had a good record for the remainder of his service as the 4th Battalion shifted toward the Ypres Salient.

As the Allies prepared for the Somme offensive that began in the early summer of 1916, Private Lifford was in Belgium with his Canadian unit as they prepared for attacks near Zillebeke and Hill 60 in June. Little is known of his exact movements in the months prior to his death, but according to his circumstances-of-death record, on June 9 John was attached to the 1st Canadian Trench Mortar Battery in the trenches at Hill 60, when he was killed instantly by an enemy shell that burst close to him. In letters later written home by fellow mates in his unit, friends expressed their grief in losing John and told how they had "assisted in his burial service." It appears his grave was later lost. John left behind his wife, Jennie, and three young children, as well as his friends and extended family. He was thirty-eight years old.

Lest We Forget

Private John Lifford is honoured on the Ypres (Menin Gate) Memorial to the missing in Ypres, Belgium.

16. Parkinson, Charles (June 15, 1916)

Private 444144, 55th Battalion, 12th Reserve Battalion, 14th Battalion (Royal Montreal Regiment)

Charles Parkinson was born on February 16, 1897, in Dogdyke, Lincolnshire, England, to West Walter Parkinson and Minnie Wilkinson. Charles came from a large family that included three sisters, Annie, Margaret, and Kate, as well as four brothers, Sydney, Alfred, Edwin, and Walter. Although there are few records explaining the family's reason for coming to Canada, a passenger list shows that the entire family arrived at Saint John from Liverpool in April 1905 aboard a ship called the *Virginian*. The document also reveals that Charles's father was a farmer destined for St. Mary's in York County. Little is known of the particulars of their life upon arriving in Fredericton, but newspapers suggest that Charles and his brothers quickly found work as mill labourers in the area once they were old enough. Records show that the family had a home at 318 Regent

Street during the war and that they had connections to the Oromocto area, as an address belonging to Minnie in that location can be found in Charles's attestation paper. It is possible that the family moved to another residence while Charles and his father were overseas. At the time of his formal enlistment in Fredericton on April 15, 1915, Charles had prior military experience serving with the local militia and he was not married. According to his attestation paper, he was seventeen years old and had blue eyes, brown hair, a dark complexion, and was five feet seven inches tall. Along with other Fredericton boys in the area, he joined the 55th Battalion. Documents suggest that, after leaving for training, Charles never returned home to family and friends.

On June 19, Private Parkinson embarked from Lévis, Quebec, aboard the SS *Corsican* for Shorncliffe, England. Upon arrival, Charles transferred to the 12th Reserve Battalion for about two months before being drafted to the 14th Battalion (Royal Montreal Regiment), which was preparing to go to France in late summer. His service record reveals that he joined the 14th Battalion on August 28 and arrived in France the next day. While Charles had only two months of training in England, he took the time to write his will, leaving everything to his mother, Minnie. According to his active service file, on September 12 he moved with his unit to the Ypres Salient, where he served until the Battle of Mount Sorrel in June 1916. Private Parkinson's service record over these eight months illustrates a soldier with an uneasy relationship with authority. On two occasions, he underwent punishment for five and then twenty-eight days for "being absent from working party without permission" and later for "insolence to an officer." Regardless, he was granted a leave of absence to England in March 1916 and returned to his unit at the beginning of April, when he was attached to a trench mortar battery.

Leading up to the Battle of Mount Sorrel, the Germans tried to secure remaining high ground in the Ypres Salient and northern France by attacking Canadian positions in the area. Their goal was to divert Allied resources from an offensive that they knew was being prepared in the Somme region to the south. As a result, 3rd Canadian Division was brutally cut down by a well-planned artillery bombardment that destroyed forward Canadian positions and killed hundreds of soldiers, including the division commander, Major-General Malcom Mercer. German infantry then captured the Canadian positions on Mount Sorrel and two surrounding hills. On June 3, the Canadians launched a swiftly organized counterattack but failed. Three days later, the Germans exploded three mines under Canadian positions and captured the village of Hooge to the north. Sir Julian Byng, commander of the Canadian Corps, was determined to take back the lost ground, and in the early hours of June 13 the Canadians attacked after a large artillery bombardment, driving off German forces and recapturing much of their lost ground. This was a significant victory for the Canadians in this important battle.

It was during this time that local newspapers revealed that Charles Parkinson had been killed instantly by a high explosive shell that also wounded two other soldiers. (By then, Charles's father, West Parkinson, had enlisted and had just reached England with the 104th Battalion.) The papers also published a letter received by Charles's mother, written by Colonel Paul P. Powis of the trench mortar battery Charles had been attached to. It reads as follows:

> We had just gone into the trenches just before the Canadians launched an attack. We had done good work, having fired 100 rounds of ammunition, when a big shell burst right alongside our position, wounding two men badly and killing your son instantly which, I trust, is a slight comfort to you when it is considered that so many fine soldiers had to stay for hours out in the front, mortally wounded, without getting the least possible assistance, as every able man had to drive on in the attack. I brought in one poor fellow who had been without food or drink for thirty-six hours, having come across him by the merest chance. Such is the price of victory, and it was indeed a splendid achievement; and your son's life has not been in vain. His comrades wish me to convey to you their deepest sympathy. Your son was not under my command long, but he always did his duty cheerfully and died like a true soldier.

At the time of Charles' death on June 15, newspapers reported that among the many items sent home to his mother was a leather case containing a number of photos of himself and his brothers and sisters. The case had been pierced by a piece of the shell that had killed him. Charles was nineteen years of age.

Lest We Forget

Private Charles Parkinson is buried at the Railway Dugouts Burial Ground (Transport Farm), near Ypres. According to the Commonwealth War Graves Commission, Charles Parkinson is one of 2,459 burials honoured here.

17. McKillop, Duncan (June 16, 1916)

Private 69673, 26th Battalion

Duncan Cameron McKillop was born on July 25, 1893, in Glasgow, Scotland, to Peter and Catherine McKillop. According to the 1901 Scottish census, Duncan had two younger brothers named David and James. His life in Scotland was typical of most families at the time, with his father working as a labourer while he and his siblings attended school. Documents suggest that his father worked as an iron moulder. On April 5, 1910, Duncan landed in Saint John after coming from Scotland aboard the ship *Cassandra*. He was twenty years old at the time and looking for work in Canada. Eventually, Duncan made his way to the area of Gagetown and then Fredericton, where he found work as a baker. On August 21, 1913, Duncan married Alberta Mount, daughter of William and Mary Mount of Fredericton. By the time war broke out in 1914, Duncan and Alberta were living at 534 King Street, but there is no evidence to suggest they had any children. According to his attestation paper, Duncan enlisted in Saint John on November 25, 1914, with the 26th Battalion. He had no prior military training and was described as having hazel eyes, light brown hair, a dark complexion, and standing five feet six inches tall. He was twenty-three at the time of his enlistment. According to his service record, McKillop remained in Canada training with the 26th Battalion over the winter of 1914–15.

On June 13, 1915, Private McKillop and the 26th Battalion sailed from Saint John aboard the SS *Caledonia*, arriving in England on June 24. He spent the next few months training with his unit in England preparing to head for the Western Front. On September 15, he left for France with the 26th Battalion and disembarked at Boulogne, France, before marching to Belgium near the area of Hazebrouck. Over the winter, Duncan remained with the 26th in the Ypres Salient in the vast trench system, participating in active engagements when in the line. There are few details of his experiences in his service record, but the war diaries of the 26th Battalion illustrate a constant routine of managing weather, rebuilding trenches, and enduring German shelling. By the summer of 1916, the 26th Battalion and Private McKillop were near Reninghelst, Belgium, and then St. Eloi, where the June war diaries describe a period of heavy bombardments of their trenches under weather conditions that were clear and warm. As newspaper reports show, it was during the Battle of Mount Sorrel that Duncan was killed after one of these German artillery bombardments, a period that also saw the deaths of other local Fredericton boys, Charles Parkinson and John Lifford. Both the *Saint John Telegraph* and the *Daily Gleaner* reported the death of Duncan, although with limited details, illustrating the close connection he had developed in both communities during his short time in New Brunswick. Duncan was twenty-four at the time of his death. His body was never recovered. While Duncan did not have any children of his own with Alberta, she eventually married another well-known soldier in the area, Henry Morris, who had returned because of injuries. Henry had also lost loved ones, including three brothers early in the war. Together, Alberta and Henry had a daughter.

18. Spare, Harry Thomas (June 16, 1916)

Lance Sergeant 69875, 26th Battalion

Harry Thomas Spare was born on September 7, 1879, in White Parish, Salisbury, England, to Lavina Emma Gregory and Thomas Spare. According to the 1891 and 1911 England and Wales censuses, Thomas had four siblings named William, Fanny, Lavina, and Amy. Few records illustrate his early life growing up in England, but census documents suggest that Harry likely had some form of early education and apprenticeship with his father, Thomas, who worked as a painter in the Wiltshire area until his death in the late 1890s. By 1901, Harry's grandmother and two cousins, Edith and Harry Gregory, had moved in and were living with the family after the passing of Thomas. By this time, Harry was working as a painter in town just like his father. In 1912, newspapers show that Harry moved to Canada and settled in Fredericton because of his mother's brother, Sergeant R.W. Gregory, who later served with the 236th Battalion, The New Brunswick Kilties. Although there is no indication Harry had military experience like his uncle, he likely chose to settle in Fredericton because of established relationships Gregory had in the area. Harry quickly made friends through work and networks formed at Christ Church Cathedral, where he attended and became an active member of the cathedral choir.

When war broke out, Harry went to Saint John and enlisted with the 26th Battalion on November 11, 1914. According to his attestation paper, he had hazel eyes, brownish red hair, a fair complexion, and was approximately five feet seven inches tall. Lance Sergeant Spare spent the winter and spring of 1914–15 in Canada training with the 26th Battalion in preparation for going overseas. At thirty-five years of age, Harry had a brother, William, who also was about to enlist. It is unclear if Harry saw any family and friends again.

On June 15, 1915, Sergeant Spare left to go overseas from Saint John aboard the SS *Caledonia*, arriving on June 24. He remained with the 26th Battalion in England over the summer until his unit was sent to France in September, less than three months after arriving. Harry spent the fall and winter of 1915–16 just south of the Ypres Salient as part of the first two Canadian divisions that had formed up in northern France and southern Belgium. In April 1916, he received an eight-day leave for rest before returning to the front lines. Although his service record indicates he was still with the 26th, newspapers suggest that he transferred to an ambulance corps unit in the months leading up to the Battle of Mount Sorrel. He might have received medical training, and was serving with the 26th's stretcher bearers. When the German army opened up an artillery barrage against Canadian positions near Sanctuary Wood and Mount Sorrel, Harry was put in the incredibly difficult role of trying to assist some of the thousands of Canadian casualties. On June 16, Sergeant Spare was helping a wounded soldier, bandaging his wounds, when an artillery shell exploded nearby his position, killing him instantly. According to a long letter written home to Sergeant R.W. Gregory by Lieutenant John Ward of the 26th, Harry's efforts, by putting his own life on the line to help others, pointed to the kind of heroism that many of his comrades admired:

> You will, I am sure like to know that Sergeant Spare's death occurred during one of the heaviest bombardments ever this war has seen. The last time I saw him alive was when he was bandaging a wounded man, who was lying on a raised bag just above the trench, and there, exposed to flying shrapnel, Spare was carrying on his work as calmly and unconcernedly as possible. I stayed with him for a few minutes and then passed on up the trench in the course of my duty. When I re-passed the spot again about an hour

later, the body of Sergeant Spare and three of his comrades lay on the raised bag. His face was very quiet and peaceful without a sign of pain or shock. From the nature of his wounds, it was evident that his death had been instantaneous, and he never could have known that he was hurt. It appears that after dressing the wounded man, he came down into the bottom of the trench where men were crouching, and a little while later, a shell bursting in the trench killed him and two of his companions. He had such a death that a soldier would choose if death must come. Of Sergeant Spare, I can say that his life was one of self-sacrifice and devotion to duty. He carried self-forgetfulness to a degree rarely found. During the last seven months I have seen him at work under all conditions and my admiration for his character has grown steadily with greater knowledge. His patience and self-control were remarkable. On working parties, where hours of waiting in the rain, followed by long marches through blackness and mud in the trenches, when things were warmest in camp, when he gave his time to instructional work, in such and every case he gave of his best. More than this no man can do, and at last he gave his life. Greater love than this hath no man. It was my duty to look through the papers found in Sergeant Spare's pockets, and you may know that he had kept many letters from his mother and yourself. All these I destroyed, as is customary. Please accept this assurance of the sympathy of his comrades.

Although records obtained through the Commonwealth War Graves Commission suggest that Harry might have been buried at some point near Zillebeke Road, given the nature of continuous fighting that happened in the Ypres Salient his final resting place is unknown. At the time of his death, Harry was thirty-six years old.

Lest We Forget

Lance Sergeant Harry Thomas Spare is honoured on the Ypres (Menin Gate) Memorial located in Ypres, Belgium.

19. Cormier, Edmond (June 28, 1916)

Private 70300, 55th Battalion, 26th Battalion

Edmond Cormier was born on May 31, 1895, in St. Mary's, Kent County, New Brunswick to Calixte Cormier and Philomène Gauvin. While information is limited on their early life together, marriage records indicate that Calixte and Philomène met while living in the Adamsville area, just south of Rogersville, and married on August 13, 1888. According to census records, they had three children: one daughter, Marie Nathalie, and two sons, Edmond and John Napoleon. Records also reveal that Philomène was only seventeen years old when she married Calixte, who worked as a farmer in the area. Together they raised their children over the next twelve years. It is at this point that few records exist to explain what happened to Edmond's mother, Philomène, as Calixte became a widower and by 1905 had remarried to a woman named Marguerite Arsenault. Marriage records show that Marguerite was a widow herself, having been married previously to a François Babinault. Documents show that she also came from the Adamsville area and had likely known the Cormier family before.

By the spring of 1905, Calixte and his family, including Marguerite, appear to have been living in the Moncton area. At some point before the war, Edmond, now a teenager and finding work as a labourer, made his way to Fredericton. Few details link Edmond and the Cormier family to Fredericton apart from the likelihood that he was working in the area and had built relationships with people through local churches. By the spring of 1915, Edmond had moved to the Chatham area, where, at age nineteen, he formally enlisted on April 23, 1915, in the 55th Battalion. According to his attestation paper, Edmond was single and had no prior military experience. He was described as having a fair complexion, blue eyes, brown hair, stood approximately five feet seven inches tall, and weighed 150 pounds. Edmond would never return home.

Private Cormier spent only a few months with his unit in Canada before leaving with the 55th for England aboard the SS *Caledonia*, arriving on June 24, 1915. He remained at Shorncliffe Camp over the next few months until joining the 26th Battalion in November and arriving at Roulles, France, on November 19. Private Cormier was active with the 26th Battalion over the winter of 1915–16 during a break in major fighting until the battles of St. Eloi and Mount Sorrel in the summer of 1916. By June, according to the war diaries of the 26th Battalion, Private Cormier was with his unit in the area of Reninghelst, Belgium, and on June 28 they relieved the 28th Battalion in the St. Eloi trench sector. Edmond's circumstances-of-death record reveals that, as he was moving with his unit into the trenches that day, he was hit in the head by a bullet and died instantly. Edmond was twenty years old.

Lest We Forget

Private Edmond Cormier is buried at the Reninghelst New Military Cemetery in the village of Reninghelst, Belgium, southwest of Ypres, which remained in use until September 1918. It contains 798 identified casualties.

20. McBean, Guy D. (July 14, 1916)

Private 709840, 104th Battalion

Guy D. McBean was born on October 9, 1895, in Taymouth, New Brunswick, to Ernest McBean and Ella Dennison. According to marriage records, Ernest and Ella were married on September 7, 1892, in Fredericton. Together they had three children: Ray, Angus, and Guy. Although few accounts exist detailing Guy's early life in Taymouth, newspapers suggest that his father owned a family farm in the area. Census records show that a sister-in-law named Isabelle also lived with the family for a short time. After spending much of his childhood working on the family farm, Guy eventually moved to Fredericton just prior to the war. While in the city, he found work as a chauffeur at the York Hotel for Harold Young and Willis McPherson. Still a teenager at the time, Guy appeared to be incredibly well liked by all who knew him in Fredericton. At the time of his formal enlistment for service in Sussex, New Brunswick, on November 23, 1915, Guy had no prior military training. According to his service record, McBean was twenty years old and had blue eyes, brown hair, a fair complexion, and was five feet five inches tall. Along with other young men from the area, he joined the 104th Battalion and soon began training in preparation for going overseas; his brother, Angus, enlisted with the medical corps. Although Guy did not sign a will, all the particulars of his service, including pay and medals, were eventually sent to his parents.

After spending the winter and spring of 1915–16 in Canada training, the 104th left from Halifax on June 28, 1916, aboard the SS *Olympic*, arriving in England on July 6. According to his service record, it appears that, during the trip across the ocean, Guy developed a bacterial infection causing severe soreness and swelling in the throat. Upon arrival he was diagnosed with diphtheria. Immediately admitted for treatment at Moore Barracks Military Hospital at Shorncliffe, Private McBean, according to his medical case sheet, was suffering from nausea and swollen tonsils so severe that he had a temperature of 105° Fahrenheit (40.5°C). After just two days at Moore Barracks Hospital, he was put directly into isolation at Folkestone, where his condition quickly worsened. McBean had the patterned symptoms of diphtheria from the very beginning, which included low-grade fever and swollen neck glands, followed by vomiting. As he suffered over the next seven days, medical personnel could not reverse the infection that had spread so quickly in Guy's body. By July 12, news of his condition had reached Fredericton, where it was revealed that he had been admitted to hospital. Two days later, on July 14, Guy passed away, unable to overcome the toxins that had infected his body. Private McBean had been on active service for less than seven months. He was twenty years old.

Lest We Forget

Private Guy D. McBean is buried at the Shorncliffe Military Cemetery, near Folkestone, England. According to the Commonwealth War Graves Commission, Guy is one of approximately 577 identified casualties in the cemetery from the First and Second World War.

21. Sherman, Laurence Shuster (August 5, 1916)

Private 7933, 7th Battalion, Royal Sussex Regiment, British Army

Laurence Shuster Sherman was born on November 9, 1884, in Fredericton to Louis Walsh Sherman and Alice Maxwell. Louis and Alice married on November 25, 1868, in Fredericton at Christ Church Cathedral. In addition to Laurence, the couple had five other children: Francis, Myra, Bessie, Stella, and Ralph. Records also suggest that a daughter, Mary, passed away shortly after birth. Their father, Louis, originally came from the United States and worked as a lumber merchant in the area. When the children were young, he abandoned the family, leaving Alice alone to raise the children along with the help of the eldest sibling, Francis. Census records suggest that, despite these setbacks, the children in the family continued to receive a good education. Myra and Bessie eventually became schoolteachers, while Francis was a well-known poet in the area. Laurence also attended school and was a member of the Christ Church community. When old enough, Laurence entered the banking business and became a branch manager for the Royal Bank of Canada in Fredericton and later in Halifax.

By the time war broke out in 1914, Laurence was already at the London office of the Royal Bank. The *Moncton Daily Times* reported that, on April 3, he had gone home for a few days before leaving from Halifax to return overseas. Although he had no previous military training, his professional skills were useful and needed to help organize the military effort in England. On September 23, 1915, Laurence formally enlisted for service with the Royal Sussex Regiment. Since this was a British unit, fewer documents remain that outline the specific details of his service and limited information regarding his general health and a description of his physical appearance. Newspaper accounts suggest, however, that Laurence had trouble getting admitted for service at first because of a series of operations that left him quite fragile; as the war went on, he was finally accepted for service.

Corporal Sherman remained in England for approximately eight months before going to France with the 7th Battalion of the Royal Sussex Regiment in May 1916. According to the regiment's official diaries, the 7th Battalion was deployed near Albert, France, for much of 1916 preparing for the Somme battles that began on July 1. The series of battles on the Somme took place between July and November and became one of the bloodiest and costliest periods for both the Allied and German armies. On the first day alone, the British suffered more than 57,000 casualties; before the Somme battles ended, they had more than 1.5 million casualties. In late July, the 7th Battalion and Corporal Sherman were in the frontline trenches near Pozières Ridge, tasked with resuming a failed attack on German trench strongpoints from the previous day. According to the war diaries, German positions were strongly held by machine guns that units had difficulty overcoming. At some point in early August, during a series of bloody attacks on these machine guns and trenches by the 7th Battalion, Corporal Sherman was wounded and evacuated to Boulogne for medical treatment. Laurence's condition worsened, and on August 5 he passed away. He was thirty-one years of age.

On August 9, news of his death was received at home, and friends and family paid their respects to "Laurie," as he was known in Fredericton. According to the *Daily Gleaner*, a letter had recently been received by Laurence dated July 22, describing the close calls he had during attacks on Pozières Ridge. At the time of his death, Laurence was unmarried and left all his possessions to his eldest brother, Francis.

22. Burns, Isaac Stephen (August 17, 1916)

Private 478824, The Royal Canadian Regiment, 193rd Battalion
(Nova Scotia Highlanders)

Isaac Stephen Burns was born on July 10, 1872, in Saint John to Daniel and Francis Burns. According to newspapers, Isaac had a brother named John, who eventually moved to Los Angeles, California. Very little else is known about Isaac's upbringing in Saint John other than that he and his family grew up in the Methodist faith. Records illustrate that Isaac was

a well-respected soldier and military man prior to the First World War, having enlisted in The Royal Canadian Regiment (RCR) at the age of just thirteen in 1884. Newspapers highlight a young man that would become very active with the RCR. When the unit was stationed in Fredericton, he became a

Family memorial of Private Isaac S. Burns,
Nashwaaksis Douglas Rural Cemetery.
Brent Wilson

member of the brass band, playing the cymbals and bass drum. He also became a star baseball player. He met a young woman during his time in Fredericton named Elizabeth Ridland. Born into a Scottish Methodist family, Elizabeth was living in Nashwaaksis with her family at the time. They married on September 25, 1895, in Fredericton, and over the next eleven years they had five children named Agnes, Victoria, Ellen, Annie, and William Arthur. Known as "Bobby" to his friends, Isaac and his family moved to Halifax in 1905, where he was stationed with the RCR at the Wellington Barracks until the outbreak of the war in 1914. He formally enlisted November 22, 1915, in Halifax with the RCR. Although he was a well-respected soldier at the time, because he was forty-four years old he remained stationed in Canada. Private Burns was five feet six inches tall, weighed 172 pounds, and had a medium complexion, brown eyes, and black hair.

Private Burns remained with the RCR in Halifax from November 1915 until the spring of 1916, when he transferred to the 193rd Battalion (Nova Scotia Highlanders). By late April, Isaac was admitted to the Rockhead Military Hospital in Halifax where doctors initially diagnosed him with "chronic indigestion." According to medical records, by July doctors had performed surgery and found him to be suffering from gastric cancer in his stomach. After hearing that nothing could be done for his condition and although doctors advised him to continue treatment at the hospital, Private Burns discharged himself on July 31 to be with his wife and family. Isaac passed away less than a month later on August 17, 1916, surrounded by family.

One day after his death, the *Daily Gleaner* reported the news of his body being transferred to Fredericton in preparation for his funeral, which would occur the afternoon of August 30 at the home of his brother-in-law, David Gorman. Isaac was buried soon after with full military honours, led by the pipe band of the 236th Battalion and a firing party from the No. 8 Field Ambulance, Canadian Army Medical Corps, from Saint John. The New Brunswick Kilties also attended while returned soldiers from Europe acted as pall bearers. Private "Bobby" Burns was buried in the Ridland family plot in Nashwaaksis. He was forty-five years old.

23. Findley, Sidney (September 7, 1916)

Private 22568, 12th Battalion, 14th Battalion (Royal Montreal Regiment)

Sidney Findley was born on September 10, 1896, in Birmingham, England, to Charles Findley and Letitia Maria Turner. While there are few details of their marriage, Charles's military record shows that they wed on July 22, 1896, just before the birth of Sidney. Census records reveal that Sidney had two siblings, a sister and a brother. The 1901 England and Wales census also indicates that Sidney's early upbringing was in Birmingham at the Turner family residence at 119 Barr Street. By the spring of 1908, Sidney had been sent to Halifax from Liverpool aboard the SS *Carthaginian* through the Middlemore Children's Emigration Homes program. He was twelve years old. Little is known about the circumstances of his upbringing and why Sidney would leave England, especially since documents highlight that his father worked as a jeweller and was a veteran of the South African War. By 1911 Sidney found himself living in New Brunswick employed as a domestic work hand for Charles and Alice Ross, of Nashwaak Bridge, who later lived at 246 Queen Street in Fredericton. In addition to having Sidney in the home, the Ross family had a daughter named Pearl. According to Sidney's attestation paper, he was only seventeen years old when he enlisted in the Canadian Expeditionary Force at the outbreak of the war. Documents confirm that he was working as a farmer in the area and that he had no prior military experience.

Sidney Findley's name is found on the Vimy Memorial to Canadian soldiers who have no known grave in France. James Rowinski

Along with other Fredericton soldiers, Findley left with the 71st Regiment contingent in the fall of 1914 under the leadership of Lieutenant-Colonel Harry F. McLeod and joined the 12th Battalion at Valcartier, Quebec, where he began training in preparation for going overseas. Standing approximately five feet six inches tall, Sidney had hazel eyes, light brown hair, and a swarthy complexion. It is unclear if he ever saw friends from the area again.

On October 4, 1914, Private Findley embarked from Valcartier aboard the SS *Scotian* for England. Upon arrival, Sidney remained with the 12th Battalion over the winter of 1914–15 for training, perhaps also having an opportunity to visit his family for the first time in eight years. Records indicate that both his father and brother were also serving with British units in Egypt, while his mother worked as a Royal Nursing Sister in England. By February 1915, Private Findley had left England and, like Charles Parkinson, transferred to the 14th Battalion and made his way to northern France and the Ypres Salient. Few details reveal his exact location during the next six months, but the 14th Battalion was engaged in battles at Festubert and Ypres, making it likely that he was fighting there as well. The spring and summer of 1915 was an active period of trench warfare and the introduction of poisonous gas brought added stress to conditions the soldiers faced. For Private Findley, any opportunity to find a break from the front was important. In late November 1915, Sidney was granted a week-long leave of absence to England. Upon his return to the front, he found himself in trouble for being absent from his billets, forfeiting three days' pay, and receiving Field Punishment No. 1 for approximately ten days. A few months later, Sidney was admitted to hospital suffering from German measles, and remained in treatment for two months. In July, he attended a grenade course at the Canadian Divisional Training School in preparation for key battles he would be part of when the Somme offensive began. Perhaps sensing that something significant would happen, Sidney signed his will on August 8, leaving everything to his mother in England.

On September 3, the Canadian Corps took over a section of the Somme front near Pozières Ridge. According to his circumstances-of-death record and the battalion's official war diary, Sidney was with the 14th Battalion on September 7 defending against enemy counterattacks when he was killed instantly. In the ferocity of repeated attacks that followed, his body was never found. On October 3, news of his death was reported in the *Daily Gleaner*. The article stated that a letter had been received at home just prior to the news of Sidney's death in which he told his mother that he "would be home soon" on leave to see her again. News was also received by the family that his father, Charles, and a brother had been injured in engagements they had taken part in. Twenty-year-old Sidney left behind his family in England as well as friends and loved ones in Fredericton.

Lest We Forget

Private Sidney Findley is honoured on the Vimy Memorial overlooking the Douai Plain from the highest point of Vimy Ridge, about eight kilometres northeast of Arras. It was designed by Canadian sculptor W.S. Alward to remember all Canadians who served during the First World War and particularly to the sixty thousand who gave their lives in France. The memorial also bears the names of eleven thousand Canadians who died in France and have no known grave.

24. Beatty, Frank S. (September 9, 1916)

Gunner/Private 85687, 23rd Battery, 12th Reserve Battalion,
2nd Battalion (Eastern Ontario Regiment)

Frank S. Beatty was born on August 13, 1896, in Fredericton to Charles Malcolm Beatty and Harriet Booker. The couple had five sons and one daughter: in addition to Frank, born the second-youngest in the family, were their daughter, Edith, the eldest child, followed by George, Henry, Ernest, and Archie. The 1911 census reveals that, prior to the First World War, George, Henry, and Edith were no longer living at their home at 322 Smythe Street in Fredericton. Little is known specifically of Frank's early life living in Fredericton; however, birth records show that his father was from Iron Bound Cove, Queen's County, New Brunswick, and was working as a blacksmith in Fredericton while raising his family. Born into a working family, with roots in the Baptist Church, it is likely that Frank was taught the importance of education and work, and so it is not surprising that, as a teenager attending school, he volunteered for three years with the local 71st York Regiment before enlisting for overseas service in the winter of 1914. According to newspapers, all five brothers joined up at some point during the war. Although Frank was only seventeen years old at the time, he was likely eager to do so, formally enlisting on December 2, 1914, in Fredericton with the 23rd Field Battery. The *Daily Gleaner* reveals that his older brother, George, enlisted with the 12th Battalion, and spent time in London with the Army Postal Service. Henry and Ernest enlisted as well, eventually joining Frank overseas, as did their younger brother Archie, who joined the 8th Field Ambulance in Saint John. Their sister, Edith, remained at home in Fredericton throughout the war. Claiming to be eighteen years old on his attestation paper, Frank, still a boy in many ways, was described as having a blond complexion, blue eyes, and brown hair. Records indicate that he would never marry, and it appears likely that he never saw his family again before going overseas.

Gunner Beatty trained with the 23rd Field Battery, 6th Canadian Field Brigade for a few months before leaving with his unit on February 23, 1915, for England. After arriving at Shorncliffe Camp, Frank transferred to the 12th Reserve Battalion, the same unit his brother George belonged to, and he would spend the next twelve months training. Given his age and also that he had been reunited with his older brother, Frank took part in many of the questionable activities frowned upon by society at the time. In the fall of 1915, he admitted himself to St. Martin's Hospital at Shorncliffe for treatment of a viral infection affecting many soldiers who were away from home for the first time. For impressionable, young, unmarried men, especially with money in their pockets, these experiences were common. Given Frank's young age, his medical record simply highlights the coping decisions of a teenager, away from home with his brothers, and how he may have been trying to fit in. On two separate occasions, he would be reprimanded for small violations while on duty, including being out of his billets while at the front and for interfering with a military officer in England. All these examples appear to paint a picture of a young teenager doing his best to deal with a difficult period of time.

Eventually, Frank joined the 2nd Battalion (Eastern Ontario Regiment) and on March 9, 1916, he arrived at Le Havre, France, with his unit. According to newspapers, his brothers Henry and Ernest also joined the 2nd Battalion during the summer of 1916 as preparations began for the Somme battles. By late August, Frank's unit had moved into the area of Pozières Ridge, near Courcelette, where 1st Division of the Canadian Corps held a three-thousand-yard (2.7 kilometre) front of trenches that had been ruined by fighting over the previous two months. Between September 3 and 11, Frank and his brothers were involved in fighting for control of Pozières Ridge, and many men of the 2nd Battalion who were involved in extensive bombing raids of enemy trenches were killed or wounded when their supply of grenades was gone. On September 9, Frank survived a frontal attack he was a part of near Courcelette, but then a German machine gun opened fire on his position, killing him instantly. Records show that Frank had just celebrated his nineteenth birthday in the trenches. While there were witnesses to his death, his body was never recovered. Newspapers reporting his death on September 22 in Fredericton reveal a family of brothers dedicating their lives to service for their country. While Frank would not survive the Somme battles, his brothers Ernest and Henry made it through, as did George and Archie. Their mother, Harriet Booker, passed away during the winter of 1920, never having had a chance to receive Frank's medals or being able to visit where her son would eventually be honoured.

Lest We Forget

Private Frank S. Beatty is remembered on the Vimy Memorial in Vimy, France. According to the Commonwealth War Graves Commission, the highest point of Vimy Ridge was the chosen location for a memorial to all Canadians who served for Canada during the First World War.

25. King, Laughlin Donaldson (September 14, 1916)

Private 101189, 66th Battalion, 8th Battalion

Laughlin Donaldson King was born on March 4, 1888, in Fredericton to Elizabeth McDonald and Edward Myles King. Elizabeth and Edward both came from the Sheffield area and married on April 24, 1871. According to census records, Laughlin had four siblings named Lillian, John, Edward, and Lee. Documents reveal that the King family lived in Fredericton for most of Laughlin's upbringing at 269 Charlotte Street. His father worked as a lumberman throughout New Brunswick and Quebec, and Elizabeth kept their home and raised their children. While few details illustrate his early life, in September of 1895 tragedy struck the family. The Fredericton *Daily Gleaner* reports that, while away in Saint-Magloire, Quebec, for work with his brother Fred, Edward suffered an accidental self-inflicted gunshot wound after falling in the woods. Fred and Edward had gone deer hunting approximately 95 kilometres into the woods of

Saint-Magloire when Edward tripped causing his gun to misfire. He died shortly afterwards. Accounts suggest that the family had been planning to move to Quebec so that everyone could be closer while Edward was working in the woods. As a result of Edward's death, the family remained in Fredericton, where Laughlin found work as a cook and underwent military training with the 71st Regiment. Eventually he left New Brunswick altogether and went out west, where, according to newspapers, the family lost contact with him for about ten years until the outbreak of the war. At the time of his enlistment in the 66th Battalion in Edmonton on September 8, 1915, Laughlin was twenty-seven years old, unmarried, and working as a cook. He had blue eyes, fair hair, a blond complexion, and was five feet eleven inches tall. Private King remained in Edmonton for training over the winter of 1915–16 while his unit made final preparations to go overseas. Records show that his brother, Lee, also enlisted. It is unclear if Laughlin ever saw friends and family from Fredericton again.

On April 28, 1916, Private King embarked from Halifax aboard the SS *Olympic* for England. Upon arrival, Laughlin transferred to the 8th Battalion, and by June 29 he had landed in France after less than a month of training in England. He was arriving at an important time in the war as the Allies were preparing for the upcoming Battle of the Somme. Canadian units were not brought into key phases of the Somme battles until September. Information on Laughlin's specific movements after arriving with the 8th Battalion on the Somme is very limited. By September, Laughlin was near Puchevillers when, according to his circumstances-of-death record, he received a gunshot wound to the abdomen that medical staff could not treat. On September 14, he passed away at No. 3 Casualty Clearing Station. News of his death was reported in the *Daily Gleaner* a week later confirming that he had succumbed to wounds after only a few months on the front line. He left behind four siblings and his medals went to his brother, Lee. Laughlin was thirty-one years of age at the time of his death.

Private Laughlin Donaldson King is buried at Puchevillers British Cemetery, in Puchevillers, France. According to the Commonwealth War Graves Commission, he is one of 1,756 identified casualties in this cemetery.

26. Charnley, John William (September 15, 1916)

Lance Corporal 445278, 55th Battalion, 42nd Battalion
(Royal Highlanders of Canada)

John William "Morris" Charnley was born on December 9, 1891, in Bacup, Lancashire, England, to Elizabeth Charnley; there are few details of John's father, who passed away when John was young. According to the 1901 census of England and Wales, Elizabeth was left a widow at the age of thirty-four to raise five children: in addition to John, there were Mary, Tom, Joseph, and William. At the time, it appears that John's paternal grandparents, William and Alice, were living with them as well. Although details are missing of his early family life, it appears that, when the children were old enough, everyone in the home worked as weavers in the local cotton mill. Over time, John became close friends with five siblings named Morris who were also working at the cotton mill. Their parents, Robert and Ellen Morris, had moved to Bacup with their large family of twelve children, some of the eldest of whom—Robert Jr., Lillian, Albert, Henry, and Edward—were John's good friends. In 1912, the Morris family decided to move to Canada to work in cotton mills in this country. Family records reveal that John asked if he could go along with the boys who had become like family to him. The Morris family agreed, and they left England for Canada in 1912, just after the sinking of the *Titanic*. They settled initially in Cornwall, Ontario, then Montreal in 1913, before arriving at Marysville in early 1914. According to newspaper accounts, the arrival of such a large family to the area looking for work at the Marysville Cotton Mill drew much interest. The Morris brothers found work at the mill, while their father was employed as a shoemaker at the H.S. Campbell shoe factory. The family attended Christ Church Cathedral

By this time, John had been adopted into the Morris family and, given how close he was to the boys, he was considered a son by Robert and Ellen. John also became incredibly close to Lillian. According to family stories, just prior to the outbreak of war, John and Lillian had fallen in love and had begun plans to marry. After Canada entered the war, John promised Lillian that they would get married when he returned from overseas. This promise is confirmed by John's naming "my Lillian Morris" as his beneficiary in his will and on his medal card showing her as his fiancée.

In July 1915, John, Robert, and Albert all went to Sussex to enlist with the 55th Battalion. Newspapers at the time confirm that their younger brother, Henry, had already enlisted the previous year and had been sent overseas. According to his attestation paper, John had blue eyes, light brown hair, a fair complexion, and was five feet eight inches tall. He was twenty-three years old. Over the next few months, the Morris brothers divided their time between training in preparation for overseas duty and spending time with family in Fredericton and Marysville.

On October 30, Lance Corporal Charnley left from Montreal for England aboard the SS *Corsican*. After more than a week at sea, John arrived with his unit on November 9. Less than a month later, he was admitted to the Canadian Convalescent Hospital in Bear Wood, Berkshire, suffering from pneumonia. He remained seriously ill at the Bear Wood facility until early 1916, when doctors finally believed he was healthy enough to be discharged for duty. After recovering, John was transferred to the 42nd Battalion, Royal Highlanders of Canada, and arrived in France on April 15. Like many Canadian units in 1916, the 42nd made its way to the Ypres Salient and northern France during the battles of St. Eloi and Mount Sorrel. By August, however, the Canadian Corps had left for the Somme region to prepare for assaults that began in late summer. During the fighting on the Somme, the Canadians had more than twenty-four thousand casualties. In early September, John and the rest of the Canadian Corps went into positions along a 3,000-metre section of Pozières Ridge, with the 42nd Battalion on the centre-left flank. On September 15, the Corps launched its first major attack on the Somme near the village of Courcelette. That evening, as John was advancing with the 42nd Battalion over open ground toward German trenches, a machine gun opened fire on his position, killing him instantly. Given the intensity of fighting during the Somme, John's body was never recovered. Shortly after his death, on October 2, the *Daily Gleaner* reported the news to the community with great sympathy to the family. By the end of the war, only one of the Morris brothers who had enlisted survived. Robert was killed at Vimy in 1917, and Albert passed away from illness in 1918, shortly after being invalided home. In July 1919, the *Daily Gleaner* reported that the "only survivor of four sons" to return home was Henry, who was suffering from significant shell shock and deafness. Although papers suggested that the Morris family had "reason to feel proud of the part they played...having given three sons for the cause of humanity," family stories reveal parents heartbroken and filled with shock after such a loss. At the time of his death in 1916, John was twenty-four years old. All of his medals went to his fiancée, Lillian.

Researching the life of John Charnley was difficult because his name is incorrectly inscribed on the Fredericton War Memorial as "John W.C. Morris," while Christ Church Cathedral, the Marysville Cenotaph, and Library and Archives Canada have him properly listed as "John Charnley."

Lest We Forget

Private John William "Morris" Charnley is honoured on the Vimy Memorial in Vimy, France.

27. Shaw, Donald Bruce (September 15, 1916)

Private 444587, 55th Battalion, 18th Battalion

Donald Bruce Shaw was born on December 7, 1898, in New Maryland, New Brunswick, to William A. Shaw and Maggie Graham, who had married on January 14, 1844. In addition to Donald, they had six children named William Roy, Irvine, Vera, Lloyd, Betty, and Hazen. The Shaw family had residences both in New Maryland, where they worked their farm, and in Fredericton at 147 Westmorland Street. When not working on the farm, the family attended St. Paul's Church and were active within the community. Given his young age at the outbreak of the war, there are few accounts of Donald's early childhood, which largely revolved around farming and the church. At the time of his enlistment on April 23, 1915, Donald belonged to the local militia. Although only fifteen years old when he joined up in Fredericton with the 55th Battalion, on his attestation paper he claimed to be three years older. He was described as having grey eyes, brown hair, and a dark complexion and was five feet seven inches tall. Newspapers indicate that he was the only one in the family who enlisted, likely because the others in the family were needed to work the farm. Over the spring and summer of 1915, Donald remained in Canada training with the 55th Battalion in preparation for going overseas. According to his service record, just prior to leaving Canada, he was at Valcartier, Quebec, with the 55th Battalion. It is unclear if he saw his family before departing.

On October 30, 1915, Private Shaw left from Montreal aboard the SS *Corsican* for England. He arrived November 9 and, perhaps because of his young age, remained in England for the next seven months until being transferred to the 39th Battalion from eastern Ontario. When a draft was called for in the early summer of 1916 for the 18th Battalion, also from Ontario, Donald went over. On June 28, he arrived in France and then Flanders, just before the opening stages of the Somme battles. Spending July and August in southern Belgium, Donald eventually shifted south and arrived at Albert, France, in September as Canadian divisions were preparing for attacks along Pozières Ridge. According to the official war diary of the 18th Battalion, on September 9 his unit marched to Albert and rested until the opening assault on Courcelette a few days later. On September 14, Private Shaw moved into trench positions as part of the 4th Canadian Infantry Brigade, with his battalion holding the right flank alongside the 20th and 21st Battalions. At 6:24 a.m. on September 15, his unit attacked the German front and achieved its objectives for the day. According to his circumstances-of-death record, at some point during the first day of fighting Donald was killed; his body was never recovered. News of his death reached home in early October. According to his obituary in the *Daily Gleaner* on October 12, it was the first news the family had received at all about Donald since leaving the previous year. At the time of his death, Donald had been overseas for only ten months. He was seventeen years old.

Lest We Forget
Private Donald Bruce Shaw is honoured on the Vimy Memorial located in Vimy, France.

28. Hobkirk, Charles Hamilton (September 16, 1916)

Lieutenant, 71st York Regiment, 64th Overseas Battalion, 25th Battalion (Nova Scotia Rifles)

Charles Hamilton Hobkirk was born on January 2, 1894, in Winnipeg, Manitoba, to Ethel Margaret Dawson and Harry Russell Hobkirk. Documents reveal that Ethel was born in Lancashire, England, while Harry was from Charlottetown, Prince Edward Island. There are few accounts detailing why Harry and Ethel were living in Winnipeg and then Toronto, but the 1891 census shows that Harry was a military instructor when they met. According to census records, Charles had three siblings named Annie, Ray, and Marjorie. Charles, Annie, and Ray were born during their family's time in Winnipeg and Toronto, while Marjorie was born in Fredericton. After being a military instructor in Ontario until 1904, Harry and Ethel moved to Fredericton when he accepted a position with The Royal Canadian Regiment, stationed in the city.

Charles's family lived at 196 Regent Street and, according to newspapers, he was a star football player throughout high school and with other area teams. The 71st York Regiment's records reveal that, in 1909, while still attending school, Charles was a member of the unit. His younger brother, Ray, also joined as a bugler once he was old enough. At the time of his enlistment for overseas service, Charles's attestation paper shows that he was working as a bank clerk for the Royal Bank of Canada at the Fredericton branch. His attestation paper also reveals that, when he enlisted at Sussex on September 15, 1915, with the 64th Battalion, commanded by Lieutenant-Colonel Henry Montgomery-Campbell, he was nineteen years old. He had blue eyes, fair hair, and a fair complexion and his height was six feet one inches, much taller than average for those days. After joining the 64th, he began training in preparation for going overseas. He would never return home.

On March 31, 1916, Lieutenant Hobkirk left from Halifax for Liverpool, England, arriving on April 9. Charles remained with the 64th Battalion over the next few months, preparing to head to the front. He signed his will on July 8, leaving everything to his father. On August 2, Charles transferred to the 25th Battalion (Nova Scotia Rifles) and departed for France a few days later, where he joined his new unit in the field during the Battle of the Somme. Few words reveal the futility and the staggering losses of the First World War like the Somme. In the summer of 1916, the British launched a major offensive against German lines that lasted for months and resulted in approximately one million casualties on both sides. Lieutenant Hobkirk arrived with the 25th Battalion in early September near the village of Courcelette. According to Nicholson's *Official History*, on the morning of September 16, a second attack by the 22nd and 25th Battalions at Courcelette was launched in broad daylight without any jumping-off point. After ten minutes of "smart bayonet fighting," his unit, with the "Fighting 26th" Battalion from Saint John in support, went straight through the town. The 25th came under heavy counterattacks over the next three days and suffered 202 casualties. Details slowly emerged about Charles's death on September 16, as letters and newspapers described him charging like a lion while leading his men. A few weeks after his death, the *Daily Gleaner* published a letter written by a Nova Scotia soldier connected with Hobkirk's unit, describing his bravery that day:

> We passed over our first line and went forward at the double through a hell of fire. But we got through, driving everything before us and dug in about 100 yards the other side of the town. Hobkirk and I raced through the streets pot-potting at fritzes; some of the beggars put up a fight but, in most cases, they put up their hands with "mercy komrade." We bombed their dugouts and captured machine guns and trench howitzers. Our battalion has received the highest praise for the most gallant charge and probably someone will write a more glowing account than I can. We held our trenches till late on the night of the 17th, when we were relieved by another battalion. We lost seventeen officers over three days; five killed, twelve wounded, and about 275 men. Poor old battalion, we made our name but at what a cost. We were twenty-four hours at one time without water and on half rations. Poor Hobkirk, he fell at the head of his platoon, a gallant solider. I can't write about it now.

Charles, only twenty years of age, left behind his parents, siblings, and friends back home.

Lest We Forget

Lieutenant Charles Hamilton Hobkirk is buried at the Courcelette British Cemetery, in Courcelette, France. According to the Commonwealth War Graves Commission, Charles is one of 1,970 fallen soldiers honoured here. The cemetery was designed by Sir Herbert Baker, an architect who designed many of the Western Front memorials.

29. McKnight, Locksley (September 16, 1916)

Lieutenant, 56th Battalion (Calgary), 49th Battalion (Edmonton Regiment)

Locksley McKnight was born on December 30, 1889, in Fredericton to John and Katherine "Kate" McKnight. According to census records, Locksley had two brothers, Ivan and Hilton, as well as a sister, Imogene "Jean." Family stories obtained through the University of New Brunswick reveal that Locksley's early education took place in local Fredericton schools and that he was well regarded in the city as one of the finest student athletes in the area. Although there are few details of his early childhood, as a young man he entered UNB in 1905, graduated in 1909, and later returned to the city in 1911 for additional coursework after becoming principal at the Andover Grammar School. Locksley then took a job at the McCauley School in Edmonton. On his departure from the province, the *Daily Gleaner* spoke highly of Locksley, describing him as "one of the best athletes in the province," a star football and basketball player at UNB, and one of the best in eastern Canada. He continued to do well in Alberta as a teacher, principal, and athlete, later joining the 101st Edmonton Fusiliers prior to the war. On October 18, 1915, he accepted a commission in Calgary with the 56th Battalion (Calgary). In a letter written home and published in the *Daily Gleaner* on November 27, Locksley records: "They gave us a great send-off at Edmonton — wonderful. Had a big shine at the school, presents from my class at the school, the teachers, ex-pupils, the boys at the house, our tennis clubs, the University of Alberta boys and some individual ones. Some of the presents were an engraved wristwatch, an autograph camera, a sword from the teachers, a complete shaving kit, a pair of field glasses, a silver and leather flask, a cane, a dance, dinners, etc. We were certainly well used."

At the time of his enlistment in Calgary, Lieutenant McKnight was twenty-five years old, unmarried, and described as having gray eyes and brown hair, and standing approximately five feet six inches tall. It is unclear if he found the time to return home to Fredericton prior to leaving, but records suggest that the community was keenly aware of everything that was happening in Locksley's life. This spoke to the close relationship he and his family had in the area.

On March 23, 1916, Lieutenant Locksley embarked on the SS *Baltic* in Halifax for England with the 56th Battalion, five months after enlisting in Alberta. According to his service record, after arrival he attended officer training for the next two months. On June 17, Locksley left for France with the 49th Battalion (Edmonton Regiment) just before the beginning of the Battle of the Somme. Over the next two months, he was in charge of a bombing section of the 49th until the Battle of Courcelette. According to his circumstances-of-death report, on the afternoon of September 16,

The ruins of the village of Courcelette during the Battle of the Somme.
LAC/PA-000710

Locksley was leading his unit over open ground to bring reinforcement for companies in the frontline trenches. Eyewitness accounts recalled seeing Lieutenant McKnight hit by sniper fire as he proceeded forward and then fall to the ground. He reportedly died instantly. Accounts from a fellow officer that afternoon, obtained through UNB, offer the following account of his death: "At the last moment, he, along with some other officers, was selected to remain behind as a reserve. Next afternoon, when they learned at headquarters that four out of five officers of 'D' Company were wounded, and that I was the only officer left and had been slightly wounded, they sent Locksley and another officer to help me out. We were in a somewhat isolated position and they had to come across an open space for a short distance. They had just started, when a German machine gun opened on them, killing them both."

News of Locksley's death reached home quickly, as papers reported that both he and another Fredericton resident, Charles Hobkirk, were killed the same day near Courcelette. Lieutenant Locksley McKnight was twenty-seven years old.

Lest We Forget

Lieutenant Locksley McKnight is honoured on the Vimy Memorial in Vimy, France. Despite being honoured on the memorial, records indicate that his body was recovered and buried just west of Courcelette on map location "57d. R.29.a.50.15, Le Sars." It is unclear, however, why it was never removed and reburied in a war cemetery.

30. Montgomery-Campbell, Herbert (October 1, 1916)

Lieutenant, 64th Overseas Battalion, 5th Canadian Mounted Rifles

Herbert Montgomery-Campbell was born on July 11, 1898, in Apohaqui, New Brunswick, to Lieutenant-Colonel Henry Montgomery-Campbell and Laura Winslow. Herbert was the only brother in a large family with four sisters: Margaret, Constance, Florence, and Annette. Although Laura was born in Chatham and Henry came from the Fredericton area, they eventually met and later married on September 10, 1889, in Fredericton surrounded by family and friends. After their marriage, Henry and Laura moved to Apohaqui, where they began an extensive farm, started a family, and became involved in the Sussex region. Prominent in local and political affairs, including as president of the Sussex Cheese and Butter Company, the Sussex Exhibition Company, and the New Brunswick Dairymen's Association, Herbert's father also came from a family with strong military roots, as was true of his mother Laura. In addition to having siblings who became actively involved during the war, the Winslow family was equally prominent in New Brunswick. As a result, the Montgomery-Campbell children grew up learning the skills of farming, tending to farm animals, and the importance of public service; they even learned horseback riding. Herbert's sisters eventually became nurses and served during the war, but his decision eventually to volunteer for service was likely influenced by parents, uncles, and aunts who had a history of active service in the military. Herbert was surrounded by military influences: in addition to his father being the commanding officer of the 8th Hussars and 64th Battalion during the war, an uncle and namesake, Brigadier-General Herbert Montgomery-Campbell, had served during the Boer War and was commanding officer of the British Army's 46th Divisional Artillery. When the war broke out in 1914, Herbert was only a teenager studying at Rothesay Collegiate School; however, the desire to serve proved too great. Although young for service, he left school at the age of seventeen and enlisted on February 5, 1916, with his father's unit, the 64th Battalion, in

Halifax, several months before Charles Hobkirk joined him. Herbert's attestation paper reveals that he had been active with the 81st Hants Regiment, belonged to the Church of England, and stood five feet seven inches tall, having a medium complexion, brown eyes, and brown hair.

On March 31, 1916, two months after enlisting, Lieutenant Montgomery-Campbell left Canada with his father's unit for Liverpool, England. Upon arrival Herbert was immediately placed in isolation suffering from scarlet fever until discharged on April 14. During the next few months, Herbert trained with the 5th Canadian Mounted Rifles (CMR) and eventually landed in France on June 18. Despite reports in local newspapers that he had joined the 4th CMR, his military records suggest otherwise, indicating that he was with the 5th at the front. He arrived just as the Battle of Somme began — three months of brutal fighting designed by the Allies to pull the Germans away from Verdun. Newspapers indicate that the young Herbert celebrated his eighteenth birthday in the trenches.

On the morning of October 1, under a constant drizzling rain, Herbert and his unit were given directions to capture Regina Trench near the village of Courcelette. Although details of his particular whereabouts are not found in his service record, Nicholson's *Official History* provides relevant information. While waiting for Zero Hour, at 3:15 in the afternoon Herbert was in an advanced position being harassed by his own artillery's shells that kept falling short of the German lines. A section of the 4th CMR had been tasked with creating a blockade to seal off the west of the trench while other units of the 4th and 5th CMR were to advance over no-man's-land against heavy machine-gun fire and barbed wire that had not been cut. Nicholson's *Official History* describes how many were killed as they moved forward. According to Herbert's own service record, he was successful in leading his company of the 5th CMR in achieving its objectives at Regina Trench that day, securing and consolidating what he could under repeated counterattacks and machine-gun fire. However, as he was "directing his men and placing himself at all points of danger to encourage them," Lieutenant Montgomery-Campbell was killed instantly alongside other men in the unit he was leading. According to the *Official*

History, all but fifteen from the 4th and 5th CMR positions were either killed or taken prisoner in less than twenty-four hours. Given how much fighting continued in the area, Herbert's body was never recovered.

News of Herbert's death reached newspapers in Saint John and Fredericton two weeks later, sending a wave of "profound sadness" throughout his home community and across the province. Known as a "general favourite" by his school friends and others who knew him, he had been away from Canada for only seven months at the time of his death. He was eighteen years old.

Lest We Forget

Lieutenant Herbert Montgomery-Campbell is remembered with honour on the Vimy Memorial in Vimy, France.

31. Loggie, Purves Primrose (October 2, 1916)

Royal Flying Corps

Purves Primrose Loggie was born on October 1, 1892, in Fredericton to Thomas George Johnston Loggie and Ada J. Purves. George and Ada married in Pictou, Nova Scotia, on January 21, 1880. George worked for the Department of Land and Mines, eventually becoming deputy minister in the department and later became a lieutenant-colonel and commanding officer with the 71st York Regiment. He also received an honorary degree from the University of New Brunswick in 1914. After their marriage, George and Ada moved to Fredericton, where they raised Purves and another son, Gerald. Eight years younger than his brother, Purves likely looked to Gerald as a role model growing up. The children likely had a comfortable and educated upbringing, as the 1901 census indicates that the family also had a domestic servant living with them named Florence Kelly. Gerald graduated from The Royal Military College of Canada in 1905 and became an officer in the Permanent Force. Purves attended the Charlotte Street School between 1898 and 1906 and then Fredericton High School until 1910. While at Fredericton High School, he was an active member of the school's rugby team. All this time the family attended St. Paul's United Church. After graduation, Purves spent one year at UNB before going to McGill University for four years to pursue a degree in mechanical engineering.

After war broke out in 1914, Purves obtained an aviator's certificate from the Curtiss Flying School, and then decided to go to England directly from Canada in the summer of 1915 in the hopes of becoming an aviator with the Royal Flying Corps (RFC). Because Purves made the decision to enlist in England, there is limited information on him. As a result, it is difficult to offer any physical description or details of his personal life in 1915. By all accounts, he appears to have been working his way into a profession much like his father with the New Brunswick provincial government when war was announced. In early August 1915, the *Saint John Standard* reported him as visiting with family in Fredericton before going overseas.

On August 31, 1915, Purves arrived in Liverpool after taking a passenger ship from Montreal. Only twenty-two years old, he became an apprentice at the Vickers-Maxim plant in Denley, England. By December, the *Daily Gleaner* reported that he had become an instructor at the plant and was trying to qualify as an aviator with the RFC. He was one of a handful of Fredericton boys who were either already qualified or in the process of becoming pilots with either the RFC or the Royal Naval Air Service (RNAS). By the middle of 1916, however, Purves had fallen ill and been hospitalized with pneumonia. Hearing this news, both George and Ada left Canada for England to be with their son. Although arriving in time to be with him in England, unfortunately Purves's condition worsened, and he passed away on October 2. He was twenty-three years old. Word of his death reached New Brunswick papers only a few days later, with the *Daily Telegraph*, *St. John Standard*, and *Daily Gleaner* all sharing the shocking news.

Bringing in wounded Canadians on a truck from the Battle of Courcelette.
National Library of Scotland Licence: CC BY 4.0

After arriving home, George and Ada found a way to honour the memory of their son. In February 1917, the University of New Brunswick announced the creation of a scholarship in his name by a generous donation from the family. Known as the Purves Primrose Loggie Scholarship, the grant, awarded annually for $1,500, would be used to support students in the applied sciences at UNB. A few months later, J. Ellis Taylor of Saint John West was the first recipient of the Purves Primrose Loggie Scholarship.

Lest We Forget
Purves Primrose Loggie is buried at East Hill Cemetery, Dartford, England. (No digital record)

32. Goodine, Neils (October 8, 1916)

Private 445588, 55th Battalion, 43rd Battalion

Neils Goodine was born on September 28, 1897, in Cambridge, Massachusetts, to Clement Goodine and Mary White. The 1901 census reveals that, after returning to Canada with his parents shortly after his birth, Neils was the eldest of three brothers, the other two being Cecil and Norman. Records also show that they had a younger sister, Ruth, who was born in 1902; she passed away at just two years of age. Little is known of his early years growing up in Fredericton with his family, but by the time war broke out in 1914, Neils had been working as a stone cutter in the area and records suggest that both his mother and father had passed away.

When Neils formally enlisted on September 1, 1915, in Sussex with the 55th Battalion, his brother Norman was noted as his only next-of-kin, with an address at 475 Brunswick Street, Fredericton. Raised in the Catholic Church and only eighteen years of age, Neils stood five feet six inches tall and had a fair complexion, blue eyes, and brown hair. Neils was not the only brother to enlist: his younger brother Cecil also left for Europe two years after Neils; the youngest brother, Norman, worked with the Western Union office in Fredericton. The young Private Goodine, reported in newspapers as having a "sterling character," would not return home to family and friends.

According to his service record, Neils left Sussex for Camp Valcartier with the 55th Battalion on September 2, 1915, where he trained for two months. On October 30, Private Goodine sailed with his unit from Quebec City for England aboard the SS *Corsican*. They disembarked at Plymouth after a ten-day crossing of the Atlantic Ocean. After spending the winter of 1915–16 with his unit training, by March 24, 1916, Private Goodine had been admitted to Moore Barracks Military Hospital at Shorncliffe suffering from pneumonia. He stayed there for thirty-four days, then was moved to the Monks Horton Convalescent Hospital in Kent, where he was discharged on May 1. By the early summer of 1916, as the Canadians were becoming more active along the Western Front, Private Goodine joined the 43rd Battalion after being with the 17th and 40th Battalions, and left for France on July 29. New Brunswick newspapers report that, throughout the next few months, Neils became more actively involved in the Somme battles. According to his circumstances-of-death record, Neils was part of the 43rd Battalion's attack on Regina Trench, the second attack by Canadians on a strongly held German position in the vicinity of Courcelette. It was after this crippling fighting that Private Goodine was reported missing on October 8. Family and friends hoped that Goodine would eventually be located in a hospital or prison camp, but a year after his disappearance Goodine was officially being presumed killed in action. In the meantime, his brother, Private Cecil Goodine, left for Camp Valcartier with the 236th Battalion a day before news of his brother's death was reported in local papers. Neils was only nineteen years old at the time of his death.

Lest We Forget

Private Neils Goodine is honoured at Regina Trench Cemetery, Grandcourt, France. The cemetery is approximately 1.5 kilometres northwest of Courcelette and contains 1,203 identified casualties.

33. Sears, George (October 8, 1916)

Sergeant 477823, The Royal Canadian Regiment

On January 24, 1890, George H. Sears was born in Sevenoaks, Kent, England, to Joseph Sears and Alice Rachel Southby. According to the 1901 England and Wales census and 1911 census of Canada, Alice and Joseph had seven children in addition to George, named Dorothy, Leonard, Stanley, Nora, Norman, Constance, and Phyllis. Although there are few accounts of their life in England, at some point prior to the war the Sears family settled in Centreville, Carleton County. George, the oldest in the family, eventually moved away to find work, and settled in Fredericton as a labourer. There he met a young woman from Pokiok named Estella Pearl Vennor, and they married on June 18, 1913. By this time George was working odd jobs in the area and had joined The Royal Canadian Regiment (RCR), stationed in Fredericton. His decision to get involved early with the military likely motivated others in his family who also became active with local regiments. When the war began, his father joined the 224th Battalion, while his three brothers all enlisted in different artillery units. For George, although his military record suggests he formally enlisted for overseas service in 1915, his experience began a year before when George and RCR were sent to Bermuda during the first few months of the war. Estella remained in Fredericton during his time away and maintained the home they shared at 100 Lansdowne Street. George eventually returned to Canada with the RCR and formally enlisted for overseas service in Halifax on August 23, 1915. He was described as having hazel eyes, dark brown hair, a fresh complexion, and was five feet nine inches tall. George was twenty-four years old at the time; it is unclear if he saw his wife again before going overseas.

On August 28, Sergeant Sears left Halifax aboard the SS *Olympic* for England. After arriving at Shorncliffe he was, according to his war service record, "severely reprimanded" for being absent for eight days. He received a fine, but George remained with the RCR in late October as they began preparations to go to the Western Front. On November 2, he landed in France and began the trip north toward the Ypres Salient in Belgium. The Canadian Corps, and George, would call this area home for much of 1915–16. Although there are no records of George's writing home to Estella or to his mother Alice, letters from his brothers Leonard and Stanley described well the realities they were facing:

> I suppose you have seen in the papers what the Canadians are doing. If you have a map, you will have a little idea of where we are. Don't look for us to be home too soon. This is a sort of

Kathleen Mavourneen trip we are on now—it may be for years and it may be forever. As you will know by this time, we have been getting it hot, and heavy around here lately, and I think myself lucky that I have still got all my pieces left. We are getting it a little easier now. I can stand it myself, but my poor old horses are nearly all in. We just came through a desperate battle with the Germans without a scratch. I suppose you have read about it all in the papers. I wish you could have heard the artillery fire. I have heard about "screaming shrapnel," and believe me it sounds like a gale of wind shrieking through a million knotholes. It is something fierce the amount of ammunition they are using in this hell-on-earth...I guess this would be a nice country to live in in peace times, but it is not very healthy just now. The death rate is pretty high and very few of them are the result of old age.

By July 1916 the Somme battles had begun in France. Whether in the Ypres Salient or in northern France, the description offered by the Sears brothers reveals much about what they were experiencing and feeling at the time. George's unit, according to accounts from the official war diary of the RCR, was ordered into the trenches in October to relieve the 42nd Battalion near Courcelette. During forward attacks on German trench lines, the RCR experienced difficulties getting through barbed wire that had not been cut by their artillery barrage. During these actions, on October 8, George was initially reported as missing; however, his circumstances-of-death record later officially reported him killed in action after attacks near Courcelette. News that he was missing reached home in late October. By November, his mother had become so desperate for information that she looked to the *St. John Daily Telegraph* "in the hope that some member of his unit at the front may get a copy of the paper and thus give her some details regarding him." More than a year would go by before official word reached home confirming that George's body had been located and identified. He was twenty-six at the time of his death.

34. McAdam, James Murray (October 12, 1916)

Gunner 85752, 23rd Field Battery, 8th Field Battery, 12th Field Battery

James Murray McAdam was born on November 25, 1894, in Fredericton to James A. McAdam and Annie Murray. While few reports detail his parents' early life together, according to census records, James came from a large family, including eight siblings named Alex, Walter, Kenneth, Wallace, Kathleen, Archie, Daisy, and Donald. By all accounts, the McAdam family was very well known in Fredericton, as James's father was the local undertaker and owner of a prominent funeral home business. For most of their lives, the family lived at 522 George Street, a heritage home that still stands today across from the Old Burial Ground. Newspapers record that James was one of the city's best-known young men and a fine athlete, "prominent in football, baseball, hockey, and basketball, and his genuine qualities were generally appreciated by his friends and acquaintances." In addition to being active in athletics, cadets, and his local church, James eventually found work as a clerk with the Bank of Nova Scotia in the city.

When war broke out in 1914, he immediately resigned his position when his employer would not grant him leave to serve with the Canadian Expeditionary Force. At the time of his enlistment in Fredericton on December 4, 1914, with the 23rd Field Battery, James was described as single and twenty years of age. According to his attestation paper, he had brown eyes, brown hair, and a blond complexion, while standing approximately five feet nine inches tall. He was not the only McAdam brother to enlist, as newspapers reveal that his brothers Walter and Alex served as well. James spent the next three months training in Canada before preparing to go overseas during the winter of 1914–15. It is unclear if he ever saw his brothers while fighting overseas, but records suggest that he never returned to Fredericton.

On February 23, 1915, Gunner McAdam left Canada for England with the 23rd Battery, 6th Brigade, arriving approximately a week later. Shortly after, he made his way to Shorncliffe, where medical records show that he was admitted to St. Andrews Hospital on March 23 to remove swollen glands in his throat. Records reveal that he spent almost two months in hospital before joining a draft going to France in late May. By June McAdam had transferred to the 8th Battery, 2nd Brigade, and was with his unit in northern France and the Ypres Salient. Over the next ten months, James stayed active with the 8th Battery until April 1916, when his personnel record reveals that he was wounded by shrapnel fire during the Battle of St. Eloi. Details of the injury reported in the *Daily Gleaner* indicate that he was "one of six men who were wounded while attending the same gun during a heavy bombardment by the Germans," and James was seen carrying a wounded comrade to a dressing station when he received his wounds. After his injury on April 21, McAdam was sent to England to convalesce until being deemed physically fit to return to the field on July 12. He returned to France a few weeks after the beginning of the Battle of the Somme, now serving with the 12th Field Battery, and stayed with them over the summer of 1916 in Belgium until Canadian units were ordered south to the Somme region. According to his circumstance-of-death record, James was killed during active engagements north of Pozières on October 12. While limited information exists to explain the particulars of his death, newspapers reported the McAdam family's loss a few weeks later, offering sympathetic words on behalf of the community. James was twenty-two years old. His brother Walter enlisted the day after James's death and was killed a year later while fighting at Passchendaele in 1917.

35. Kitchen, Stewart (November 6, 1916)

Sergeant 85736, 23rd Field Battery, 48th Howitzer Battery

Stewart Edward Kitchen was born in Fredericton on February 20, 1895, to Harry Allen Kitchen and Susan Annie Porter. Harry, who was from the Prince William area, and Susan, who was born in what is now Miramichi, were married on March 9, 1888, in Fredericton in front of friends and family. In addition to Stewart, there were two older brothers, Gordon and Roy. Newspaper accounts indicate that Stewart had a younger sister named Pearl; however, there no records of her birth. The Kitchens lived in the Parish of Kingsclear, outside Fredericton, and Stewart was educated in local schools before entering the University of New Brunswick as a forestry student. Apart from these limited pieces of information, very few details exist of Stewart's early life in the area. By the time he enlisted in the 23rd Battery on December 2, 1914, with a number of other university students, he was twenty years old and had three years of cadet corps training, ensuring he was not completely unprepared for the harshness ahead. According to his attestation paper, Stewart was a relatively short young man standing five feet four and half inches tall, weighing 130 pounds, and had brown hair, blue eyes, and a blond complexion. Stewart belonged to the Baptist Church and was unmarried. After enlisting, Sergeant Kitchen left for Valcartier with his unit in preparation for overseas duty. He remained in Canada for another two months before leaving for England; it is unclear if he ever saw his family again.

According to his service record, Sergeant Kitchen sailed for England with his unit on February 23, 1915, and held in reserve at Shorncliffe for the next few months. At the end of May, Stewart was drafted to France with the 48th Howitzer Battery, 2nd Brigade, Canadian Field Artillery as a reinforcement. He remained in the field for almost a year until receiving a ten-day leave of absence to England in January 1916. This might have been his first real chance to relax since arriving in Europe. According to his active service form, on January 25, 1916, he returned from leave to his battery, where he remained for the next eight months until being attached to 1st Canadian Divisional Train, Canadian Army Service Corps on September 28, 1916. After a short period in the fall of 1916, Stewart "ceased to be attached," and rejoined the 48th Battery soon after in the Somme region. As the Somme battles continued, Stewart was active as a gunner near Albert for the month of October. On November 6, it is believed that Stewart was repairing a dugout nearby his position during a lull in fighting when an enemy shell fell close by, killing him instantly. Newspapers reveal that he was the third UNB student to have sacrificed his life for his country and that he was one of the most popular young men in college. At the time of his death, Stewart was twenty-two years old.

Lest We Forget

Sergeant Stewart Kitchen is buried in the Bapaume Post Military Cemetery, Albert, France. The cemetery was designed by well-known architect Charles Henry Holden. According to the Commonwealth War Graves Commission, the cemetery contains 410 burials of First World War soldiers, 181 of them still unidentified. The cemetery lies on two hills, which at the time were called Tara Hill and Usna Hill. Bapaume Post Military Cemetery is on the west side of Tara Hill and the southwest side of Usna Hill. These hills within the town of Albert fell into German hands from March to August 1916.

36. Hanning, James Talmage (November 27, 1916)

2nd Lieutenant, No. 9 Squadron, Royal Flying Corps

James Talmage Hanning was born on February 15, 1887, in New Maryland to James Hanning Sr. and Jane McElveny. There is limited information on when James and Jane married, but census records reveal that they had five children: besides Talmage, there were John Edward, Mary, Robert, and Bessie. In 1886, at age nine, Bessie fell ill with diphtheria and passed away. Their father followed five years later from heart failure, leaving Jane a widow raising four children. After her husband's death, the family took up residence in Fredericton on Charlotte Street, where Jane ran a local store, and later at 217 St. John Street. In 1895, according to the *Daily Gleaner*, to her friends' surprise, Jane married James Bird, a former city councillor and lumberman in the area. All of Jane's children attended local schools as well as St. Paul's Presbyterian Church. After graduating from Fredericton High School, Talmage attended the University of New Brunswick, where he qualified as a civil engineer and land surveyor before moving out west to work on the Canadian Pacific Railway. Talmage then went on to work for the CPR, and newspapers suggest that he was part of the early developments in Canadian aviation, managing proposed flight projects across the Atlantic Ocean prior to the war. When war broke out in 1914, his skills as an engineer and aviation expert made him a good fit for the Royal Flying Corps (RFC). While still out west, Talmage, or "Tal" as his brother called him, went to Ottawa for a meeting with Colonel Guthrie, and was quickly granted an opportunity to obtain a commission in the RFC. Before going overseas, Talmage visited his hometown and family one last time in early 1916.

Hanning paid his own way to England on a passenger ship and enlisted in the RFC on January 15, 1916, at the age of twenty-seven. According to RFC records, he had brown hair, brown eyes, and a medium complexion and stood five feet ten inches tall. Tal's brother, Edward, also enlisted, choosing to serve as a signaller with the Canadian Engineers before joining the RFC. He received the Military Cross for actions during the war. Prior to the war, Edward had graduated from the Provincial Normal School as a teacher and had taught in St. Stephen and schools out west prior to enlisting.

Although there are few official records of his active service during the war because Talmage had enlisted with the RFC, not the Canadian Expeditionary Force, newspapers offer important details of his time while overseas. As the Battle of the Somme began in early July 1916, Tal was active in artillery observation and reconnaissance missions in the air, and continued this work until the Somme ended in November. Late that month, the plane he was flying in went missing behind German lines. Newspaper articles reported him as missing, but months went by before Tal's brother, Edward, wrote home explaining to his mother what had happened and why:

> I have made many enquiries about Tal all the time from every pilot and observer that I have met. I had at last met an observer who was in No. 9th squadron and also in Tal's flight. (The squadrons are divided into flights). He was a great friend to both Tal and Strauss and the news he has is anything but good. I hesitated to write the news to you. He has no definite news but has made enquiries everywhere after the machine failed to return and finally found a major who was in an observation post, observing for the artillery at the time. This major saw the machine come down, and from the way it fell they gave up hope for them as a wing fell off the machine. One of the officers in the machine was seen to fall out. He was supposed to be the observer as he would not be strapped in. There is no doubt of the observer's fate and has been reported officially killed. It looks very much as if there was not a chance in the world for Tal. I did not want to write this, but when your letter arrived saying to let you know at once even if I got bad news. I decided to write all I have found out. Tal went out on military observation that morning and after having a few hours over the German lines, he returned to the aerodrome, reporting

that it was impossible to see the target owing to the low clouds. Although it was a rotten day, and everybody realized that it was an impossible day, he was sent out again in the afternoon. Tal apparently decided to do the work at all costs and came down to a low altitude, about 1000 feet, and the machine was brought down by a machine gun fire from the ground. It fell close to the German frontline trenches. The wreckage of the machine was found when the British advanced, but the ground was so torn up with shell fire that no information could be got from it. I have had strong hopes for Tal, mainly owing to your dreams of him being alive, but the news does not look at all good.

This observer had flown with Tal many times and said that he had the reputation of being their stoutest pilot. On one occasion a six-inch shell passed through the tail of his machine, carrying away half of the tail, but in spite of the fact that the machine was almost unmanageable, he continued on till his work was finished before returning. One of the observers won a Military Cross with a bar to it while flying as Tal's observer, so Tal must have done at least as much as he did. But Tal is just the sort to give the other fellow all the glory. Another time this observer that I met was flying next to Tal's machine in a bombarding raid on a German, just behind their lines. They came under heavy shell fire and four shells burst together, almost making a direct hit on Tal's machine. He saw it go into a spinning nosedive straight for earth and supposed that Tal and Strauss were done for, but shortly after reaching the aerodrome, they came in with a riddled machine, but uninjured. Tal had succeeded in getting it under control again.

If Tal is gone mother, you have the satisfaction of knowing that he has been able to kill several hundred Huns besides getting valuable information. There is of course the slimmest chance that he may have landed without being killed, but it is really a very slight one. I am trying to get the name and address of the Major who saw it and expect to be able to, although this observer has forgotten it. I will then write him and get his story in full.

I certainly don't like to write this letter, but I believe it would be your wish that I do so. But you must look on it from the brighter side, whether Tal is alive or dead he has done much more than most people do in a lifetime and he had done it well.

According to details received from his brother's letter and RFC reports, 2nd Lieutenant James Talmage Hanning was killed by machine-gun fire at 2:40 p.m. on November 27, 1916, while carrying out a reconnaissance mission at a very low altitude behind German lines in the area of Bapaume, France. Tal was twenty-seven years old and unmarried. His body was never recovered.

Lest We Forget

2nd Lieutenant James Talmage Hanning is honoured on the Arras Flying Service Memorial, near Arras, France. According to the Commonwealth War Graves Commission, he is one of approximately 1,000 airmen of the Royal Naval Air Service, the Royal Flying Corps, the Australian Flying Corps, and the Royal Air Force from the First World War killed on the Western Front and who have no known grave. (No digital record)

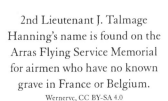

2nd Lieutenant J. Talmage Hanning's name is found on the Arras Flying Service Memorial for airmen who have no known grave in France or Belgium.
Wernervc, CC BY-SA 4.0

Canadian machine-gun crews at Vimy. LAC/PA- 001017

Chapter Three

1917

The Canadian Corps continued offensive operations on the Western Front throughout 1917. In April, the Canadians captured Vimy Ridge in a costly battle. In the second half of August, they took Hill 70 and the city of Lens. Then, near the end of October, they were drawn into the Third Ypres campaign, where, in a series of hard-fought attacks over treacherous ground, they captured the ruined town of Passchendaele and surrounding high ground, whereupon offensive operations were suspended in Belgium for the winter. Heavy casualties and declining voluntary enlistment compelled the Borden government to introduce conscription in August, which caused serious political division within the country.

37. White, Walter James (January 23, 1917)

Private 477991, 71st York Regiment, 12th Battalion, The Royal Canadian
Regiment, 7th Canadian Trench Mortar Battery

Walter James White was born on December 7, 1895, in Fredericton to James and Bertha White. According to newspaper records, his father was a member of the militia's 71st Regiment and became the bandmaster of the 12th Battalion after he enlisted for overseas service, illustrating the likely influence of the military on Walter at a young age. Although few accounts detail Walter's early life in Fredericton, records show that he lived with his brother George and his parents in a house on Campbell Street before the family moved to 258 Brunswick Street. When Walter was old enough, he worked as a printer for the local newspaper and was a member of the 71st Regiment. He was also reportedly an accomplished clarinet player in his spare time and attended the Roman Catholic Church in Fredericton. His service record shows that Walter stood five feet three inches tall, weighed 116 pounds, and had blue eyes, blond hair, and fair skin. He completed training in Valcartier with the 12th Battalion in the late summer of 1914, then went to Bermuda with The Royal Canadian Regiment (RCR). Upon his return to Canada in July 1915, Walter signed up for overseas service with others in the RCR in Halifax, and left for England aboard a passenger ship a few days later. His younger brother George had also decided to enlist at the tender age of fifteen as a bugler around the same time. Walter was twenty years old and single.

In early September 1915, Private White arrived in England with the RCR and trained at Salisbury Plain with other Canadians until November. Almost immediately after arriving, Walter was given "168 hours of detention for not complying with orders," the likely result of difficult conditions for Canadians waiting to go to the Western Front. Although many soldiers throughout the war succumbed to a variety of illnesses and diseases or had extended periods of hospitalization, others endured training and bided their time in local communities. Receiving an admonishment or punishment was not uncommon for soldiers waiting to get into the fight.

On November 2, Walter left for France with the 7th Canadian Trench Mortar Battery and arrived in the Arras region. His records appear to indicate that he stayed in this area for more than a year, likely shifting north into southern Belgium to support actions when ordered. His medical records show that, in April 1916, Walter spent time in hospital getting treatment for German measles and then again in May for a sprained ankle. Overall, his service record does not reveal significant injuries reported early in the war.

The set-piece battles of the Somme devastated both the Germans and Allies in the late summer and autumn of 1916, but Private White was one of the lucky ones to make it through to the winter of 1916–17. Only weeks into the new year, however, on January 23, 1917, Walter was near Neuville-Saint-Vaast with his unit, just southwest of Vimy and north of Arras, when a bomb exploded near his position, killing him instantly. He was twenty-two years of age and left everything to his mother, Bertha. Writing home to family, his cousin, Private Harold White, shared how Walter died.

Lest We Forget

Private Walter White is buried and remembered with honour at the Ecoivres Military Cemetery in Mont-Saint-Éloi, France, which contains 1,728 Commonwealth burials from the First World War.

38. McManamin, E. Francis (March 17, 1917) Military Medal

Private 22611 (CEF)/720423 (BEF), 12th Battalion, 1st Dorset Regiment,
7th Battalion, Royal Munster Fusiliers

E. Francis McManamin was born on April 2, 1883, in Fredericton to Edward and Mary McManamin. According to the 1891 and 1901 censuses, Edward and Mary had a large family of nine sons: in addition to Frank, there were Philip, John, Mark, William, Thomas, Joseph, Stephen, and Herbert. The second-oldest son, John, passed away at the age of twenty-three in the winter of 1895 after a long illness. For Frank, one of the youngest in a family of all boys, the death of his older brother likely had an influence on his upbringing. Details of his early life are limited, but newspapers suggest that Frank became a prominent athlete in Fredericton and later in Cape Breton playing a variety of sports, including hockey, basketball, baseball, and rugby. As a teenager, he enlisted with the 4th Canadian Mounted Rifles and went to South Africa during the Boer War. After returning, newspapers suggest that he worked as a clerk in the Federicton area before moving west to Edmonton; two brothers, Thomas and Philip, also were working out west before 1914. And so, prior to the Great War, Frank's many life experiences helped prepare him for military service once again.

When war broke out, Frank immediately enlisted and left for Valcartier, where he joined the 12th Battalion and met up with an old friend from Fredericton, Robert Phillips. The two had known each other since the Boer War, and accounts in newspapers suggest they remained close as they prepared to go overseas to England. According to his attestation paper, Frank enlisted on September 23, 1914, in Quebec and was described as having blue eyes, black hair, and a fair complexion. At the age of thirty-one, he stood approximately five feet ten inches tall and was unmarried. He was not the only brother to enlist, as newspapers reveal that Stephen and Herbert joined the Royal Flying Corps and the 140th Battalion, respectively. Although it is unclear if Frank saw family before going to

England, while overseas he wrote letters home frequently to family and friends. Many of these letters found their way into newspapers, providing an interesting window into his experiences during the war.

On October 3, 1914, Private McManamin left Quebec for England aboard the SS *Olympic*, arriving more than a week later on October 14. Despite being a veteran of the Boer War, Frank appears to have had difficulty adjusting to life with the Canadian Expeditionary Force once at Salisbury Plain. During his first few months with the 12th Battalion, he was repeatedly charged for being absent without leave, for "creating a disturbance," "breaking out of barracks," and "being in possession of a pass believed to be a forgery." According to newspapers, Frank and Robert were both discharged and sent to Liverpool en route for Canada. Both eluded their military escort, but were later arrested and sent back to Salisbury Plain. While still at Salisbury, they were successful in getting released to join a regiment going to France. When they were unable to join another Canadian battalion, they chose to enlist with the Dorsetshire Regiment of the British Army. Two weeks later, Frank and Robert were in France.

As a result of his joining a British unit, there are limited details of Frank's exact movements during the war; however, because Frank wrote home so much, his letters provide important details regarding his service. On March 28, 1915, he wrote:

We are getting along all right now and had three goes at the Germans. I had two close shaves. A bullet grazed my cheek and left a mark an inch long. The other one was when a big German mortar shell burst just in front of the trench and pretty nearly buried us all. I wish you could have seen it. I had to laugh for about an hour. I would like to tell you about what's going on here, but we're not allowed to. The trenches are full of water and it is very cold. We spend hours in them and then we go to what are known as dugouts, just behind the trenches. We go up tomorrow for a ten-day stay and then we are to get a long rest. I hope so. I want you to send me a number of copies of the Gleaner as far back as you can get them. We like to get the news from

Fredericton. It just snowed here yesterday, and it was just like one of those old timers in Fredericton you know around the first of March. I think the north pole must be shifted over here now.

By this time, Frank was in northern France and preparing to head to the Ypres Salient with his unit. In May, he wrote home again describing engagements near Hill 60 in Belgium, where, he said, "it was hell let loose...I never want to see anything like it again." He explained in a letter that Robert wanted everyone to know he was doing alright, but in fact he was killed that same day, and his body was never found. A few months later, Frank accompanied the 7th Royal Munster Fusiliers to Serbia, in the Balkans. On December 8, the *Daily Gleaner* shared news of a letter sent to his father in which Frank offers "Just a few lines to let you know I am well and getting along all right. I have got back at the front and now just a few hundred yards from the firing line. We may be going into the trenches today."

Over the next year, he continued to write home, often sharing bits of news of his time in the Balkans, and later partially explaining how he received his Military Medal for engagements while in Greece. Tragedy then struck the family. On March 16, 1917, Frank was engaged in a bombing raid, sent out to guide his unit into enemy lines at night. As he was leading the raid, a German machine-gun turned on him. According to accounts in newspapers, although he was able to retreat, his body was hit so many times it was impossible that he would ever recover from the wounds. After being treated throughout the night, Frank passed away the next morning.

News of his death reached papers across the province by early April and later the London press in England. On April 3, St. Dunstan's Church held two masses in which the congregation was asked to offer prayers for the family. In a letter written home a year later to family, Captain J.D. Black offered that Frank wanted everyone to know that "his last thoughts were of home and he asked me to send word to you to let his family know the facts of his death. I know it will be a great bereavement, but I am sure that his family will be proud and know that, although he is gone, he died a hero. Let everyone know that I share in their sorrow…he was a great pal." At the time of his death, Frank was thirty-three years old.

Lest We Forget

Private E. Francis McManamin is buried at the Struma Military Cemetery, located near Kalokastro, Greece, in the Struma Valley. According to the Commonwealth War Graves Commission, there are 908 identified casualties in this cemetery.

39. Winslow, Jasper Andrew (March 22, 1917)

Captain, 71st York Regiment, 12th Battalion, 3rd Divisional Ammunition Column, Canadian Field Artillery

Jasper Andrew Winslow was born on February 28, 1875, in Fredericton to Emma Barbara Winslow and Edward Byron Winslow. According to records, Jasper belonged to a large and well-respected New Brunswick family that included eight children. He had five brothers, Wentworth B., Rainsford Hannay, John James Fraser, Francis Edward, and Robert Napier, as well as two sisters, Elizabeth Caroline and Marguerite. Although there are few specific accounts detailing his early life growing up in Fredericton, Jasper and members of his family all received access to schooling at a young age. As well, the family was closely connected to the Christ Church Cathedral congregation. When war broke out in 1914, most of the Winslow brothers, as well as a sister, enlisted and offered their service to support the British war cause in Europe. Rainsford eventually succumbed to injuries received in the autumn of 1918 while overseas. Robert Napier served with the American Expeditionary Force and John was part of an intervention force in Russia after the war.

Around the time of his enlistment, records illustrate that Jasper was a tall man for the time, standing six feet, and that he had a dark complexion and brown eyes and hair. Given his family's close ties to the local church community, he belonged to the Church of England. He had previous experience with the 17th Duke of York's Royal Canadian Hussars and the 11th Argenteuil Rangers, both from Montreal. At the time of his enlistment on September 25, 1914, he was working as an accountant, was unmarried, and was immediately attached to the 12th Battalion under Lieutenant-Colonel Harry McLeod before going overseas. In many ways, Jasper was the ideal soldier of the time, with tremendous experience in both civilian and military life. He was thirty-nine years of age.

Winslow's unit sailed aboard the SS *Scotian* from Quebec City on October 3, 1914. Once in England, Jasper spent time training in Shorncliffe and at Bramshott Camp in Hampshire over the winter before qualifying for the rank of lieutenant in January 1915. He remained attached in reserve to the 12th Battalion until being sent to France in the summer of 1916 with 3rd Divisional Ammunition Column, Canadian Field Artillery. In February 1917, he was offered a commission as captain. His service record indicates that he was with his unit in southern Belgium and northern France until March 17, 1917, when he contracted a grave case of pneumonia and was admitted to No. 22 Casualty Clearing Station as a result of his condition. Newspapers reveal that he was not alone during this time, as his brother Rainsford was with him. It was an incredibly busy time for the Allies as they began preparations for the attacks on Vimy Ridge that would soon follow during the Battle of Arras. Just five days after being admitted, medical records reveal, Jasper's condition quickly worsened. Doctors could do little to save him, and he died on March 22. He was forty-two years old, and he left everything to his brothers.

Lest We Forget

Captain Jasper Winslow is buried and remembered with honour at the Bruay Communal Cemetery Extension, approximately 26 kilometres northwest of Arras. The French Army handed this part of the line to Commonwealth forces in March 1916, creating the 22nd Casualty Clearing Station. Nearly half of the burials here are from the Canadian Corps, which occupied this sector from early 1917. There are 412 Commonwealth burials from the First World War.

40. Neilson, William Alexander (March 29, 1917)

Private 696985, 175th Battalion, 31st Battalion

William Alexander Neilson was born on January 28, 1886, in Fredericton to Alexander Todd Neilson and Annie Susan Shanks. Documents obtained through the Provincial Archives of New Brunswick reveal that Alexander came to Canada from Scotland in 1882, and shortly thereafter he met his soon-to-be wife, Annie. Although she was from Waterville, Maine, her parents had roots in Ireland and Scotland. As a result, while we have little first-hand information regarding how they met, that Alexander and Annie both had ties to Scotland likely had some influence on the relationship that blossomed between them. From all accounts, the Neilsons were a larger-than-average family and were incredibly hard working, typical of many families at the time. Although they frequented between Saint John and Fredericton, at the time of their marriage on March 7, 1884, they owned a farm close to Burton. During and after the war, they lived near Victoria Mills. Given that their first child, James, was born on April 6, 1884, it is likely that Annie was pregnant during their wedding, something that was not uncommon. Together, Annie and Alexander had twelve children before the First World War. Apart from William, the names of the other children were James, Alexander, Donald, Lily, Maude, Arthur, Blanche, Janet, Hazel, Gordon, and Angus.

Born the second child in the family, William Alexander grew up learning the skills of farming and hard work, eventually moving to western Canada, where he continued working in that capacity prior to the war. Newspapers reveal that William, or Alexander, as he was often referred to in records, enlisted in Calgary with the 175th Battalion on July 16, 1916. Although he had no previous military experience, his attestation paper illustrates many of the qualities the Canadian Expeditionary Force was looking for: William had extensive experience in labour and farming, was single, by all accounts healthy, and, although he was slightly older than most recruits at thirty years of age, at five feet ten inches he was taller than most as well. William was described as having blue eyes, brown hair, and a fair complexion. Over the next three months, William remained at Sarcee Camp in Calgary training with the 175th until making his way to Valcartier and then to Halifax, where his unit made final preparations before going overseas. It is unclear whether he had the opportunity to see his family one last time.

Private William Alexander Neilson sailed from Halifax aboard the SS *Saxonia* on October 3, 1916, arriving at Liverpool seven days later. After spending the fall of 1916 training at Seaford Camp in Sussex, the 175th was eventually consolidated into the 31st Battalion and left for Le Havre, France, on January 19, 1917. William was arriving at an important time for the Canadian Corps, as the Vimy sector became flooded with Canadian units in preparation for the Battle of Arras — in particular, the Vimy Ridge assault the corps would lead in April.

In the months leading up to the assault, German lines were constantly harassed by Canadians coordinating raids and shelling in an effort to obtain critical information on German defences. By early March, the official war diary of the 31st shows, William was in and around St. Eloi before moving forward to the Neuville-St-Vaast area with his unit. The diary reveals that snow and rain increasingly made conditions difficult for everyone in the region. Despite the cold weather, the 31st continued preparations and raids on German front lines. News of British and French success at Bapaume and Péronne had reached Canadian units by this time, and by March 24 the 31st Battalion was instructed to move out of range of German shells harassing nearby villages. According to records, on March 29, 1917, William was taking part in attacks with his unit northeast of the village of Écurie when a German shell landed close to his position. William's circumstances-of-death report suggests that, while taking part in forward attacks on German lines, he was hit by shrapnel and died instantly. News of his death did not reach New Brunswick until a month later, with reports in Saint John papers stating incorrectly that he had been killed on April 9 and the *Daily Gleaner* revealing his name on casualty lists. Overseas for only five months, William had just celebrated his thirty-first birthday.

41. Thompson, Cyprian Alfred (April 8, 1917)

Lieutenant 23071, 38th Dufferin Rifles, 12th Battalion, 4th Battalion, 36th Reserve Battalion, The Royal Canadian Regiment

Cyprian Alfred Thompson was born on April 18, 1893, in Halifax according to his attestation paper, to Alice G.G. Thompson and Herbert H. Thompson. Newspapers suggest, however, that Cyprian might have been born in England and came to Canada with his mother after the death of his father. At some point after arriving to Canada, Cyprian and his mother eventually moved to Fredericton and occupied a residence at 776 Queen Street. While few details account for his early life with his mother, records show that, after graduating from Fredericton High School, Cyprian pursued studies at the Collegiate Institute in Brantford, Ontario, and later worked as a bank clerk in the Bank of Montreal at Grand-Mère, Quebec. At the time of his enlistment in the 12th Battalion at Valcartier in September 1914, Cyprian was unmarried, approximately five feet nine inches tall, with fair skin, blue eyes, light hair, and was a member of the Church of England. He had previous military experience with the 38th Dufferin Rifles at Brantford and, as an educated man with desirable leadership qualities, he eventually would be elevated to the rank of lieutenant with the 36th Reserve Battalion in the summer of 1916. Cyprian was twenty-one years of age when he left Canada from Quebec. He would never return home.

Cyprian Thompson boarded the SS *Scotian* on October 4, 1914, with the 12th Battalion bound for England, and arrived shortly after at Shorncliffe Camp. Cyprian remained held in reserve with the 12th for half a year until early 1915. In the spring of 1915, he was attached to the 4th Battalion and proceeded to France with them. According to the *Daily Gleaner*, in October 1915 Thompson was reportedly buried alive by a bursting German shell; after being dug out, he was held for nine days with a field ambulance unit behind Allied lines.

In many ways, Cyprian's official service record presents evidence of a soldier dedicated to service even when faced with tremendous physical and mental trauma. His medical history documentation also points to a developing medical and military culture still learning how to treat conditions soldiers had never experienced before. After less than twelve months of service on the Western Front, Cyprian was twice diagnosed with shell shock in the fall of 1915, only to be returned for duty, and then readmitted to military hospitals a total of ten times. Of course, given the involvement of the 4th Battalion in key battles such as Mount Sorrel and the Somme in 1916 and later at Vimy Ridge in 1917, Cyprian's experiences would have been incredibly traumatic. While on medical discharge for treatment of shell shock and in the opinion of the medical board needing "a fairly long rest," in August of 1916, he was granted the temporary rank of lieutenant with the 36th Reserve Battalion and was later attached to The Royal Canadian Regiment (RCR). Interestingly, Cyprian's medical record also reveals that, although suffering from what was described as "nervous dyspepsia" in the fall of 1916, he was eager to get back in line, claiming that "the above condition has practically disappeared and ... [he was] feeling fit again."

Lieutenant Thompson returned to France with 3rd Canadian Division in November and remained with the RCR through the winter under the command of Colonel Clarke Hill until the 1917 spring attacks near Arras and at Vimy Ridge. It was there that Lieutenant Thompson became an integral part of the four-day assault by all four Canadian divisions against German positions. More than 10,600 Canadians were killed or wounded during the fighting, with the first two days claiming the highest number of casualties. Newspapers reported, however, that Cyprian died on Easter

Sunday, April 8, 1917, a day before the formal assault on Vimy Ridge, without details as to how he died that fateful day. Lieutenant Thompson was only twenty-two years old, just ten days short of his birthday. Records reveal that Cyprian's mother was the only surviving member of the family.

Lest We Forget

Lieutenant Cyprian Alfred Thompson is buried at Ecoivres Military Cemetery, in Mont-St-Éloi, France, a few kilometres southwest of Vimy. According to the Commonwealth War Graves Commission, the cemetery contains 1,728 Commonwealth burials from the First World War, of which Canadians are the overwhelming majority. Plots V and VI contain the graves of men killed in the capture of Vimy Ridge in April 1917.

42. Bull, Charles Henry (April 9, 1917)

Private 445113, 55th Battalion, 26th Battalion, The Royal Canadian Regiment

Charles Henry Bull was born on August 22, 1891, in Woodstock to Helen Neales and Charles Bull, both of whom were from the Woodstock area. Charles was almost thirty years older than Helen when they married on June 27, 1888. Besides Charles, they had a daughter, Julia Helen. According to records, in May 1892 both parents contracted pneumonia and passed away a week later, leaving their young children in the care of family. The 1901 census reveals that Helen and Charles lived in the care of their aunts, Rose and Julia, in Woodstock until they reached the age to be on their own. Charles's links to the Fredericton community likely began through his mother's family, as he had an uncle, Reverend Dean Neales, and an aunt who lived in the area, in addition to the family he had been living with in Woodstock. It is likely through these connections and his time with The Royal Canadian Regiment (RCR) that he met a young woman from Fredericton named Dorothy Clara Wandless. Dorothy came from a large family with brothers who eventually served during the war as well. Charles and Dorothy married just after the outbreak of war on September 21, 1914. According to records, Charles had been employed as a chauffeur and grocer and lived at 350 Church Street with his wife. On September 18, 1915, Dorothy gave birth to a baby girl named Dorothy Helen Bull; however, Helen would never meet her father as he had already left for Europe. According to his attestation paper, Charles enlisted for service in Sussex on June 26, 1915, with the 55th Battalion. He had previous experience with the RCR and stood five feet eight inches tall with a medium complexion, blue eyes, and brown hair. Charles never returned home to his family.

After enlistment, Private Bull travelled to Camp Valcartier with the 55th Battalion, from where his unit left for England on October 30, 1915, arriving at Plymouth on November 9. He spent all of 1916 in England training with a variety of units. At one point, Charles was on a farrier course learning how to manage horses while in the field, work he was likely skilled at doing. Records reveal that he signed his formal will during this time naming his wife as sole beneficiary. On January 4, 1917, he joined the 26th Battalion before transferring to the RCR, and had headed to France by February. Although the time soldiers spent in the field varied greatly, it was common for many to become a casualty sooner rather than later in the trenches.

After arriving with the RCR, Private Bull and his unit began preparations for the Vimy Ridge attacks that would come shortly after. For Charles, it would truly be trial by fire, as he would be thrown into a fierce fight without having any field experience on the front in weather that was cold, wet, and windy. As the Vimy Ridge Easter weekend attacks approached, orders were given to commanding officers to relay to their units. Charles soon learned that the RCR, part of 3rd Division's 7th Brigade, would begin their attack at the centre of the ridge, an area that was steeper with closer objectives. As Zero Hour came on the morning of April 9, and the RCR went forward along with the PPCLI and 42nd Battalion, Private Bull advanced without hesitation. It was here that Charles was reported missing after action on the first day of attack. Months went by before information from witnesses in the field reported seeing Charles and many others nearby him killed instantly, "blown to pieces" by an enemy shell. Official news of Private Bull's death was not reported in newspapers until mid-June, when his family's hopes of his being alive "were shattered by the telegram which came this morning." Private Charles Henry Bull was twenty-seven years of age, leaving behind his wife and daughter. After the shock of Charles's death passed and the war was finally over, Dorothy remarried a man named Clement Breneol in the fall of 1920.

Lest We Forget

Private Charles Henry Bull is remembered at La Chaudière Military Cemetery, located at the foot of Vimy Ridge. According to the Commonwealth War Graves Commission, the cemetery contains 594 identified casualties.

43. Gartley, Raymond Medley (April 9, 1917)

Private 709226, 104th Battalion, 5th Canadian Mounted Rifles

Raymond Medley Gartley was born on July 27, 1897, in St. Stephen to Gertrude Agnes Bennet and Henry Osbourne Gartley. Raymond was the eldest of the couple's three children; the others were his twin sisters, Martha and Mary, born in 1899. The 1911 census shows that Martha and Mary later went by their middle names Elsie and Elva. Raymond's father was a farmer and labourer from the area, and his mother was from Fredericton, born into a Loyalist family. Records suggest that, at a very early age, Raymond's father passed away, causing the family to move from St. Stephen back to Fredericton, where they had a home at 262 Regent Street. As the eldest child, it was likely important for Raymond to find employment, and so he began working as a bellhop at the Queen Hotel in Fredericton. Newspapers reveal that he became well known to the public and was a general favourite with anyone who met him.

By the time war came, for young Raymond as for so many other young men, the pressure and excitement to join likely became too great. According to his attestation paper, Raymond enlisted with the 104th Battalion in Sussex on October 25, 1915. Young Gartley was only eighteen years of age, unmarried, had no prior military experience, and stood five feet six inches tall. He had a fair complexion, blue eyes, and brown hair. After enlisting, he trained over the winter of 1915–16 with other Fredericton boys who had enlisted with the 104th, not leaving to go overseas until the spring of 1916. Raymond would never return home to Fredericton and his family.

Private Gartley left Canada with the 104th from Halifax aboard the SS *Olympic* on June 28, 1916, just as the Somme campaign was about to begin. His unit arrived at Liverpool on July 6, and he continued to train over the summer and fall. By early December, Raymond had joined the 5th Canadian Mounted Rifles (CMR) at Witley Camp in Surrey, and on December 7 headed to the Western Front. Just before leaving, Raymond named his mother in his will as sole beneficiary. Over the winter of 1916–17, Raymond shifted with his unit to the Arras region in preparation for the Vimy Ridge attacks that would begin in April. According to the official war diary of the 5th CMR, Private Gartley was held in reserve as support for the 1st, 2nd, and 4th Mounted Rifles as they went forward during the early morning attack on Vimy Ridge on April 9. At 5:30 a.m., while in position, the 5th reported: "Intense artillery bombardment...one continuous roar that causes the ground to tremble and there is mingled with it the roar of the guns and the swishing and screeching of the shell-filled air. [Sixty] guns are covering our own advance, forming a rolling barrage."

Private Gartley's role early on in the Vimy Ridge attack was to provide material and structural support to ensure attacking units had the resources to obtain their objectives. This could involve moving to the forward lines as a working party digging dugouts or advancing to provide additional ammunition and supplies to sustain the attack. If casualties became too great, it could mean replacing units altogether. At some point during the first day of the Canadians' assault on Vimy Ridge, Raymond was killed; his body was never recovered. On Tuesday, April 24, the *Daily Gleaner* reported the news of his death among the names of other well-known boys from Fredericton who were either killed or missing. While Vimy Ridge eventually became known as a great victory for Canadians and the Allies, the news brought tremendous grief for families who had lost someone. Raymond Medley Gartley was nineteen years old.

Lest We Forget

Private Raymond M. Gartley is remembered with honour on the Vimy Memorial, in Vimy, France.

44. Yerxa, Guy Randolph (April 10, 1917) Military Cross

Lieutenant, 71st York Regiment, 50th Battalion (King's Own Calgary Regiment)

Guy Randolph Yerxa was born on February 15, 1890, in Fredericton to Randolph Yerxa, also of Fredericton, and Mary E. Torrens, of Fairville, near Saint John. Although Guy's father was from Fredericton, records suggest that his early life was spent on the family farm in the area of Keswick. Mary came from a large family that had residences in Fredericton, New England, and Ireland. There are few details of how Randolph and Mary met, but they exchanged vows during a quiet ceremony in Fredericton on August 30, 1887. According to marriage records, at different times they occupied a shared residence at 527 King Street with family. In addition to Guy, the couple had two other children named Gladys and Roy. Together, the couple moved a few times. For a time, Randolph found work as a grocery clerk in Boston, and both Guy and Roy attended Edgerly School in the Boston area. After the family returned to Fredericton, Guy quickly became a popular young man in the area and was well liked by all who knew him. He served for two years with the 71st York Regiment and was employed as a surveyor for the Royal Bank of Canada before moving to Calgary to work with the Immigration Works of the Interior Department.

When war broke out in 1914, Guy enlisted with the 50th Battalion, known as the King's Own Calgary Regiment, in December. At the time, he was twenty-four years of age and was described in his attestation paper as single, five feet nine inches tall, with blue eyes, fair skin, and dark hair. During his time in Calgary, he met a young woman named Louise King, the daughter of the city's postmaster, and the two became quite close. According to newspapers, Guy was a non-commissioned officer quickly working his way up the military ranks prior to leaving for overseas duty. He remained in Canada training for the next twelve months. It is unclear if he ever saw his family in Fredericton again.

On October 27, 1915, Guy embarked from Halifax aboard the SS *Orduna*, arriving in England on November 4. He completed his training at Bramshott Camp and accepted a commission as lieutenant on June 20, 1916. Before embarking for Le Havre, France, on August 10, 1916, Guy was given a six-day leave of absence, possibly an opportunity to celebrate the birth of his son, Randolph. Although his service record indicates he was unmarried at the time of his enlistment, it appears that at some point he and Louise had gotten married in Canada. Louise was also pregnant.

Upon arriving in France, Guy was quickly recognized for his excellent work in the field, and later was being considered for additional appointments. His promotions appear to speak to the kind of person Guy was and the respect he had earned among his commanding officers. Many of those he served with during this time would later express deep admiration for him, his character, and how he was an essential part of the battalion he served with. In January 1917, Guy was granted another ten days' leave of absence to England. Although there is limited evidence, it is possible that Louise had come to England to introduce Guy to his newborn son. By February, his battalion was stationed near Souchez, France, where troops were given orders, plans, and objectives each week in preparation for what was to come during the attack on Vimy Ridge. Leading up to the attack, Yerxa was involved in coordinated assaults on enemy trenches to obtain important information and to wear down German soldiers. These raids were part of a much larger effort to train and plan for Vimy. Guy's service in the winter and spring of 1917 earned him the Military Cross, awarded for his work in a raid on enemy trenches on March 21, 1917, and, according to the *London Gazette*, "for conspicuous gallantry and devotion to duty leading his men to the enemy second line with great courage and skill under heavy fire. Later, he personally superintended the collection of the wounded and set a splendid example throughout."

A few weeks later, on April 9, Lieutenant Yerxa was an integral part of the four-day assault by all four Canadian divisions against German positions on the coveted Vimy Ridge, just north of Arras. More than 10,600 Canadians were killed or wounded during the four days of fighting, with the first two days claiming the highest number of casualties. It was here, on April 10, that Guy lost his life. A fellow officer with the 50th Battalion, Lieutenant Stewart Moore, recalled that he had been killed during their first attack on German positions, while Lieutenant-Colonel L.F. Page offered that, although Guy was killed leading his men into action, his sacrifice helped Canada and the Allies to win one of their greatest victories of the First World War. In letters written home a week after his death, Guy's fellow officers shared their sympathies and condolences:

> As an old friend and brother officer of Lieut. G.R. Yerxa, I want to write and express to you my most sincere sympathy in his death. As you are no doubt aware, we have for the past four weeks been giving Germans particular problems, and your husband was killed in our first attack. His body was recovered and buried, but unfortunately, owing to censorship rules I am unable to give you the exact location at the present moment. He has always acted with splendid dash and courage, and his death is regretted by all of us. Yours sincerely, Lieut. Stewart Moore.

> It is with the deepest regret and sympathy that I write to tell you of the death of your husband, Lieut. G.R. Yerxa, of my battalion. He was a splendid officer, very efficient and very keen on his work and just shortly before his death had done excellent work in a raid into enemy trenches... [I]f there is anything I can do for you I sincerely hope you will write and let me know as I am entirely at

your service. Again, offering you the deepest sympathy of myself and of my officers. Very sincerely yours, Lieut. Col. L.F. Page.

Guy was twenty-six years old at the time of his death, leaving behind his wife, newborn son, and extended family. Although his fellow officers indicated through letters where his body was buried, his grave has never been found.

Lest We Forget

Lieutenant Guy Randolph Yerxa is memorialized and remembered with honour on the Vimy Memorial.

45. Morris, Robert Jr. (April 11, 1917)

Private 445282, 55th Battalion, 4th Canadian Machine Gun Company

Robert Morris Jr. was born on June 28, 1890, in Warwick, Birmingham, England, to Robert Morris and Ellen Collier. According to the England and Wales census, Robert Jr. had eleven siblings named Letty, Albert, Lilly, Henry, Edward, Maggie, Thomas, Nellie, Harold, Clemet, and Mona. Records also show that he had a foster brother named John Charnley, a young man from England who had been friends with him, Albert, and Henry. While family stories suggest that the Morrises had come to Canada primarily looking for job opportunities in the early 1900s, the 1911 census of England and Wales suggests they might have gone back to England briefly before coming to work at the Marysville cotton mill. After the war, the family moved to May's Landing, New Jersey.

Apart from family stories, few details highlight Robert's life in Fredericton. Records suggest, however, that he worked as a weaver at the Marysville mill and that he had prior experience in England doing similar work. Newspapers suggest that the large family was well known in both the northside and southside Fredericton communities. At the time of his enlistment in Sussex on July 28, 1915, Robert was unmarried and was described as having blue eyes, brown hair, a fair complexion, while standing five feet six inches tall. Along with his brothers, Albert and John, he joined the 55th Battalion. Family stories suggest that their younger brother Henry had been the first of the Morris boys to go off to war. As Robert's attestation paper reveals, he had no prior experience in the military, suggesting that his decision to join was influenced by his brothers and by the example of Henry, who was already fighting overseas. At the age of twenty-five, Robert made his way to Valcartier for more training in the summer, and he and his brothers were all together as they prepared to go overseas a few months later.

On October 30, 1915, Robert Jr. and his two brothers left Montreal aboard the SS *Corsican* for England, arriving on November 9. Robert remained with the 55th and then the 36th Battalion in England over the winter of 1915. In April 1916, he was attached to a machine-gun unit. According to his service record, that summer Private Morris left with the 4th Machine Gun Company for France. Records appear to show that, after arriving in England, the three brothers finally went their separate ways toward the front. The Battle of the Somme had just begun, and it is likely that Robert headed to northern France and the Ypres Salient with his unit. There are few details in his service record about where he was over the winter of 1916 until February 21, 1917, when he was admitted to hospital for a week due to an undisclosed illness. He continued with the 4th Machine Gun Company in the months leading up to Vimy Ridge and the Battle of Arras. It was a significant period of time in the war, as the four Canadian divisions trained and fought together for the first time. When the Battle of Vimy Ridge began on April 9 and over the next few days, Robert was with his company north of Thelus. On April 11, according to his circumstances-of-death form, Private Morris was on duty when he was "instantly killed by an enemy shell." News of his death reached local newspapers in Fredericton on May 3, indicating that he had died the Wednesday after Easter. In a letter written to his father, Captain J.G. Weir

Among "the Boys" commemorated by the Devon Memorial is Private Robert Morris Jr. The memorial is now located in Devon Middle School. Brent Wilson

shared the following: "Robert had safely gone through the attack of the 9th of April but was instantly killed by a shell while standing at duty in the gun pit beside one of the guns. You and your family will have the deepest sympathy of the officers and men of the company."

His foster brother, John, had been killed months earlier during the Somme. After their deaths, as well as those of other soldiers from the northside, including Fred Tylor and James Stickles, the northside community created a fund so that a memorial tablet could be made for the "brave young men of St. Mary's parish who have paid the supreme sacrifice." Today, that memorial tablet, once in a local church, now resides in the entrance of Devon Middle School. At the time of his death, Robert was twenty-seven years old.

Lest We Forget

Private Robert Morris Jr. is buried at the Bois-Carré British Cemetery located in Arras, France. According to the Commonwealth War Graves Commission, Robert's is one of 449 names honoured here.

46. Boddington, Albert Henry (April 14, 1917) Military Medal

Sergeant 90209, 28th Field Battery, 6th Brigade, Canadian Field Artillery

Albert Henry Boddington was born on December 22, 1880, in Birmingham, England, and grew up a member of the Church of England. According to records, Albert, like Sidney Findley, came to Canada as a part of the Middlemore Children's Emigration Homes program, which saw children from around the British Commonwealth brought to Canada to live for a variety of reasons and circumstances between 1870 and 1948. In the summer of 1897, when Albert was sixteen years old, he sailed to Halifax on the *Assyrian* from Liverpool along with 107 other children. Four years after arriving, the 1901 New Brunswick census reveals that Albert was boarding with William Rosborough's family in Prince William and Dumfries, likely working on their farm. Ten years later, on July 29, 1908, Albert married Lily May White and together they moved to Fredericton and occupied a residence at 108 Northumberland Street. Albert found work at the Waverly Hotel, but eventually joined the Fredericton Fire Department. Census records reveal that Albert and Lily had their first daughter, Violet Josephine, in March 1909 and their second daughter, Vera Patricia, on October 20, 1910. According to his attestation paper, Albert had participated in three peacetime militia camps between 1906 and 1908. He enlisted on March 30, 1915, in Fredericton with the 28th Field Battery. He stood five feet seven inches tall, weighed 152 pounds, and had fair skin, blue eyes, and brown hair. Albert was thirty-four years of age when he went overseas.

On August 18, 1915, Gunner Boddington landed in Plymouth, England, before arriving in France four months later on January 18, 1916, disembarking at Le Havre with the 7th Brigade, Canadian Field Artillery. Almost immediately after being sent to France, Albert was promoted to sergeant, and a few months later was transferred to the 6th Brigade before being granted a leave of absence from the field on March 25, returning eight days later. Although few details exist of his exact movements during the war between June and November 1916, he was heavily involved in actions on the Somme in November when Albert was awarded the Military Medal for bravery in the field. According to the official citation found in his service file:

> Near Courcelette on November 18th, 1916, Sergt Boddington displayed great gallantry and devotion to duty at the taking of Desire Sapp support trench. When a telephone line which had been laid forward from the Battery O.P. [observation post] after the advancing infantry was cut beyond repair this N.C.O. on his own initiative, worked his way forward twice under a heavy fire to a point whence he brought back timely and important information.

A few months later, on April 9, 1917, Sergeant Boddington was part of the four-day assault by all four Canadian divisions against German positions on Vimy Ridge. On April 14, the final day of the successful Canadian assault on the ridge, Albert was killed. According to a letter sent to his wife, Lily, Albert had been hit by shellfire from an enemy gun, killing him instantly. Accounts from those who witnessed his death · suggest he was trying to select a position for their battery. In a letter written home to Lily, Captain S. Oke, chaplain of the 2nd Brigade Artillery, offered words of support:

> I know just how hard it will be to take up the old duties when your heart is so heavy and sore, but it is better that you should do so for your sake, for the sake of his children, and for his sake. We laid his body away this morning in the pretty cemetery at Ecoivres, where many others have their last resting place. The service was attended by a large number of men from the brigade to which he belonged, and a suitable cross was set up to mark the place. I trust that you will accept my most sincere sympathy in the great loss you have sustained.

At the time of his death, Albert was thirty-nine years old, leaving behind Lily and their two daughters, Violet and Vera. Today, a plaque located outside the old Fredericton fire department station on King Street bears Albert's name and those of other Fredericton firemen who perished during the war.

Lest We Forget

Sergeant Albert Henry Boddington is buried in the Ecoivres Military Cemetery in Mont-St-Éloi, France. In addition to the 1,728 Commonwealth burials from the First World War, there are also 786 French and 4 German war graves.

Fredericton Firemens' Memorial on the former Fire Hall on King Street; included among the names are Sergeant Albert H. Boddington, Murray Rutter, and William Smith. James Rowinski

47. Kelly, Lloyd Robert (May 2, 1917)

Private 817492, 140th Battalion, 26th Battalion

Lloyd Robert Kelly was born on September 3, 1896, in Kingsclear, New Brunswick, to Benjamin Kelly and Annie Elizabeth Poore. Benjamin was born on October 14, 1856, and Annie on June 26, 1866; both were from New Brunswick. According to marriage records, Benjamin and Annie were married in July 1888 and together they had four sons, Gerald, Leslie, Whitman, and Lloyd, as well as two daughters, May and Hilda. Lloyd was the second youngest in the family. Growing up just outside Fredericton, Lloyd and his family were familiar with most other families in the area either through work, church, or school. Lloyd married Eva Ella Milton, who had been born in Norfolk, England, on November 29, 1915; Lloyd was nineteen and Eva was listed on the marriage certificate as eighteen, although records found elsewhere suggest that she might have been as young as sixteen.

According to his attestation paper, Lloyd enlisted with the 140th Battalion on December 3, 1915, in Sussex. He had no prior experience in the military, but his skills as a farmer would be useful in Europe. Lloyd stood five feet five inches tall and had a medium complexion, with blue eyes, and dark brown hair. The couple likely knew at the time of his enlistment that Eva was pregnant and that she would have the baby while he was away. She gave birth to a little boy in the fall of 1916, and Eva named him Lloyd, after his father. They likely had a chance to spend time together before Lloyd left in 1916; he would never return.

Private Kelly trained with his unit in Canada before leaving from Halifax for England on September 25 aboard the SS *Corsican*. The 140th arrived at Liverpool on October 6 and, on October 29, with very little time for additional training, Lloyd transferred to the 26th Battalion at the front. Lloyd finalized his will two days before leaving, naming Eva as his sole beneficiary. Unlike so many others who had arrived before him, Lloyd did not have the benefit of extended training in England and would have had to learn quickly while in the field. Private Kelly likely considered himself lucky that his first test did not come during the Battle of the Somme; he arrived at the front in late November after active operations ended over the winter of 1916–17. The break did not last long, however, as Canadians began preparing for their upcoming attack on Vimy Ridge. While fighting with 2nd Division's 5th Brigade during the April 9 attack at Vimy, Private Kelly and the 26th Battalion made good progress, achieving their objectives as they advanced behind the barrage of Canadian artillery fire. Units followed behind and pushed forward as the 26th dug in to keep ground that had been won. Despite substantial losses, Private Kelly and the Canadians kept moving forward and contributed to a significant victory at Vimy. By May, the 26th was still in the area of Neuville-St-Vaast, according to battalion war diaries. Although there are reports of enemy shelling and German counterattacks, what exactly happened to Lloyd on May 2 is still largely unknown. His circumstances-of-death record simply reveals that he died from wounds while receiving medical attention at No. 6 Casualty Clearing Station. Private Kelly was twenty-one years old, and left behind his wife, Eva, and a son he would never meet. Eva Kelly eventually married Christopher Patrick Sullivan from Fredericton in the fall of 1918.

Lest We Forget

Private Lloyd Robert Kelly is buried with honour at Barlin Communal Cemetery Extension, Barlin, north of Arras, France.

48. White, Oscar (May 3, 1917)

Private 22644, 71st York Regiment, 12th Battalion, 1st Battalion

Oscar White was born on March 20, 1886, in Fredericton to Samuel M. White and Mary White. According to the 1911 census, Oscar was the second oldest in a family with five daughters and two sons occupying a home at 655 George Street. His younger brother's name was George, and his sisters were Sadie, Eva, Beatrice, Dorothy, and Margaret. At the time of his enlistment, Oscar was single and working as a labourer in Fredericton. He is described as having blue eyes and a fair complexion. Oscar's service record also suggests that prior to the war he was a member of the 71st York Regiment, and was five feet eleven inches tall, weighed 165 pounds, and belonged to the Baptist Church. At the time of his enlistment on September 23, 1914, in Valcartier with the 12th Battalion, Oscar was twenty-eight years of age. It is unclear if he ever saw his family before going overseas.

Private Oscar White departed from Valcartier for England on October 3, 1914, along with many other Fredericton boys, aboard the SS *Scotian*, arriving a little more than a week later. He spent the winter of 1914 in England training with the 12th Battalion until being drafted into the newly formed 1st Infantry Battalion from Ontario on August 23, 1915. Like many other Canadian soldiers, Oscar endured some of the worst horrors of the Great War as well as the harsh winter on Salisbury Plain the first year the Canadians were in England. Oscar's military service was defined by illnesses, wartime trauma, and injuries sustained in the field. Even before leaving England after being drafted into the 1st Battalion, he had been admitted to military hospitals at Bristol and Newcastle with a variety of ailments. Typical of many service personnel, Oscar was treated on numerous occasions for viral infections that were all too common among men and women living in such close and stressful living quarters. Two months after he joined the 1st Battalion, he fell sick to painful illnesses that did not stop until a year later. As well as being sick throughout

La Targette British Cemetery, Neuville-St-Vaast, France.
Commonwealth War Graves Commission

most of his service, he also suffered from shell shock in the spring of 1916. He was returned to the field in the Ypres Salient, however, only a month after being diagnosed. Almost immediately upon his arrival back to his unit, Oscar suffered a gunshot wound to his left eye, forcing him to be readmitted to hospital. Newspapers indicate that he returned to England for treatment for a few months while receiving medical support for his injury. During his total service attached to 1st Canadian Division, Oscar was active in the Second Battle of Ypres, the Battle of the Somme, and later at Vimy Ridge; however, upon his return to the field for a final time after being injured, Oscar's fate was officially called into question. On May 3, 1917, he was reported wounded and missing in the Villers au Bois region, northwest of Arras. He was presumed to have died of wounds sometime in May 1917. He was thirty-one years old. Newspaper reports of Oscar's war service reveal a family with very little information as to what had been happening with Oscar throughout his time overseas. By the time he was reported missing and officially killed in action, the family likely had prepared for the worst.

49. Clarke, Charles Edward (May 4, 1917)

Gunner 90228, 28th Battery, 5th Brigade

Charles Edward Clarke was born on October 20, 1897, in Saint John to Whitney and Lavina A. Clarke. Charles had two brothers, Ray and Clarence, as well as a sister named Ada Blanche. As he was growing up, the family lived at 21 Dorchester Street in Saint John before moving to Fredericton. Records do not indicate their reasons for moving away from Saint John, but pay documents confirm that Whitney, Charles's father, had died at some point prior to Charles's military service and that one of his brothers had left Canada with an infantry unit in the summer of 1916. Records suggest that Charles lived with his sister, brother, and mother at 589 York Street in Fredericton and that his family moved to 366 Saunders Street at some point during or after the war. Prior to his enlistment, Charles was employed as a shoemaker. According to the *Daily Gleaner*, three years before he enlisted, he had "joined the George Street Church and had been very active in youth work in the church and was a general favourite." Without any prior military experience or training, Charles enlisted with the 28th Field Battery in Fredericton on March 30, 1915, the same day Albert Boddington signed up. Charles's attestation paper reveals that he was eighteen years old, unmarried, stood five feet seven inches tall, and had blue eyes and brown hair. Although Charles would write letters home to his mother, his legal next-of-kin, he never returned to see his family again.

On June 12, Clarke arrived at Shorncliffe, England, along with the 28th Field Battery, and spent the next six months training. He was transferred to the 8th Howitzer Brigade on October 1, 1915, at Otterpool, Northumberland, and then to the 6th Howitzer Brigade before leaving for France on January 18, 1916. His service form reveals that, just five days earlier, he went missing from his unit for an evening—likely taking one last opportunity to relax before heading to the front. On May 22, he was taken on strength by Canadian 2nd Division's 5th Brigade, Canadian Field Artillery. Charles spent the next year with the division in Belgium and northern France. On April 25, 1917, after the successful capture of Vimy Ridge, Charles wrote to his mother from the area to tell her about what was happening. The letter appeared in the *Daily Gleaner*.

Dear Mother, just a few lines again to let you know that I am well. I received your parcel O.K. and was much pleased to get it. The cake was in great condition when it reached here. I intended writing before, but we have been awfully busy lately. We have to work all day and are out most every night with ammunition until the small hours of the morning, so you see we don't get much time to ourselves. I am sorry to have to tell you that Cleve York has been killed. I was in the burial party. We buried him today. I have not seen Jim for about a month but will try and see him soon. I was not far from Cleve when he was killed, and I think his death was caused by the shock of explosion from a Hun shell, as we could not find any marks on his body. We have been getting very poor rations, but these last few days they are better. Of course, there is no shortage of food, but there are so many different things to come up to the line that the transports and Army Service Corps have about all they can handle. Well, mother dear, this is certainly an awful war, but we are all in hopes it will end this summer, as we do not like to spend another winter in this country, as you know it is a lot worse here in winter. How are Roy and Viola? Tell them both to be good and we will soon be home to see them. Well, mother, I really must close for this time. Lots of love to all...Charlie or, "Deacon," as the boys all call me. P.S.—I am glad to tell you that I am still trusting in God and I feel sure he will take care of me. Charlie.

A little more than a week later, on May 4, nineteen-year-old Charles Edward Clarke was killed in the vicinity of Vimy. The notification of Charles's death came to his mother, Lavina, the same day she received the letter he had written home.

Lest We Forget

Gunner Charles Edward Clarke is buried in La Targette British Cemetery, located to the southwest of Neuville-St-Vaast, France. According to the Commonwealth War Graves Commission, the cemetery, formerly known as the Aux-Rietz Military Cemetery, was designed by Sir Reginald Blomfield, the designer of the Menin Gate Memorial, and contains 638 First World War burials, 41 of them unidentified. There are also three Second World War burials, two of which are unidentified.

50. Osborne, Hubert Patterson (July 7, 1917)

Captain, 71st York Regiment, 104th Battalion, Royal Flying Corps

Hubert Patterson Osborne was born on April 28, 1894, in Belleville, Ontario, to Major William James Osborne and Evelyn Beatrice Osborne. According to census records, Hubert was the eldest of four children, the others being Gordon, Frank, and Margorie. His father was actively involved in the military while growing up in Ontario and later New Brunswick. According to newspapers, William Osborne belonged to the 49th and then 15th Battalion (Argyle Light Infantry) while living in Belleville. Eventually rising to the rank of captain, in 1897 the family moved to Fredericton, where he joined the 71st Regiment, rising later to major. In addition to his involvement with the 71st Regiment, he was active in city politics as an alderman on council, manager of the Fredericton Business College, and board member of the YMCA and Fredericton Board of Trade. The family lived at 221 Charlotte Street. Given the involvement of his parents in the community life of the city, Hubert naturally became active himself and was well liked. For some time, he served with the 71st Regiment as a staff sergeant. After high school, Hubert attended both Mount Allison University and the University of New Brunswick, and then moved to Toronto to study law at Osgoode Hall with his uncle, Judge Phitten. When war broke out in 1914, he immediately returned to Fredericton, and on December 8, 1915, he enlisted in Sussex with the 104th Battalion before going to Halifax to qualify for a commission as a captain. His father and brother Gordon soon also enlisted, with Major William Osborne joining the 55th Battalion and Gordon enlisting with the 9th Siege Battery in Saint John. Like many others from Fredericton and around the province,

Hubert spent the next few months in Canada training in preparation for going overseas. It is unclear if he saw his family again over the winter and spring of 1915–16 before he left. At the time of his enlistment, Hubert was twenty-two years old and unmarried.

Captain Hubert Osborne enlisted with the 104th Battalion and later transferred to the Royal Flying Corps, where he served as an observer. PANB F2943

CAPT. HUBERT OSBORNE.

On June 28, 1916, Captain Osborne left Halifax aboard the SS *Olympic* and arrived in Liverpool on July 5. While in England, Hubert decided to join the Royal Flying Corps and obtained a transfer from his Canadian unit so that he could begin training at the flying school during the winter of 1916–17. According to letters sent home, he was assigned to the 63rd Squadron while in England and was planning to go to the Middle East. However, the decision was made to transfer all Canadians to No. 58 Squadron, which ultimately meant that he would be going to France instead. For the next few months, Hubert remained in England taking practice flights and preparing for the time when he would cross the Channel. On July 3, 1917, he arrived in France at the Belgian border as part of No. 21 Squadron and was partnered as an observer in a plane flown by a veteran pilot named George Leckie.

Despite the attraction of flying in a plane during the First World War, it was one of the most dangerous places to be. The typical time of a pilot in the Royal Flying Corps and later the Royal Air Force (RAF) was often not very long. On the morning of July 7 at 7:30 a.m., just four days after arriving at the Western Front, Captain Osborne was performing artillery observation with Leckie over German lines when they came under attack. According to Lieutenant Stewart M. Goodeve, a friend with No. 21 Squadron, their plane was hit from the ground by enemy fire; eyewitness accounts suggest that, as the machine began a nosedive, Hubert was seen attempting to correct its fall. At that point both he and George were hit by additional machine-gun fire and the plane crashed behind Allied lines. When his body was recovered, it was found that he had been shot through the heart. In letters of condolences sent home from superior officers and printed in the *Daily Gleaner* a few months after his death, many shared sincere sympathies for the family's loss:

> In the few days your boy was with the squadron, he became very popular and won the hearts of all by his open frankness and his consideration for others. Believe me, we all miss him terribly, and his friends here wish me to send you their deepest sympathy. Hubert died as I know he would wish to – doing his duty

splendidly. He was considered one of the best by all his pals and friends. Believe me, their graves are having all possible care. Major Good has had crosses made from a propeller and these will be placed on the graves tomorrow. May God comfort you and Major Osborne in your sorrow.

At the time of his death, Hubert was twenty-three years of age, leaving behind both of his parents and his siblings, Gordon, Frank, and Marjorie.

Lest We Forget

Captain Hubert P. Osborne was buried with honour at the Perth Cemetery (China Wall), in Zillebeke, Belgium. According to the Commonwealth War Graves Commission, 2,791 servicemen of the First World War are buried or commemorated in this cemetery. There is also a dedication to him on the family plot in the Fredericton Rural Cemetery.

51. Hanson, John Clarence (July 14, 1917)

Lieutenant, 71st York Regiment, 104th Battalion, Royal Flying Corps

John Clarence Hanson was born May 23, 1893, in Sussex to Rupert Douglas Hanson and Gussie Price. His parents married on September 28, 1892, in Sussex. Rupert was working in the area as a schoolteacher when he met Gussie, who came from Petitcodiac. According to records, John was an only child in a small family heavily involved in education in the province. After working for a time as a local schoolteacher, Rupert eventually moved the family to Fredericton, where he took up the position as Inspector of Schools. Given his work, Rupert often travelled throughout New Brunswick; as a result, newspapers reveal, John's early education began in the Bathurst and Chatham Grammar Schools. In 1909, he enrolled at the University of New Brunswick and upon graduation in

1913 won the alumni medal for the best Latin essay and the Governor-General's medal for efficiency in science. After graduating, "Jack," as his friends called him, moved to Albert County, where he was a schoolteacher and then principal of the Riverside Consolidated School. His service record reveals that he belonged to the local militia and had three years of experience with the 71st York Regiment at Camp Sussex. While John moved away for his teaching career, his parents remained in Fredericton, where they had a home at 818 Charlotte Street. When war broke out in 1914, John received a commission as a lieutenant with the 104th Battalion. He remained in Canada for training with the 104th until 1916, and during that period, newspapers reveal, he formed a close bond with two other officers from Fredericton, Hubert Osborne and Royden Barbour. All three had enlisted with the 104th and had ambitions of becoming pilots once overseas. It is unclear if John ever saw his family again before leaving for England.

On June 28, 1916, Lieutenant Hanson embarked from Halifax aboard the SS *Olympic* for Liverpool. According to his military service record, he stayed in England during the remainder of 1916 and eventually requested permission to join the RFC. After passing all the necessary courses, in late March 1917 he was assigned as an observer to No. 55 Squadron, described by newspapers as "one of the best fighting squadrons equipped with the newest machinery." Before going to France, the three Fredericton boys, John, Royden, and Hubert went to London on pass, and John and Hubert had their photos taken and placed in lockets to send home to their mothers. By June 10, John had landed in France alongside pilot officer Second Lieutenant H.E. MacFarlane. Newspapers suggest that, throughout his service, he routinely wrote home. In July 1917, his parents received the following letter:

Dear parents, well, my first show is over. We did not see any signs of a Hun machine. Cooke, my Canadian friend who joined the squadron around the time I did, has five shows to his credit. I'm beginning to fear that he will get his wing before I do. Mine is bound to come through before long. The weather has turned fine and warm again. I had to get up at 8 o'clock this morning because the sun was so hot, but now I am getting the benefit of a lovely breeze. All I wore yesterday was a pair of shorts and a shirt. It sure is a contrast. In the air, it is difficult to keep my hands warm. As you can imagine, stiff, cold fingers is an awful nuisance, so I usually sit on my hands and beat them together. One of these days I will find the right rig to keep warm and then I will be the Jake. There have been some tanks in the neighbourhood for training, so I want to try and set an eye on them. While I would not mind having a ride in one, they say driving one is very much rougher than a football match and it is possibly true. They are just starting the harvest here and the populations hate the tanks most cordially. Well, I really must stop as I have another letter to write. Lovingly, Jack.

A few days after writing home, Jack and his crewmate were asked to perform a test flight on a new Rolls-Royce aircraft. According to Major J.S. Baldwin, on the morning of July 14, 1917, they were testing the plane near the aerodrome when the machine nosedived into the ground. Both officers were killed. Accounts written home and published in newspapers offer that "it was impossible to say why the accident occurred...and that it seems such a waste of a useful officer. Your son was doing exceedingly well in his squadron and was a good observer." Jack was admitted to hospital for treatment, but there was little doctors could do. A few months after his death, the Brunswick Street Baptist Church held a memorial service in honour of John and two others who had been killed overseas, Stewart Kitchen and Stanley Edgett. At the time of his death, John was twenty-four years old.

Lest We Forget

Lieutenant John Clarence Hanson is buried at the Longuenesse (St. Omer) Souvenir Cemetery, in St-Omer, France. According to the Commonwealth War Graves Commission, there are 3,390 identified casualties in this cemetery. John and his pilot are buried beside each other.

52. Gough, Walter Ernest (July 16, 1917)

Private 709834, 104th Battalion, 5th Canadian Mounted Rifles

Walter Ernest Gough was born in Fredericton on May 8, 1894. He was the second eldest of a large family that resided at 63 Shore Street in Fredericton. Walter's parents were Isabelle Amelia (Sturgeon) Gough and James Wellington Gough. Isabelle originally came from White Rapids, in northern New Brunswick, and James was from Fredericton. The 1911 census reveals that Walter had four brothers and two sisters: James Percy, Norman, Kenneth, and Robin, and Barbara and Jean. All three older brothers in the Gough family, James Percy, Walter Ernest, and Norman, eventually enlisted for service during the war. Little is known of his early life prior to enlisting, Walter's attestation paper reveals that he worked as a shoemaker at the Hartt Shoe Factory in Fredericton and that he was not married. According to the *Daily Gleaner*, Walter was known as one of the best amateur baseball players in the city and was a popular young man. At the time of his enlistment, Walter stood five feet eight inches tall, had a dark complexion, gray eyes, and his hair was brown. The Goughs were Presbyterians and had close ties to local churches. Only twenty-one years old with no military experience Walter arrived in Sussex on November 23, 1915, to enlist with the 104th Battalion. While training with the 104th, newspapers reported that, as he was boarding the train for Sussex to go overseas, he heard the news that his younger brother, Norman, had been wounded in France. Only a few weeks earlier, Walter and his family had also received the terrible news that his brother James Percy had died on May 7. It had been just one day before Walter's birthday.

Only one month after his brother's death and news of Norman's injuries, Private Gough embarked from Halifax on June 28, 1916, with the 104th Battalion aboard the SS *Olympic*. In November, his New Brunswick battalion was absorbed into other units, and Walter joined the 5th Battalion Canadian Mounted Rifles (CMR). Newspapers report that Walter, eager to get to the front, volunteered to help reinforce the 5th CMR along with two chums from Fredericton, Harry "Dutchy" Lynn and Frank Merryweather. They all trained together in England with the 5th CMR until leaving for the front in late November. Both Harry and Frank would be wounded the following year; Walter, or "Tid"[1] as he was known to friends, would not be as fortunate. After arriving in France following the Somme battles, the 5th CMR made their way to the Arras region near Vimy, where Walter remained over the winter of 1916–17 and during the series of battles in and around Arras in the spring. During the Vimy Ridge attacks, the 5th Battalion, serving with the 8th Brigade, was used as support for the 1st, 2nd, and 4th CMR. After Vimy Ridge, the Canadians were involved in a series of attacks intended to push back the Germans beyond the Vimy and Lens areas. According to the 5th CMR war diary, heavy enemy shelling was reported throughout this period, as were exchanges between enemy and Allied planes near Lens by mid-July. While Walter was engaged in the area with his unit, heavy shelling continued on trench lines, and explosions were observed near railway embankments. Although few details explain the particulars of what happened to him, Walter

Fredericton Boy Killed

"Ted" Gough, Killed in Action.   H. C. Lynn, Wounded.   F. Merryweather, Wounded.

Private Walter E. Gough (at left) enlisted in the 104th Battalion and was serving with the 5th Canadian Mounted Rifles when he was killed in action near Vimy Ridge on July 16, 1917. PANB F2943

---

1   Gough was identified as "Ted" in a photograph that announced his death. It was routine for variations of nicknames for individuals to occur often due to human error in the creation of records.

was reported killed in the area of Avion and Méricourt, just southeast of Lens, on July 16, 1917. He was only twenty-three years old.

53. Smith, William Harold (August 5, 1917)

Gunner 301259, 36th Field Battery, 11th Howitzer Brigade, 9th Howitzer Brigade

William Harold Smith was born on April 8, 1893, in Iden, Sussex, England, to Edward and Beatrice Smith. The Smith family eventually came to live in Fredericton and occupied a residence on Carleton Street. Edward and Beatrice had a large family: in addition to William were three sons, Albert, Hugh, and Donald, and three daughters, Dorothy, Daisy, and Marjory. There are few records detailing William's early life growing up in Fredericton, but at the time of his enlistment in 1915, he was unmarried and worked as a chauffeur in the area. According to his service record, William had blue eyes, a medium complexion, dark brown hair, and his family were Methodists. He was also described as being a tall man for the time, standing at five feet eleven inches. In addition to working as a chauffeur, William was a volunteer fire fighter with the Fredericton Fire Brigade. Like so many others his age, he put his home life on hold to do his part in the war, enlisting for service on November 22, 1915, in Fredericton.

Just twenty-two years old, William went overseas as a gunner with the

36th Canadian Field Battery, leaving for England on February 26, 1916, aboard the SS *Missanabie*, disembarking nearly two weeks later, on March 13. In May, after two months of training, he was transferred from the 11th to the 9th Howitzer Brigade, which left for France on July 13. While engaged with enemy artillery in the field, William was badly gassed; three months later, he contracted albuminuria, a type of kidney disease. Given the living conditions and changing season, William caught a severe cold that quickly developed into tuberculosis. According to records, he was taken to England in November 1916 and was admitted to a military hospital due to his poor health and degenerating lungs. His lungs had been so badly compromised by the gas, however, that nothing could be done for him, and he was sent home to Canada in March 1917 in the hope that being in the climate of his own country would be beneficial. The *Daily Gleaner* reported that William arrived March 28 and was able to walk downtown that day and the next, where he was always warmly greeted by his friends, noting that he was one of the most popular boys in town. According to reports, he practically lived outside during the last few months of his life in a tent made for him in his garden, where every attention could be given to him by family and friends. He died on Sunday, August 5, 1917, at twenty-four years of age. He was the first local soldier to return and die at home. On the day of his funeral, William's casket, draped in the Union Jack, was carried from his house to the hearse, where six returned men acted as pall-bearers. William was given a military funeral and firing salute by members of the 236th Kilties at the Fredericton Rural Cemetery. He was much loved by family and community, and his funeral was one of the largest ever seen in Fredericton at the time. His name appears on the memorial plaque installed on the old King Street Fire Station, along with Albert Boddington's.

Lest We Forget

Gunner William Harold Smith is buried in the northwest corner of Fredericton Rural Cemetery along the Woodstock Road. His grave is commemorated with both a CWGC headstone and one set up by the family.

54. Grant, Percy Winslow (August 15, 1917)

Private 817478, 140th Battalion, 26th Battalion

Percy Winslow Grant was born on December 26, 1896, in Fredericton to Neville and Aurella Grant. According to marriage records, Neville and Aurella married on July 3, 1895. They had four children and occupied a residence in downtown Fredericton at 332 Church Street, while their extended family lived at the Mouth of Keswick. Percy was the eldest in the family, followed by his two sisters, Eva and Annabelle, and a younger brother named Julius, or "John," as he was referred to in newspapers. According to the 1911 census, just prior to the war, the family was still living on Church Street, along with Percy's maternal grandmother, Felicia Morse. Although there are few accounts detailing his childhood growing up in Fredericton, local newspapers reveal that Percy's family was well known and had strong connections in the community — his father, Neville, was lauded as one of the best men in Fredericton. Newspaper accounts provide insight into Percy as a member of one the most respected Black families in the area, but few military records highlight its significance within the context of the First World War. Just prior to the war, Percy's father worked as a labourer and cleaner for the Canadian Pacific Railway, while his mother worked at home raising their family. Neville passed away on October 12, 1912, after a battle with cancer.

At the time of Percy's enlistment in Sussex on September 28, 1915, with the 140th Battalion, his attestation paper shows that he was working locally as a labourer and that he had no prior military experience. While pictures published by the *Daily Gleaner* in 1917 draw attention to his African ancestry, Percy's personnel records give little attention to this, describing him as having blue eyes, brown hair, and a fair complexion and standing five feet five inches tall. It is this inaccuracy in the record that clouded important details regarding the possible experiences he might have had as a Black soldier serving with local units. Just prior to leaving for overseas in early September 1916, Private Grant named his mother as his sole beneficiary in his will, a process records show he would have to repeat four more times while serving with the Canadian Expeditionary Force.

On September 25, 1916, Private Grant left from Halifax for Liverpool on the SS *Corsican*, landing on October 6. Upon arrival, Percy remained with the 140th Battalion, but then spent the next four months training over the winter with the 13th Reserve Battalion RCR and the PPCLI. According to his active service record, on February 17, 1917, Private Grant was transferred to the 26th Battalion and arrived at Le Havre, France, a week later. Percy and the 26th Battalion took part in the Battle of Vimy Ridge two months later, widely considered a defining moment for the Canadian Corps at a critical point in the war. There are few details of Private Grant's experiences during and shortly after Vimy, but he remained with the 26th Battalion over the next few months as the unit continued to push forward, pressuring the German line. Throughout, Percy stayed with the "Fighting 26th" and was involved in coordinated

The Christ Church Cathedral Memorial that includes the name of Percy Grant. James Rowinski

attacks near Lens on August 15, the beginning of the Battle of Hill 70, which lasted until August 27. According to Percy's circumstances-of-death record, he was killed on the very first day of action at Hill 70; his remains were never found. In a vicious series of attacks and repelling of German counterattacks, the Canadians eventually prevailed at Hill 70 against five divisions of the German 6th Army, while suffering thousands of casualties.

News of Percy's death reached home August 29. The following day, the *Daily Gleaner* reported his death, revealing the significance of his being the first African Canadian New Brunswicker to be killed in the war. At the time of his death, Percy was twenty years old, a fact that also illustrates he was only seventeen when he enlisted, two years younger than he had attested to. The significance of Percy's African ancestry is particularly important to highlight and remember so that stories about Canada's military past do not remain limited in scope, but rather serve to represent the experiences of all who lived and sacrificed during such a trying time in our country's history.

Lest We Forget

Private Percy Winslow Grant is remembered on the Vimy Memorial, located in Vimy, France.

55. Osgood, Giles Dever (August 15, 1917)

Lieutenant, 74th New Brunswick Rangers, 140th Battalion, 26th Battalion

Giles Dever Osgood was born on August 14, 1883, in Fredericton to Margaret Ann Laferty and Giles Osgood Sr. Census records show that Giles had five siblings named Harry, Sarah Jane, Mabel, Alice, and Eliza Osgood. For much of his early life, Giles lived with his family in Fredericton, where his father was employed at a local bank, while his mother worked as a provider and homemaker. Newspapers also reveal that Giles came from a military family, his father having once served with the British Army overseas during the Boer War. In 1906, Giles's father passed away, leaving his mother a widow and likely affecting the early childhood of all siblings in the home. By all accounts, Giles appears to have been incredibly popular locally and an active member of the community for most of his young life. Newspapers report that he was a popular employee at the Oak Hall establishment. After his father's death, however, Giles took a job in Saint John with Scovil Brothers. Later, he left his job in Saint John to accept a position with the Sussex Mercantile Company as a manufacturing agent and salesman, then as a representative for the Maritime Hat and Cap Company of Moncton.

The year of his father's death marked another important part of his life: his marriage. According to marriage records, Giles married Edith Hazel Bell on May 10, 1906, in Saint John. Edith was from the Saint John area and, although little is known of how they met, the nineteen-year-old Edith was likely charmed by the older Giles. Together, Giles and Edith moved to Sussex, where they had two sons, Winston Mersereau Osgood and Bryne Fenwick Osgood.

By the time war broke out, Giles had very little military experience, although records suggest he belonged to the 74th New Brunswick Rangers. Newspapers also reveal that, when Giles first applied to the recruiting office, he was informed he was physically unfit for service and would have to undergo a medical procedure if he wanted to serve overseas. His medical records suggest it might have been a stomach hernia. After his operation, Giles reapplied for service in the winter of 1915 with the 140th Battalion. This time his application was accepted. Osgood promptly went to Halifax for officer training, where he was granted a commission as lieutenant in the Canadian Expeditionary Force. At the time of his enlistment on November 28, 1915, Giles was thirty-two years old and was described as having blue eyes, brown hair, medium complexion and standing five feet six inches tall. He spent the winter of 1915–16 in Valcartier with the 140th Battalion, and he went back to New Brunswick in the summer of 1916 to sign his formal will at Saint John before going overseas.

On September 25, 1916, Lieutenant Giles D. Osgood embarked from Halifax aboard the SS *Corsican* for Liverpool, arriving October 6. On October 28, after less than a month of training, Giles landed in France with the 60th Battalion, just as the Battle of the Somme was drawing to a close. Over the next few months, Giles often wrote home, with his letters usually being printed in New Brunswick newspapers. His service record reveals that he had a small case of laryngitis in February 1917. By early spring 1917, Lieutenant Osgood was with the 5th Canadian Mounted Rifles as they prepared for the Vimy Ridge offensive, and then later with the 26th Battalion. Two months before Vimy Ridge, Giles wrote home to his friend W.H. Plummer:

Dear Bill, your welcome letter from the 5th came to hand a few days ago, and I was glad to get it, as I had begun to think you had forgotten where I lived. We are now in rest billets for about three weeks getting a general brush up! We work about two hours a day and are having a very good day compared to trench life. We are billeted in a good-sized town and the people are very kind and are most anxious to do all for our comfort. There seems to be plenty of everything in the eating lines here, despite the so-called sub-blockade, but prices are fairly high but from what I can see, that applies to every country. I am enclosing a little parody on the sunshine of my soul. I found it in one of the letters the boys were sending out, and I thought it was pretty good. You know if a fellow gets wounded badly enough to get sent back to a hospital in England, which is called a "blighty," they think he's pretty lucky. About the sub-warfare, don't worry about it, as John Bull has the situation pretty well under hand and ships are arriving and sailing over here just the same as usual. Many thanks for the parcel which you say is coming along. I will advise you when it shows up. You have certainly had some weather home this winter. I guess our cold weather is over. The last few days have been nice and sunny and very similar to weather we get home about the last of April. We are having a great time trying to parley French. I think if I were to stick around one of these French towns for a while, I might pick up quite a bit of it. At present, I have to rely on my batman. As he talks good French, and he is my interrupter at the billet where I sleep. I tell you it certainly is a pleasure to roll into a nice soft bed at night with real white sheets. If you get the record you will find part one of my letters to Mrs. Robinson, but where they say trench fever it should read trench feet. There is trench fever over here but what causes it the M.D.'s don't seem to know. It isn't serious, as a rule. A man may have a very high fever for a few days and then he is as well as ever again after. I expect we will get back in the line again before to the big push, which is bound to come pretty soon. We just got word that fritz has withdrawn on quite a large frontage, which means he is shortening up his line. Looks as if he didn't have any more men than he knows what to do with. Write me again soon. — Giles.

After being taken on strength with the 26th Battalion in May 1917, Giles stayed in northern France as the Canadians continued to push the German line back beyond the Arras sector. For the next few months, Osgood was with his unit as they prepared for the coming Battle of Hill 70. According to his circumstances-of-death record, Giles was near Lens on the opening day of the attack, August 15, 1917, when he was killed moving forward with his unit. His body was never recovered. News of his death spread quickly in local papers a week after his death, offering condolences to his wife, children, and extended family. Giles was thirty-four years old.

Lest We Forget

Lieutenant Giles Dever Osgood is honoured on the Vimy Memorial, in Vimy, France.

56. Parsons, William E. (August 15, 1917)

Lance Corporal 709189, 71st York Regiment, 104th Battalion, 26th Battalion

William Ernest Parsons was born August 24, 1888, in Fredericton to John Herbert Parsons Sr. and Ella Lorena Wells. According to census records, William was the eldest of his seven siblings, the others being Annie, Bessie, John H. Jr., Edward, Dorothy, Aldon, and Robert. The Parsons family lived at 559 Brunswick Street and his father worked as a restaurant keeper in Fredericton. At a young age, "Billie" Parsons, as William was known around Fredericton, was one of the most promising musicians in the city, having spent most of his upbringing active with the George Street Baptist Church, the Fredericton Brass Band, and later with the 71st Regiment Band. William eventually was employed as a pressman with the *Daily Gleaner* and became prominent working with youth organizations and teaching Sunday school. By all accounts, William was incredibly well liked and well known by many in Fredericton largely due to these endeavours. Although he was not married at the time of his enlistment on September 25, 1915, William's service record suggests that, prior to the war, he might have proposed to a woman named Lillian V. Currie, of Carleton Street. Since Lillian and William lived close to each another, attended the same church, and Lillian was named in his will and would receive his service medals, it is likely that they had made plans to get married after he returned. Although William had no experience in the military outside of being a musician with the local regiment, he joined the 104th Battalion in Sussex alongside his father and two brothers, John H. Jr. and Edward, and began training to go overseas. According to his attestation paper, William was twenty-seven years old and stood five feet seven inches tall, having hazel eyes, light brown hair, and a fair complexion. He wrote home constantly throughout the war, but his active service record reveals that he never saw his family and friends again after the spring of 1916.

On June 28, 1916, Private Parsons, his brother Edward, and his father embarked together from Halifax on the SS *Olympic* for Liverpool, arriving on July 5. William stayed with the 104th Battalion in England, requesting that he be made a training instructor and help with the war effort in England alongside his brother and father. For the next twelve months, William remained in his position with the 104th until news reached him that Edward had been buried alive and had almost died. This likely had an effect on William. Active and anxious to go over to France "and get a taste of real war," according to the *Daily Gleaner*, William put in a request on April 14, 1917, for a rank reduction to go to the front with the 26th Battalion. Now a lance corporal, Parsons joined the 26th on April 20, 1917. Although there are few details of his exact activities over the next few months, William remained with the battalion in the Arras area in the months leading up to the August attacks on Hill 70. On August 9, William wrote home to his family to say he was going up the line the following day. On the morning of August 15, the opening day of the Hill 70 battle, the 26th Battalion attacked a German line called the Norman trench system. At some point during the attack, Lance Corporal Parsons was reportedly killed instantly after a German shell exploded near his position. William was twenty-nine years old.

News of his death reached the pages of the *Daily Gleaner* in late August, the story indicating general grief from a community that had known him well. On September 9, an evening memorial service was held at the Baptist Church to honour William's life and sacrifice. According to the *Daily Gleaner*, his former pastor, Reverend J.E. Wilson of Woodstock, conducted the service alongside members of the Fredericton Brass Band. As the Monday paper reported a day after his memorial service, "the George Street Baptist Church was packed to the doors Sunday evening by the friends, acquaintances and former associates of William Parsons," suggesting an impressive turnout of community members and friends paying their last respects to an admired young man.

Lest We Forget

Lance Corporal William Parsons was buried with honour at the Rue-Petillon Military Cemetery in Feurbaix, France, which holds 893 identified casualties.

57. Semple, Joseph (August 15, 1917)

Private 742998, 115th Battalion, 26th Battalion

Joseph Semple was born on May 27, 1884, in Saint John to James Semple and Mary Galbraith. Records indicate that James and Mary had married in Saint John in 1878. In addition to Joseph, there were six other children in the family: Henry, Rebecca, James, Samuel, Grace, and Mary. The family grew up at 192 Waterloo Street in Saint John and later Paradise Row, where their father worked as a police constable for the city. Although little is known of his childhood, census records show that, as a child, Joseph attended school and later became a well-known travelling food salesman in the province. His connection to Fredericton began when he worked for the Willet Fruit Company, a job that brought him to the area where he became a popular young man with those he encountered. It was during his time working between Saint John and Fredericton that he met Vita Irene Brewer of Fredericton. Joseph was twenty-six and Vita two years younger. They married in November 1910 and lived at 52 Durham Street in Saint John; records suggest they did not have any children prior to the war. Joseph spent seven years with an artillery unit in Saint John. At the time of his wartime enlistment in Saint John on March 18, 1916, he was thirty-two years old and described as having a dark complexion, blue eyes, and black hair, and standing five feet eight inches tall. According to his service record, after joining the 115th Battalion, Joseph stayed in Canada for a few months before being transferred overseas to England.

On July 23, 1916, Private Semple left from Halifax aboard the SS *Olympic*, arriving at Liverpool on July 31. A month after arriving at Bramshott Camp, Joseph was promoted to sergeant of his unit. By October, however, he had reverted back to the rank of private so he could join the 26th Battalion to be with his brother-in-law when it took a draft of men to the Western Front. Perhaps realizing that he might not return, on September 26 Joseph wrote his will naming his wife as sole beneficiary.

Less than a month later, on October 23, Joseph landed in France just as the Somme battles were slowly coming to a close.

Over the winter of 1916–17, the area in and around Arras became home for Joseph and the 26th Battalion. While in the field, he was attached to the paymaster's department, perhaps because of his work-life experience as a salesman. It is unclear if he took part in the four-day Vimy Ridge assault in April 1917; perhaps his recordkeeping skills were needed given the thousands of casualties that resulted. A few months later, he rejoined the 26th Battalion at the front as it prepared for engagements at Hill 70. In August, General Sir Arthur Currie, commanding the Canadian Corps, developed a strategy to remove the German army from an area it had controlled since the beginning of the war. Beginning on August 15, Joseph and the 26th Battalion took part in coordinated assaults leading to Hill 70's capture on the first day. Although headlines in local newspapers appeared convincing—"Canadians smashing at coal city today, now a death trap for Germans"—the reality was that, over the next few days, the Canadians lost approximately nine thousand men during repeated German counterattacks. Joseph was one of these early casualties. According to his circumstances-of-death report, while going forward on the first day of the assault, August 15, he went missing and was never found. Newspapers at home quickly reported what happened. When Vita received the confusing news at her parent's home in Fredericton, she was upset by the "uncertainty of the meaning of the conflicting messages," but his death was confirmed soon after. Joseph was thirty-three years old.

In January 1919, Vita married Frank Archibald Rowan. Although the war was over, she was harassed for moving on with her life so soon. Reports surfaced that Joseph actually had survived and was coming home only to find that his wife had remarried. These claims, which were challenged by family and friends, showed how common it was for women to be judged harshly for trying to cope after such a loss—necessity forced many to remarry.

Lest We Forget

Private Joseph Semple is honoured on the Vimy Memorial, in Vimy, France.

58. Slater, Nathaniel William (August 23, 1917)

Private 709288, 104th Battalion, 5th Canadian Mounted Rifles

Nathaniel William Slater was born on April 9, 1895, in Cambridge, Massachusetts, to Alice May DeWitt and William Ainsworth Slater. Nathaniel's father was from England and his mother came from Blissville, New Brunswick. Prior to Nathaniel's birth, his parents had been living in New Brunswick, William having come to Saint John, where he found work as a stonemason. Although it is unclear how they met, according to marriage records, they had a quiet wedding at the home of a friend in Juvenile Settlement on October 27, 1892. After their marriage, the couple moved to Cambridge, where William was employed as a stone-cutter. Records suggest that Nathaniel was their only child. A year after he was born, his mother became sick with typhoid and passed away at the age of twenty-six. Eight years after her death, William remarried a woman named Isabella Dor, who had also been previously married and lost a spouse. Records suggest that, during this time, Nathaniel lived with his father's sister, Sarah Ann Slater and her husband, William B. Eastwood, in Hoyt. Nathaniel's military service record describes Sarah as his foster-mother. A brother of William's named John also lived in the area. These accounts appear to explain why William moved Nathaniel to New Brunswick after Alice's death to be close to family.

According to Nathaniel's attestation paper, prior to the war he was working as a farmer in the area with family and had begun attending the Brunswick Street Baptist Church. On September 24th, 1915, Nathaniel enlisted at Sussex with the 64th Battalion before being transferred to the 104th. His attestation paper also reveals that he had a fair complexion, hazel eyes, and brown hair, and was five feet eight inches tall. Only twenty years old at the time, "Nat," as he was called by his friends, joined others from the area and began training and preparations for going overseas. He spent the winter of 1915–16 in Canada before his unit went overseas.

On June 28, 1916, Private Slater embarked from Halifax aboard the SS *Olympic* for Liverpool. Arriving on July 5, he remained with the 104th in England until being transferred to the 5th Canadian Mounted Rifles (CMR) in November. Before arriving in France with the 5th CMR, Nat wrote his formal will, leaving everything to Sarah, his aunt and foster-mother. According to his active service record, he arrived in France on December 4, 1916, just after the Battle of the Somme had concluded. Arriving in the area of Arras with the Canadian Corps in the winter of 1916–17, Nathaniel was part of preparations leading up to the attack at Vimy Ridge. After action at Vimy, the 5th CMR shifted northward toward the area of Lens. On August 23, 1917, Private Slater was in frontline trenches that had been taken over from the Germans a week earlier during operations at Hill 70. According to the official war diaries of the 5th CMR, at approximately 3:00 a.m. on the morning of August 23, Slater's position was hit by artillery shells and the barrage continued all day long. At some point Nathaniel was killed, although details of his death have not survived in the records. The following Saturday, his father received a message from Ottawa that his son had died during actions at Lens. Reports of his death were revealed by the *Daily Gleaner* on September 20, indicating "extreme sympathy" from everyone in the community who knew him. Nathaniel was twenty-two at the time of his death.

Lest We Forget

Private Nathaniel William Slater was buried with honour at the Dud Corner Cemetery, located in Loos-en-Gohelle, France. According to the Commonwealth War Graves Commission, there are 684 identified casualties in this cemetery. Nathaniel also has a memorial marker placed in the Hoyt Baptist Cemetery in New Brunswick.

59. Peoples, Earle Milford (August 29, 1917)

Corporal 817525, 140th Battalion, Princess Patricia's Canadian Light Infantry

Earle Milford Peoples was born on October 20, 1898, in Newbury, Carleton County, New Brunswick. According to records obtained through the Provincial Archives of New Brunswick, Earle's father was Charles Bruce Peoples, but little is known of his mother. Newspapers suggest that she passed away when Earle was an infant. As an only child to a widowed father, Earle lived for a time with his grandparents, George and Hannah, as his father was often away finding work. As Earl grew up in Kingsclear, his grandfather worked as a local shoemaker. By the time he was twelve years old, Earle and his father were living in Fredericton as boarders in the Orchard residence. Charles was employed as a barber and Earle was apprenticing as a plumber. Records suggest that they lived at 363 Charlotte Street and had close ties to the downtown community and Wilmot Church. Although little is known of the particulars of his early life, Earle had no military experience or training prior to the war. At the time of his enlistment at Sussex on November 23, 1915, he attested to being twenty-seven years old, single, and working as a plumber's assistant. Earle was described as having blue eyes, light brown hair, a fair complexion, while standing approximately five feet eleven inches tall. In truth, the young man was only seventeen when he enlisted, as his medical history sheet and birth records clearly show when he joined the 104th Battalion, and later the 140th as a private. Over the next few months, Peoples remained in New Brunswick at the Provincial School of Instruction in Saint John, where he received promotions to the rank of lance corporal and then corporal by the summer of 1916. Earle signed his will in early September, leaving everything to his father, but it is unclear if he ever saw his father and friends again before going overseas.

On September 25, 1916, Corporal Peoples left Halifax aboard the SS *Corsican* for Liverpool. His service record indicates that he arrived on October 10, and after only a month of training, joined the Princess

Patricia's Canadian Light Infantry (PPCLI) at Seaford Camp in late November. By early December, Earle was already in France in the Arras sector with the PPCLI preparing for the assault on Vimy Ridge in April. After the success of Vimy, Earle remained with his unit in the same area, taking part in actions designed to push back the German front line. By August, he was in and around Lens and part of actions at Hill 70, the critical battle led by Canadians trying to gain important high ground in the area. According to his circumstances-of-death record, Corporal Peoples was with his unit on August 27 when he received gunshot wounds and fractures to both legs, as well as his arms. He was evacuated quickly to No. 7 Casualty Clearing Station for treatment of "dangerous wounds," but medical personnel were unable to help him. Earle passed away on August 29, two days after being admitted. By September 4, newspapers had reported his death with much sympathy for his father and highlighted that Earle was only nineteen at the time. Earle had been overseas for less than a year.

Lest We Forget

Corporal Earle M. Peoples is buried at Noeux-les-Mines Communal Cemetery, located south of Bethune, France. According to the Commonwealth War Graves Commission, Earle is one of 198 burials.

60. Bonnar, Herbert Little (October 15, 1917)

Private 817974, 140th Battalion, 26th Battalion

Herbert Little Bonnar was born on July 25, 1883, in Fredericton to James Bonnar and Mary Anne Good. According to the 1901 census, James and Mary had three sons: James, Edward, and Herbert. Although few records shed light on Herbert's early life, documents do show that his father was a farmer in the Marysville area, just north of Fredericton, and that Herbert eventually worked as a mill hand and cotton weaver at the local mill. During this time, he became close to a local Marysville girl named Jennie Manzer, who was four years younger than Herbert. By the summer of 1906, Jennie, only eighteen years old, and Herbert, twenty-two, married in Marysville. That fall Herbert and Jennie had their first child, a girl named Alice. Two years later, Jennie gave birth to another girl, Mabel. Their only son, Milster, was born in 1912. In 1906 Herbert's eldest brother, James, married a relative of Jennie's named Bessie Oldenburgh, and in 1919 Edward married Elizabeth Humphrey, from Saint John. Long before the war, the Bonnar brothers' father had passed away, leaving their mother a widow.

When war came to Fredericton, all three brothers enlisted for service. According to his attestation paper, Herbert enlisted at the age of thirty-two in Saint John on March 17, 1916, with the 140th Battalion. Although Herbert had no military training, his skills and trade as a labourer would come into good use overseas. Private Bonnar stood five feet five inches tall and had a medium complexion, brown eyes, and brown hair. While it is likely that Herbert wrote letters home to his family, especially his wife and children, he would never see them again once he left Canada for England.

Private Bonnar remained with his unit in Canada until leaving from Halifax on September 25, 1916, aboard the SS *Corsican*. On October 10, the 140th Battalion arrived in Liverpool, where Herbert then joined the RCR and a month later the PPCLI Base Depot. Over the winter of 1916–17 and following spring, Private Bonnar was transferred through a number of units before joining a reinforcement draft for the 26th Battalion as it was preparing to go to France in August. The summer of 1917 found the "Fighting 26th" active during the battles of Hill 70 and Lens, places where the Canadian Corps improved its ability to gain and hold territory while units from behind carried forward. Although casualties were always felt in the ranks, this strategy allowed units to be more effective when dealing with counterattacks. It is here that Herbert would see his first bit of action as a member of the 26th, coming into the field after Canadians had captured an important position from the Germans at Hill 70. By

September, Private Bonnar was near Neuville-Saint-Vaast, just north of Arras, with his unit. According to the official war diary of the 26th Battalion, by the middle of October Bonnar's unit had replaced the 22nd Battalion in the frontline trenches. On the day of his death, a heavy enemy barrage opened up on the frontline and supporting trenches where he was located during the early morning hours of October 15. Enemy shells hit exactly where Herbert was positioned, causing shrapnel wounds to his face, eyes, legs, and arms. He was evacuated to No. 42 Casualty Clearing Station, where medical attention was administered, but he did not survive. Private Herbert Bonnar was thirty-five years of age and left behind his wife, Jennie, and three children. News of his death reached Fredericton newspapers by October 22, and a brief report shared that he had died in a London Hospital, although his service record shows he died in France.

By March 1919, Jennie had married Bliss Alfred Lewis from Salisbury and relocated there with her children. Jennie received Private Bonnar's medals and plaques in honour of his service. Herbert's brothers, Edward and James, both survived the war and returned to Fredericton.

Lest We Forget

Private Herbert Little Bonnar is buried at the Aubigny Communal Cemetery Extension, located in Aubigny-en-Artois, fifteen kilometres northwest of Arras. According to the Commonwealth War Graves Commission, this cemetery is the site of the No. 42 Casualty Clearing Station, where wounded soldiers were buried after they died. There are 2,778 identified casualties that include British Commonwealth, French, and German war graves.

61. Brewer, Storey Connor (October 30, 1917)

Private 709003, 71st York Regiment, 104th Battalion,
5th Canadian Mounted Rifles

Storey Connor Brewer was born on July 4, 1898, in Smith's Corner, New Brunswick, to Holland Brewer and Carrie Allen. Although various records have conflicting birthdates for Storey, the 1901 census appears to be correct and is reflected above. When looking at the Brewer family, one cannot ignore how loss played a role in the lives of the children and parents, as they all experienced the trauma of losing a family member at some point. Storey lived in Burtt's Corner with his family, the eldest brother to Harold Magnus and Vera Pearl. He also had three siblings who passed away at a very young age. According to records, on December 3, 1912, Ervine F. died at the age of five months and Storey's mother, Carrie, passed away only a short time later in 1913. Storey's father, Holland Brewer, a labourer and mill worker by trade, married Margaret Rachel Jones on December 26, 1917, only a short time after losing his eldest son. Then, in 1918, twins Margaret and Mary died only one day after their birth to Holland's second wife, Maggie.

Records suggest that the Brewers were Irish Baptists and grew up experiencing the hard-working life of rural New Brunswick. When Storey enlisted for service in Saint John on November 4, 1914, he was working as a shoemaker, in all likelihood with other Fredericton boys at the local Hartt Shoe Factory. Only sixteen years of age and single, Storey was five feet six inches tall and had blue eyes, light brown hair, and what was described as a dark complexion. Although Storey claimed on his attestation paper to have prior military experience with the local 71st York Regiment, his early entry into service would not be an easy transition. After enlisting for service in the fall of 1914 with the 26th Battalion, Storey's young age likely played a role in his subsequent discharge after being in Saint John during the winter of 1914–15, although his service form does not give the reason for his discharge. He soon re-enlisted with the 104th Battalion on October 13, 1915, at Sussex. He trained with his unit over the winter of 1915–16 and was promoted to the rank of lance corporal.

Almost two years after enlisting for service, Storey left with the 104th Battalion from Halifax for England on June 28, 1916, aboard the SS *Olympic*. After a week-long trip across the Atlantic, he arrived with his unit at Liverpool on July 5. He spent the next few months in training at Witley Camp. By late August, his rank had reverted to private when he joined the 5th Canadian Mounted Rifles (CMR). His service record reveals his being "admonished" in early September for failing to obey an order; however, such occurrences were not rare among young men away from home for this first time. Prior to leaving for the front, he named his father, Holland, as his next-of-kin in his will. He arrived for duty in France on February 26, 1917, and took part in all the 5th CMR's engagements over the next nine months. By the fall of 1917, Private Brewer was with his unit near Ypres, involved in operations pushing the German line off and beyond Passchendaele Ridge. On the morning of October 30, at approximately 5:50 a.m., noted in Nicholson's *Official History* as a clear but very cold and windy day that brought rain in the afternoon, Private Brewer was part of the 5th CMR's frontal assault on the left flank that made the best progress of any unit that day. After only an hour and a half of fighting that morning, observers could see enemy parties in full retreat, joining large numbers who were withdrawing in disorder along roads running north from Crest Farm and Mosslemarkt. It was during the fighting at Passchendaele that Private Brewer went missing sometime over the next two days and was never found again. He was officially reported to have been killed sometime between October 30 and 31. His body was never recovered. Private Storey Brewer was only eighteen years of age.

News of his death reached home in local papers, but with limited information about what actually happened to Storey. By November 27, newspapers were reporting a Sunday memorial service held in the community church at Burtt's Corner in his honour. Reverend H.E. Cooke delivered the address to a community paying its last respects to a young

Private Storey C. Brewer's name on the York County Cenotaph at Mactaquac, New Brunswick.
James Rowinski

man described as a brave young soldier. Three years after his death, Storey's father passed away. As Holland Brewer was named as the only next-of-kin, there was no beneficiary to receive Private Brewer's medals after the war.

Lest We Forget

Private Storey Connor Brewer is remembered with honour at the Menin Gate Memorial on the eastern side of Ypres. He is also named on his parent's grave marker in the Burtt's Corner Cemetery. Private Brewer is the only individual whose name appears on three community cenotaphs (Mactaquac, Stanley, and Fredericton).

62. Smith, Alfred Moses (October 30, 1917)

Private 709925, 104th Battalion, 5th and 6th Canadian Mounted Rifles

Alfred Moses Smith was born on November 18, 1895, in Fredericton to Oliver Thomas Smith and Elizabeth Wright Rosborough. According to the 1901 census, Alfred was the fourth child born to Oliver and Elizabeth but their only son. Together with his parents and three sisters, Nellie Elizabeth, Annie A., and Mary B., the Smith family lived at 218 George Street in Fredericton, where their father worked as a shoemaker. Few records exist regarding his early life in Fredericton, but Alfred's elder sisters, Nellie and Annie, both married prior to the war and were living in Saint John and Devon. As a teenager, just before enlisting, Alfred had been working locally as a bookkeeper and was a well-known and very popular young man. When he enlisted on December 8, 1915, at Sussex with the 104th Battalion, Alfred was unmarried and only twenty years of age. According to his attestation paper, Private Smith was described as five feet eight inches tall with fair skin, blue eyes, and light brown hair. With no prior military training or experience, Alfred's choice to fight in the war was likely encouraged by other Fredericton boys doing their part for their country. It is unclear if he ever saw his family again, as he would never return after leaving for England.

Private Smith trained with the 104th Battalion over the winter of 1915–16 and into the spring until leaving from Halifax aboard the SS *Olympic* on June 28, 1916. He disembarked at Liverpool on July 6, and spent the next few months training until being transferred to the 5th Canadian Mounted Rifles (CMR) in November. By December, seven months after arriving, Private Smith was in northern France and Belgium with his unit and over the next few months fought at Vimy Ridge and battles that followed. By early September 1917, Alfred was in Belgium and was hospitalized with a case of trench foot, the result of his extended time in the trenches. He was discharged after only a week of treatment. As the Canadian involvement in the Battle of Passchendaele began, Private

Smith was with the 5th CMR on the morning of October 30, a day that was clear and cold, but windy and raining in the afternoon. According to Nicholson's *Official History*, from the early morning hour of 5:50 a.m. until approximately 7 a.m., Alfred's unit had difficulty getting through the swampy ground of an area known as the Woodland Plantation; however, they made some of the best progress of all units that morning and were relieved that evening. Private Smith was reported missing, however, after failing to report back. His service record does not include a report indicating he had been injured while fighting, although this is likely the case. Soon after his disappearance, New Brunswick newspapers reported him missing in the field with the hope that he might be found. On November 30, however, those hopes turned to sadness when the Smiths received official notification of his death in the field. Private Alfred Moses Smith's body was never recovered. He was twenty-one years of age.

Lest We Forget

Private Alfred Moses Smith is remembered with honour at the Menin Gate (Ypres) Memorial in Ypres, along with 54,393 Commonwealth soldiers who have no known grave in Belgium.

63. Webster, Lawrence Fitzgerald (October 30, 1917)

Lieutenant 70041, 26th Battalion, 5th Canadian Mounted Rifles

Lawrence Fitzgerald Webster was born on November 24, 1885, in Fulbourn, Cambridge, England. According to the 1911 census of England and Wales, he had a younger sister named Jessie Florence Webster who was ten years younger than Lawrence, who was listed as being twenty-five years of age. His mother was Martha Ellen Webster, from London, and his father was Harris Webster, from Cambridge. Documents show that Lawrence was a short man, standing approximately five feet five inches tall, and had spent time working for his great uncle as a student. It is also noted in records that he had a dark complexion, hazel eyes, and brown hair. His family belonged to the Church of England. Lawrence arrived by himself in Saint John on April 26, 1913, aboard the ship *Empress of Britain*. Ship documents reveal that he was coming to Canada to work in the farming industry after spending time as a merchant in Cambridge. His father had worked as a clerk. Saint John newspapers point out that he became quite well known in the province a very short time after arriving, working as a poultry expert in Fredericton at the Experimental Farm. Prior to enlisting at Saint John on November 4, 1914, with the 26th Battalion, Lawrence had five years of service with a British cavalry force in England called the Imperial Yeomanry, which had served in South Africa during the Boer War. In the fall of 1914, Lawrence likely felt the pull of serving his home country once more. At the mature age of twenty-nine, experienced and unmarried, he began training with the 26th Battalion over the winter of 1914–15.

Lawrence did not sail with his unit from Saint John until June 13, 1915, stopping briefly in Halifax on June 15, and continuing on the SS *Caledonia* for the long trip across the Atlantic to England. According to his service record, the 26th arrived on June 24, and Lawrence was confirmed in the rank of sergeant three months later, on September 3. The 26th went to France in September, disembarking at Boulogne five months after the Canadians had first experienced the use of chlorine gas on the Western Front. Over the next two years, he served with the 26th and then the 5th Canadian Mounted Rifles (CMR), and perhaps the most interesting feature about his service documents is that at no time do they indicate Lawrence was ever admitted to hospital for any illness or injury. Despite this, newspapers stated that he had been wounded in 1916 and went back to England in September, where he received a commission as lieutenant with the 5th CMR. Three months later, on December 1, 1916, Lieutenant Webster went back to France with the 5th CMR; according to newspapers, he was now one of the last few remaining members from the original 26th Battalion. Lawrence eventually took part in the Vimy Ridge assault, although his unit was held in reserve throughout the attack. After the success of Vimy, Lawrence was granted time away from the front line for approximately ten days, returning on July 21, 1917. After moving to the Ypres area in the late fall, Webster led men of the 5th CMR throughout a series of attacks in and around Passchendaele during which he was killed on October 30, 1917, and never seen again. Webster was thirty-one years of age.

Lest We Forget

Lieutenant Lawrence F. Webster is honoured on the Menin Gate Memorial in Ypres, Belgium.

64. Atkinson, Alexander Wardlow (November 6, 1917)

Private 742421, 71st York Regiment, 115th Battalion, 26th Battalion

Alexander Wardlow Atkinson was born on December 18, 1892, in Fredericton to Alexander and Mary Atkinson. According to the 1901 census, Alex had two sisters, Nellie May, who passed away at age ten in the winter of 1904, and Nina. Alex also had a stepsister, Annie Wilson, the daughter of Mary, who likely came from a previous relationship. Annie eventually married Lewis G. Hastings in 1907 and together they had a son named Wardlow. According to his attestation paper, Alexander worked as a shoemaker and lived with his family at 236 King Street in Fredericton just prior to enlisting. Records suggest that his father had passed away sometime before 1915, while the 1911 census reveals that his mother was no longer living with the family, as she had moved to 60 Lower Beechwood Avenue in Dublin, Ireland. Alex named his stepsister, Annie, as his next-of-kin, given that she and her young son were also living at the home on King Street despite her recent marriage to Lewis. She later relocated to Toronto and her sister, Nina, moved to Massachusetts. Alex stood approximately five feet seven inches tall, had dark hair, blue eyes, and what was

Canadian stretcher bearers evacuating the wounded during the
Battle of Passchendaele. William Rider-Rider/LAC/PA-002140

described as a "ruddy" complexion, with tattoos on both forearms. He was twenty-two years old and had two years of experience with the 71st York Regiment when he enlisted on January 12, 1916, at Saint John.

Newspapers indicate that Alexander Atkinson had been at Camp Valcartier for two years prior to enlisting with the 115th Battalion in Saint John. He embarked from Halifax with his unit on the SS *Olympic* on July 23, 1916, arriving in Liverpool on July 31. Alexander was in and out of the Connaught Military Hospital in Aldershot, Hampshire, for the next two months before being transferred to the 112th Battalion. The Western Front had just experienced some of the most horrific fighting to date during the Somme battles, and new reserve units were needed to replenish battalions on the front line. By February of 1917, Alexander had moved to the 13th Battalion, Royal Highlanders of Canada (The Black Watch) before rejoining a New Brunswick unit in the spring, this time with the "Fighting 26th." He proceeded overseas to France with the 26th in May and stayed in northern France and Belgium for the remainder of his service. The Passchendaele campaign began in late July and continued until November, and it saw Alexander's unit active throughout the final stages. For those who fought in and around the Ypres Salient, it became known as the "Battle of Mud." Few battles were more gruesome than Passchendaele, which saw more than 15,654 Canadian casualties as the battlefield itself became a death trap. It was during this fighting that Alexander was instantly killed by machine-gun fire on November 6, the day Passchendaele Ridge was captured by the Canadians despite terrible losses. Alexander was twenty-three years old. His body was never recovered.

Lest We Forget

Alexander Wardlow Atkinson is remembered with honour on the Menin Gate in Ypres, Belgium.

65. Colwell, George Stanley (November 6, 1917)

Private 742948, 115th Battalion, 26th Battalion

George Stanley Colwell was born on November 24, 1896, in Jemseg, Queens County, to James A. Colwell and Margaret Isabelle Currie. Stanley, as he was often referred to in records, grew up with his family in Upper Jemseg (Cambridge Narrows), where his father owned a farm. His father also spent time in the port of Saint John managing steamboats to help the family. Altogether the Colwell family included three sons and two daughters, named Albert, George Stanley, Frank, Ida, and Louise. As a result of his father's connection to Saint John, Stanley was employed on a tugboat as a cook once he was of age to work in his early teens. In addition to Stanley, other members of the family built working relationships with Saint John through their father: sister Ida worked as a stenographer and Albert became an engineer on the Valley Road. According to records, Frank and Louise, the two youngest, were at home working the farm just prior to the war. Stanley enlisted on March 13, 1916, in Saint John with the 115th Battalion. While newspapers report him enlisting a year earlier, his service record shows that this formally happened in early 1916. According to his attestation paper, Stanley was nineteen years of age, unmarried, and had no military training or experience. He was described as standing five feet six inches tall, with a dark complexion, blue eyes, and black hair. In the spirited emotion of the time, newspapers speak of his choice to leave home for Europe "not in any adventurous spirit, but with a firm and deep conviction that he should respond to his country's call." While we may never know his true intentions, he never returned home to his family and friends.

Private Colwell trained with the 115th Battalion in Saint John briefly before being sent off to Camp Valcartier in early June 1916. Before leaving for Quebec with his unit, Stanley spent time in a Saint John Military Hospital being treated for tonsillitis. After being in Valcartier for about a month, the 115th left Quebec for Halifax, from where they sailed to England on July 23, 1916, aboard the SS *Olympic.* They arrived in Liverpool on July 31 after an eight-day crossing of the Atlantic Ocean. Private Colwell spent the next year in England training with a variety of units, including the 115th, 112th, and 13th Battalions, primarily at Bramshott Camp. His medical history sheet reveals that he was admitted to hospital on January 26, 1917, to undergo treatment for a fractured ankle. After investigating the incident, however, doctors found out that Stanley had injured himself while involved in a wrestling match with a friend — a sign of young men still trying to enjoy themselves while they waited their turn to head to the front. He spent almost three months in hospital before being discharged and being taken on by the 26th Battalion as reinforcement. After landing in France, Private Colwell headed to the northern French-Belgian border where the "Fighting 26th" had been involved in the Battle of Hill 70 near Lens. The 26th then shifted north to Ypres to relieve other units that had been a part of the Passchendaele attacks in

October. According to the 26th's war diaries, on November 3 they went into the line to replace the 28th Battalion near Passchendaele. It was here on November 6 that Stanley died. According to his circumstances-of-death record, while he was in a support line on the last day before he was to be relieved, Private Colwell was hit in the head by a piece of shell and died instantly. Only one week earlier, on October 30, Stanley had written home to his sister, Ida, sharing news that he believed his unit would be part of an important movement by Canadians and that he likely wouldn't be able to write again for a while. Unfortunately, his letter ultimately proved to be true, as news reached home of his death. A community memorial service was held at the Baptist Jemseg Church soon afterwards, in which Reverend A.W. Brown lead a sermon opening with the text, "Greater love hath no man than this; that a man lay down his life for his friends." Private George Stanley Colwell was twenty-one years old. His body was never recovered.

Lest We Forget

Private George Stanley Colwell is remembered with honour at the Ypres (Menin Gate) Memorial in Ypres, Belgium.

66. McAdam, Walter (November 7, 1917)

Corporal 1257848, 9th Canadian Siege Battery

Walter McAdam was born on October 6, 1898, in Fredericton. His parents were James and Annie Murray McAdam, who lived at 522 George Street. Walter grew up in the Presbyterian Church and attended Fredericton High School. He was a prominent athlete and well-respected rugby player at school, and while in England he played on the Canadian rugby team against some of the best New Zealand squads. According to census records, Walter had three brothers named Murray, Alex, and Donald. All four sons, including Walter, eventually chose to enlist in the Canadian Corps. At the time of his enlistment in the fall of 1916, he was unmarried and had no children. According to his attestation paper, Walter stood five feet eight inches tall, weighed 170 pounds, and had blue eyes, light hair, and fair skin. Walter had just left school and had turned eighteen, the legal age for enlistment, when he joined up on October 13 in Fredericton with childhood friend Allen Wetmore to go overseas with the 9th Canadian Siege Battery as a gunner. Walter never returned.

On March 4, 1917, Corporal McAdam embarked for England from Halifax, arriving in Liverpool twelve days later. He spent the majority of time training, being moved between reserve units and often remaining only a month in each location. Finally, in October 1917, Walter was drafted into the 4th Siege Battery along with other local New Brunswick boys, including Allen Wetmore, landing at Boulogne on October 18. A few days after arriving, he became part of a reinforcement draft in Belgium. The Third Battle of Ypres had been ongoing since July, and the Allies were preparing a new offensive in and around Passchendaele. After being on active duty at the front for less than a month, Walter was killed alongside other members of his battery on November 7, only a few days before the battle ended. In the following letter written home to his mother from Captain G.B. Wetmore, Walter's last moments are described in detail to offer solace to his family: "Last night while the detachment your son was commanding was in action, an enemy shell fell in the midst of them, killing your boy, my cousin Allen Wetmore, also of Fredericton, and four others instantly... in the case of all six, they never could have known what happened or suffered a moment's pain and will be buried side by side... [H]e was one of the finest types of people and was to have been a corporal and before long a sergeant."

Walter was just eighteen at the time of his death, and the second son in the family to lay down his life: Walter's older brother, James Murray McAdam, was lost during the Somme battles in the fall of 1916.

Walter McAdam is buried at the Potlijze Chateau Grounds Cemetery, in Ypres, Belgium.

67. Wetmore, Allen Rainsford (November 7, 1917)

Gunner 1257849, 9th Canadian Siege Battery

Allen Rainsford Wetmore was born on July 2, 1898, in Fredericton. According to his attestation paper and the 1901 census, he lived at 731 Brunswick Street with his mother, Ida Kathleen, his father, Andrew Rainsford Wetmore, and his younger sister, Margaret, all of whom were born in New Brunswick. Before Allen enlisted with the 9th Siege Battery in Fredericton, October 13, 1916, he was a student at Fredericton High School, which was later moved to the present location of George Street Middle School in 1924 before its final relocation to Prospect Street. According to his service record, Allen was five feet seven inches tall, weighed 140 pounds, had blue eyes, light hair, and a fair complexion. He belonged to the Church of England. Allen was eighteen years old when he joined the 9th Siege Battery and, according to documents, it is likely that he was close friends with Walter McAdam, also a member of the 9th. Like many people growing up in Fredericton at the time, they lived close to each other when they were both students at FHS and enlisted for service on the same day. They were also in the same units throughout the war. Allen never returned to his family and friends.

Private Wetmore left Halifax on March 4, 1917, and arrived in Liverpool on March 15. According to his active service record, he remained in England training until he was taken on strength as a reinforcement and attached to the 4th Canadian Siege Battery during the Third Battle of Ypres at Passchendaele. The Canadians participated in an attack on the village itself to regain what was thought of as important strategic ground, although many later believed the location held very little tactical importance. Allen had been in the field on active duty for only twenty days since landing at Boulogne on October 18, 1917. He was killed sometime during the three days before the battle ended on November 7, along with five others from the original 9th Siege Battery. In a letter written home to family that was printed in newspapers, Captain G.B. Wetmore described the death of his cousin, explaining that, "in the case of all six they never could have known what happened or suffered a moment's pain... They are buried side by side in one of the many little plots of crosses so common in this poor, unfortunate country." Allen Rainsford Wetmore was only nineteen years old.

Lest We Forget

Allen Rainsford Wetmore is memorialized at the Potijze Chateau Grounds Cemetery, outside Ypres, Belgium. According to the Commonwealth War Graves Commission, he is one of 850 casualties in the cemetery, many of whom fought in the Third Battle of Ypres campaign. It was located behind the Allied trenches and remained intact during the entire war.

68. Patterson, Miles B. (November 10, 1917)

Sergeant 430114, 48th Battalion, 3rd Canadian Pioneer Battalion, 7th Battalion

Miles B. Patterson, known to his friends as "Cy," was born on October 2, 1887, in Fredericton. He had grey eyes, a dark complexion, and dark brown hair. Miles was the youngest son of Saunders D. Patterson, a farmer and carpenter from Kingsclear Parish, and Maria Ann Cliff. According to the 1901 census, Miles had one sister named Mina and two older brothers named Everett and Ward. Together, the Patterson family occupied a dwelling at 157 Aberdeen Street, although records reveal that a residence was also maintained by someone in the family at 207 Smythe Street. The 1911 census confirms that Miles was living in Vancouver with his brother Everett, while his elder brother Ward was living in Alberta after graduating from the University of New Brunswick in 1903. Ward had moved to Calgary to study law and would enlist with an Alberta Battalion, earning a commission as lieutenant during the war. Miles, working as an electrician at the time, enlisted on March 15, 1915, at the age of twenty-seven, with the 48th Battalion in Victoria, British Columbia. Upon joining up, Miles claimed to have had some prior military experience. Standing five feet nine inches tall, Miles was the ideal civilian soldier with a professional trade, life experience, and maturity, as well as the physical stature to endure what awaited him in Europe. Miles's brother, Lieutenant Ward H. Patterson, returned home in 1919, but Miles would never see his family again.

Sergeant Patterson's unit, the 48th Battalion, sailed from Canada on July 1, 1915, and arrived at Shorncliffe, England, on July 10. The fall and winter were particularly hard on Miles as he was in and out of hospital with a variety of ailments between October and January. In January 1916, the 48th was reconstituted as the 3rd Canadian Pioneers and left for France on March 9. In the newly formed unit, Miles was promoted to lance corporal, corporal, and eventually sergeant once in the field, where his unit was active in the Ypres Salient and during the Somme battles. On September 9, at the Somme, Miles was wounded in the face and in his right eye by shrapnel fire, but after spending time in the hospital, he was sent back to his unit on October 5. For the next five months, Miles remained with the 3rd Pioneers until admitting himself to hospital for five days for reasons unknown. On May 8, 1917, Miles was transferred to the 123rd Battalion, Royal Grenadiers, where he helped facilitate the flow of troops and goods, and worked on roads and fortifying the front lines. On July 9, Miles put in a request to join the 7th Battalion from British Columbia, likely wishing to rejoin his British Columbia infantry mates in the line. He was granted his first and only ten days' leave of absence to Paris. Upon returning to northern France, he remained with the 7th through the summer and fall as the Passchendaele offensive began. On November 10, as the 7th Battalion was actively pushing the Germans beyond the Passchendaele Ridge northwest of the town, the early hours of the morning brought heavy shellfire upon his unit, and Miles was seen wounded in the field. A letter written home by his brother, Ward, reveals the confusion the family was feeling at the time Miles went missing:

> Dear Mother and Father, I have a very difficult letter to write. Until two days ago I had, for the past five weeks, been constantly up the line or in support absolutely unable to move about to get more information about Miles. Two days ago, I visited his battalion and learned that on November 10th, after Miles was wounded, he was taken to the advanced dressing station, had his wound dressed and was sent back out along with other wounded casualties…they have never since been heard from. I am wretchedly sorry to have to write this to you, but there is no good object served by keeping news back or by keeping you in suspense. It is well known that at Passchendaele a great number of the wounded were killed and buried or lost on their way out of the line. I am very sorry to have written you before raising false hopes. For my own part, I have not the slightest doubt that Miles was killed while on the way out from the lines and his platoon commander and his comrades have also no doubt about it. I have talked to men and officers about Miles and have learned that he was very popular and was a general favorite. His loss is mourned sincerely, and his platoon officer said that Miles was "simply one of the best." That is the highest praise that can be given, and it means much, especially when the standard here is wonderfully high. There are a few whom the officers and men especially respect and admire and of these they say, "He is one of the best." Miles lived a pure, clean, life and he died a hero fighting for a great cause. Your affectionate son, Sergeant Ward.

Miles was one of the many thousands whose bodies were never recovered. He was thirty years old at the time of his death.

Lest We Forget

Sergeant Miles B. Patterson is remembered on the Menin Gate Memorial in Ypres, Belgium. The war came to an end exactly one year and a day later after his death.

69. Connolly, John E. (November 15, 1917) Military Medal

Sergeant 478055, The Royal Canadian Regiment

John E. Connolly was born on June 11, 1891, in Liverpool, England, to Joseph and Margaret Connolly. According to the 1901 England and Wales census, John was the eldest of five children, the others being a younger brother Joseph and three sisters named Mary, Margaret, and Francis. While little is known about his early life in England with his family, documents obtained from Library and Archives Canada suggest that John came to Canada as part of the Middlemore Children's Emigration Homes program. Records reveal that, by October 1903, John had arrived in Quebec City on his way to Montreal aboard the ship *Bavarian* through the Catholic Emigration Association. Arriving with ten other boys from Liverpool, the thirteen-year-old likely was sent to Canada for work or simply for opportunities that many believed existed in Canada at the time. Over the next ten years, John made his way from Montreal to New Brunswick, where he met Grace Smith, the daughter of Robert W. Smith, and sister of Archibald Smith, who himself would pay the ultimate sacrifice during the Great War. It is not known how they met, but on October 24, 1913, John and Grace, both twenty-three years of age, married in Fredericton. By this time, John had been serving with The Royal Canadian Regiment

(RCR) when it was stationed in Fredericton, and he was also working as a wool puller in Fredericton. John and Grace were living at 270 Saint John Street, but early on in the war Connolly left for Bermuda with the RCR for garrison duty before returning to Canada and leaving for England in the fall of 1915. John formally enlisted for service in England at Shorncliffe Camp on October 5, 1915. His attestation paper describes him as standing five feet eight inches tall, with hazel-coloured eyes, light brown hair, and a fresh complexion. John also had distinct tattoo markings on his right and left forearms. He was twenty-five years old at the time; records do not reveal if he and Grace had any children together.

John Connolly's record of service shows that he arrived with the RCR on November 11, 1915, at Boulögne, France, only a month after formally signing up for overseas service. He spent all of 1916 with the RCR, active in key battles his unit was a part of during that time. By October 1916, Sergeant Connolly's active service record reveals that he lost eight days' pay for being "late falling in on parade" and for "drunkenness while on parade." Given the conditions many Canadians were experiencing at the time, especially being away from loved ones, John's discipline violations might well be understood. After a ten-day leave of absence in late 1916, John returned and received three successive promotions over a span of four months, from lance corporal to corporal and finally to sergeant by May 1917. Remarkably, Sergeant Connolly had no reported illnesses or injuries during his service.

By July 1917, after Canadian successes at Vimy Ridge and other key fights that followed, Sergeant Connolly was awarded the Military Medal, recommended by his commanding officer for bravery while in the field with his unit (*London Gazette*, 30172, July 7, 1917). By the fall of 1917, Sergeant Connolly was in Belgium with the RCR, active in engagements in and around Ypres and Passchendaele. John's circumstances-of-death report reveals that, on November 15 at approximately 8 a.m., he was killed instantly by an enemy shell while with his company in the support line at Passchendaele. His body was never recovered. Sergeant John Connolly was twenty-seven years of age. News of his death in Fredericton was met with initial confusion because the telegram his widow, Grace, received showed another soldier's regimental number, and for a time there was hope that he was still alive. By December 3, however, Grace, now living at 643 Charlotte Street, finally received official notification that it was her husband who had died.

Lest We Forget

Sergeant John E. Connolly is remembered on the Menin Gate Memorial in Ypres, Belgium. His name is engraved on panel 10.

Chapter Four

1918

During the fifth year of the Great War, the Canadian Corps saw the end of the trench stalemate on the Western Front and the return of mobile operations. On March 21, the Germans began a series of offensives that lasted until July, throwing back the Allies in Belgium and northern France. In July, the Allies took the offensive, including the Canadians at Amiens in early August, followed by the 100 Days Campaign that saw the Canadians advance systematically through German lines beginning east of Arras, through the Canal du Nord and Cambrai, then swinging north to Valenciennes and eventually reaching Mons in southern Belgium when the Armistice took effect on November 11 ending the fighting on the Western Front. Canadian airmen continued to fly with the British air services, which amalgamated on April 1 to form the Royal Air Force. At home, conscription took effect and New Brunswickers who were called up joined the 1st Depot Battalion in Saint John and later Sussex. Some went overseas and saw action before the war ended.

70. Wright, Alfred James (February 23, 1918)

Corporal 326857, 58th Howitzer Battery

Alfred James Wright was born on November 12, 1883, in East Bergholt, Suffolk, England, to Mary Ann and Robert Wright. James had four siblings, one brother and three sisters. His sisters were Agnes, the eldest in the family, Florence, and Rosa; his younger brother's name was Charles. Although few records reveal how he came to live in Fredericton, newspapers highlight how he was well liked in the Fredericton community. Prior to enlisting, he worked as a clerk at the Lorne Hotel in Fredericton, where he also lived. According to the *Daily Gleaner*, Alfred was highly respected by many people and was involved in local activities while employed by Thomas Feeney, owner of the Lorne Hotel, who would also receive Corporal Wright's war service pay during his service. Described as quiet, unassuming, and greatly admired, he was a member of the Anglican Church during his three years working for Feeney. At the time of his enlistment on April 17, 1916, with the 58th Howitzer Battery, Alfred's attestation paper described him as standing five feet seven inches tall and weighing 170 pounds. He was also described as having a dark complexion, brown eyes, and brown hair. When he enlisted in Fredericton, Alfred was thirty-two years old, a member of the local militia, and unmarried. Only a few days before leaving for England, James signed his last will naming his mother, Mary Ann Wright, as his beneficiary. He would never return to Canada.

Private Wright embarked for England from Halifax on September 11, 1916, with his unit aboard the SS *Metagama*, disembarking in Liverpool on September 22. On September 30, he was appointed to the rank of acting bombardier at Milford Camp, part of the larger Witley Camp in Surrey, for about four months before being transferred to the reorganized 58th Battery, 14th Brigade in January 1917. Alfred continued training with the 14th Brigade until proceeding to Le Havre, France, on August 7. Just prior to leaving, in July, Alfred was confirmed in the rank of corporal. Service records show that he remained with his heavy artillery unit during the fall of 1917 and winter of 1917–18. By January 1918, the 58th Howitzer Battery was located in and around the city of Liévin, a coal-mining town near Lens, that had been completely ruined by fighting. Corporal Wright was with the 14th Brigade on February 21, when he was dangerously wounded by a piece of shrapnel that pierced his abdomen after an enemy shell casing exploded nearby. The war diary of the 14th Brigade reveals that the day Corporal Wright was injured, enemy fire was active and increasing due to good visibility. According to his commanding officer, "Hun propaganda sheets from aeroplanes states that the Canadian Corps will be wiped out in 72 hours!" While German propaganda would be proven wrong by the fall of 1918, Alfred was unable to recover from his wounds and passed away at a nearby Casualty Clearing Station two days later on February 23. Alfred was thirty-four years of age.

News of Alfred's death reached Fredericton quickly, and by April a letter had been received by his employer, Thomas Feeney, describing what had happened to Alfred. Written by Sergeant C.E. Maimann on February 26 and reprinted in the *Daily Gleaner* on April 3, the letter reads as follows:

> Dear Mr. Feeney, it is my painful duty to let you know that your former employee, Corp. A.J. Wright, died in the early morning of Feb. 23rd, as the results of wounds received on the morning of February 21. I was close to Jimmy when he was hit by a small bit of shell casing, in the stomach, and helped care for him until the M.O. [medical officer] arrived. Jim was one of our best corporals and for a long time was a Bdr. [bombardier] in my sub-section. Little else I cannot say, save that the boys miss him a great deal. But such is the luck of war. I have some mail of Jim's from Fredericton and am returning it to your address. I know he will be missed, but it can't be helped, and our hearts are with those in Fredericton who miss him a great deal more than we do. With best wishes to all, I am yours sincerely.

71. Smith, Walter Bruce (February 26, 1918)

Private 709689, 104th Battalion, 26th Battalion

Walter Bruce Smith was born on June 1, 1892, in Moncton. He was the eldest child of Ida May Smith and Fred B. Smith, who, according to the 1901 census, also had a daughter named Mildred K. and lived at 154 Regent Street in Fredericton along with the children's grandmother, Henriette Smith. According to his attestation document, Walter had a fair complexion, light brown hair, and blue eyes. He stood five feet four inches tall, about the average height of a middle school student today. At the time of his enlistment, he had a job as a teller in Fredericton at the local Bank of Nova Scotia branch. Walter's family raised him into the Baptist faith. On November 9, 1915, he enlisted in Sussex with the 104th Battalion. He was twenty-three years of age.

Walter spent approximately a year in training in Canada with the 104th Battalion before he embarked from Halifax aboard the SS *Olympic* on June 28, 1916, arriving in Liverpool on July 6. Typical of individuals attached to reserve battalions, Walter trained in England in a variety of camps for nearly a year until August 1917. He also spent time in a military hospital between January and April 1917 after an operation to treat a hernia. Walter's leadership qualities were recognized early on, as he was quickly promoted to the rank of lance corporal and later corporal, during which time he was with both the 104th and 13th Reserve Battalions until finally being attached to the 26th Battalion on August 24, 1916. At this point his rank reverted to private. Walter proceeded to the 26th Battalion on the Western Front in late summer, where he would stay throughout the fall of 1917 and winter of 1917–18. His record indicates the likelihood of his involvement with the 26th during the Battle of Passchendaele. After surviving the horrendous fighting conditions of his six months of service with the 26th, Walter was killed in action on February 26, 1918, just prior to the German Spring Offensive. Newspapers reported his death in March 1918, but the details surrounding his death remain largely unknown. Walter was twenty-six years of age. In his written will, he bequeathed everything to his father, who suffered a stroke in the fall of 1952 and never recovered.

Lest We Forget

Private Walter Bruce Smith is buried at the Aix-Noulette Communal Cemetery Extension, in Aix-Noulette, France, just west of Lense. Among 749 Commonwealth burials of the First World War, 61 of them unidentified; there are also 502 French burials.

72. McKee, Harry Hazlett (April 25, 1918)

Private 820938, 141st Battalion, 43rd Battalion

Harry Hazlett McKee was born on January 18, 1881, in Fredericton to Samuel H. McKee and Jane Armour. According to archival records, Samuel and Jane married on April 16, 1869, in Fredericton. In addition to Harry, they had six other children named Maggie, Sarah, Elsie, Samuel, Alex, and Hamilton. The McKee family was well known in the Fredericton area, as was the Armour family. According to local newspapers, Samuel worked locally as a prominent mason and businessman, while Jane worked at home raising their children. Newspapers and records suggest that Harry was the grandson of a United Empire Loyalist originally from Saint John, and that his father and brothers were active members of local and regional Masonic orders and organizations, such as the Scottish Rite of Saint John and the Royal Order of Scotland. Harry eventually attended the University of New Brunswick and later worked as a clerk for his father's family business. While growing up and working in the Fredericton area, Harry became close to a young local girl named Minnie H. Adams. They married on June 5, 1902. Records indicate that both Harry and Minnie were Presbyterian. Four years later, on December 28, 1906, Harry and Minnie welcomed the birth of their daughter, Marion. Census records reveal that, after her birth, Harry moved to western Ontario and then Winnipeg for work while Minnie and Marion resided in Fredericton with family at 459 Brunswick Street. He had no prior military experience when he enlisted in Winnipeg on December 15, 1915. He spent the next six months training with the 42nd Rifles until being held in the summer of 1916 as a deserter after attempting to re-enlist under the alias James Valentine White. There are no details to explain what happened to Harry in Winnipeg, but he eventually would be accepted back into the ranks under his actual name after signing a "solemn declaration" in December 1916 in Ontario. According to his service record, Harry was thirty-four years old, claimed to be single, and had brown eyes, brown hair, and a fair complexion, while standing five feet six inches tall. On March 2, 1917, while training with the 141st Battalion in Port Arthur, Ontario, Harry finally signed his will naming his wife Minnie as his beneficiary. It is unclear if he ever saw his wife or daughter again.

On October 4, 1917, Private McKee embarked from Halifax aboard the SS *Metagama* for Liverpool. Upon arrival on October 17, Harry was taken on by the 11th Battalion and then the 43rd over the winter of 1917–18. According to his active service record, he had approximately four months of training before landing in France with the 43rd on March 17, 1918, arriving just before the German army unleashed its Spring Offensive near St-Quentin on March 21. The Germans used a lethal combination of trench mortars and various gasses delivered by artillery fire into the Allied lines, damaging supply lines and the Allies' morale. A month after arriving, Private McKee was with his unit near Villers-Bretonneux, just outside Amiens, when, on April 22, he was dangerously gassed and admitted to No. 23 Casualty Clearing Station for treatment. According to his circumstances-of-death record, Private McKee passed away three days later, on April 25, as a result of his injuries.

News of his death reached Minnie and family by May 2, and the *Daily Gleaner* and *Telegraph Journal* reported his death a week later. He was thirty-six years of age and left behind his wife and twelve-year-old daughter Marion. On April 16, 1925, seven years after Harry's death, Minnie married Thomas Archibald Mills. She passed away on February 17, 1934.

Lest We Forget

Private Harry Hazlett McKee is buried at the Lapugnoy Military Cemetery, in Lapugnoy, France. According to the Commonwealth War Graves Commission, Harry is one of 1,332 burials honoured here. The cemetery was designed by Sir Edwin Lutyens.

73. Parsons, John Herbert (May 5, 1918)

Private 709412, 104th Battalion, 26th Battalion

John H. Parsons was born on February 28, 1894, in Fredericton to John H. Parsons Sr. and Ella Lorena Wells. According to census records, John had seven siblings, named William, Annie, Bessie, Edward, Dorothy, Aldon, and Robert. Little is known about Parsonses' marriage and early life together except that they occupied a home at 559 Brunswick Street and John Sr. worked as a restaurant keeper in Fredericton. A large family, the Parsons children also grew up with their grandmother in the home, who, according to the 1901 census, had been living with them for a time. At a young age John Herbert found work as a store clerk in the city and had close ties with the Wilmot Church community. Prior to the outbreak of the war, he had no experience in the military and records show that he was unmarried. According to his attestation paper, he had blue eyes, fair hair, and a fair complexion and stood five feet nine inches tall. John enlisted on October 5, 1915, in Sussex with the 104th Battalion and, along with his brothers Edward, William, and eventually his father, John Sr., he began training in preparation for going overseas. Private Parsons remained in Canada over the winter of 1915–16 and spring of 1916. Newspapers reveal that, in December 1915, his father volunteered at the local recruiting station. Just under the military age limit, John Sr., joined his sons as they left Canada in 1916.

On June 28, 1916, Private John H. Parsons embarked from Halifax aboard the SS *Olympic* for Liverpool, arriving on July 5. John remained with the 104th Battalion and was appointed corporal while beginning work in a military hospital in England. Over the next year and a half, he worked in London with his father. He spent much of 1917 in England as a member of hospital staff, using his skills as a clerk until reverting back to the rank of private to join the 13th Reserve Battalion and then eventually the 26th Battalion. Just prior to leaving for France, he signed his will leaving everything to his mother. According to his active service record, John arrived in France on November 18, just as the Battle of Passchendaele was coming to a close, likely motivated to be at the front, where his brother, William, had been killed a few months earlier. John spent much of the winter of 1917–18 in the Arras sector until May 1918, when he received a series of gunshot and shrapnel wounds to his chest and back. According to his circumstances-of-death record, he was transported to No. 1 London Field Ambulance on May 5, 1918, but medical treatment could not heal his complicated wounds. News of his death reached home quickly, with the *Daily Gleaner* reporting much sympathy from the community for the family, having also lost another son a year earlier. Private John Herbert Parsons was twenty-four years of age.

Lest We Forget

Private John H. Parsons is buried in the Dainville British Cemetery, located just outside of Arras, France. According to the Commonwealth War Graves Commission, the cemetery has 131 burials of those killed in nearby sectors of France. The cemetery was designed by British architect W.H. Cowlishaw.

74. Goodine, Harry E. (May 13, 1918)

Private 3257719, 1st New Brunswick Depot Battalion

Learning about Harry E. Goodine's life prior to and during the Great War period was difficult because information in the archival records is not complete and at times contradicts Private Goodine's military service record. Documents suggest, however, that Harry Goodine was born on May 8, 1892, in Springhill, Nova Scotia, to Laurence Marshall Goodine and Madeline Marshall. York County marriage records reveal that Laurence and Madeline married on September 8, 1882, in New Brunswick, but had lived for some time in Nova Scotia before returning

Recruits like Private Harry E. Goodine joining the 1st New Brunswick Depot Battalion in Sussex. Courtesy of Harold Wright

to York County prior to the war. Very little is known about Harry's mother, but it is believed she passed away prior to Harry's service, because she is not named in any military records. It is also difficult to know if Harry had any siblings, but his service record points out that his father was a widower at the time of his enlistment and that Harry had been working as a farmer in Doak Settlement, York County. As a result, it is likely that, as part of a farming family, Harry probably had siblings in either Nova Scotia or New Brunswick or both. Harry's service record shows that he was recruited into service under the *Military Service Act* (1917) and called up in a draft for service on April 24, 1918. At the time, Harry was working just outside Fredericton as a farmer, was unmarried, and belonged to the Roman Catholic Church. He stood five feet four inches tall, weighed 150 pounds, and had blue eyes, brown hair, and a medium complexion.

Private Goodine arrived in Saint John with the 1st New Brunswick Depot Battalion in late April 1918. After reporting for duty, Harry signed his formal will on May 4 naming his father as his beneficiary. According to his medical history documents, the next day, May 5, he admitted himself to the St. James Military Hospital in Saint John complaining of coughs, headaches, chills, and general soreness. For the next week his condition, now identified as pneumonia, continued to worsen, and doctors also noted information given by Harry that he had been experiencing asthma attacks for years. By May 12, Harry was experiencing tremendous pain and fever, and doctors had written in his medical file that his condition was critical. Private Goodine passed away a day later on May 13, at approximately 3 p.m. Harry's body was moved by train to Fredericton the day of his passing, while newspapers in Fredericton and Saint John reported that he would arrive the following evening for funeral preparations. Out of the millions of casualties that resulted from the First World War, historians suggest that approximately one-third of those were caused by disease or illness. Harry was twenty-seven years of age.

Lest We Forget

Private Harry Goodine is buried in the Fredericton Rural Cemetery Extension, located along the Woodstock Road in Fredericton. He is one of twenty Canadian soldiers identified here by the Commonwealth War Graves Commission.

75. Morris, Albert (June 2, 1918)

Private 445283, 55th Battalion, 9th Canadian Machine Gun Company

Albert Morris was born on December 2, 1893, in Birmingham, England, to Robert Morris and Ellen Collier. According to newspaper records, Albert, Robert, and Ellen had a large family: in addition to Albert there were eleven other children, named Letty, Robert Jr., Lilly, Henry, Edward, Maggie, Thomas, Nellie, Harold, Clemet, and Mona. They were also the adoptive parents of a boy named John Charnley, who was close friends with Albert, Henry, and Robert. Family stories suggest that like many others from England, the Morrises came to Canada primarily looking for job opportunities in the milling industry. After arriving, they initially found work in Ontario and Quebec before moving to Fredericton for employment at the Marysville cotton mill in 1910. In addition to his mill job, Robert supported the family as a local shoemaker; his sons, including Albert, eventually found jobs as labourers at the Marysville mill and the local shoe factory. Few details highlight the specifics of Albert's adolescence in Fredericton, but newspapers suggest that the Morris family was well known and had particularly close connections to both the northside and southside Fredericton communities.

When war broke out in 1914, Albert's younger brother Henry was the first of four Morris boys to enlist. Although Albert's service record reveals that he had no prior military training, his father had been active with the militia in England, so the desire to enlist likely was strong in the family. At the time of his enlistment in Sussex on July 28, 1915, Albert was twenty-two years old and unmarried. According to documented family stories and their individual service records, John and Robert Jr. accompanied Albert to Sussex, where all three enlisted together. Albert was described as having brown eyes, dark brown hair, a fair complexion, and standing five feet five inches tall. Along with other boys from the area, including his brothers, Albert joined the 55th Battalion and began training with his unit. After making their way to Valcartier for more training in the summer of 1915, all three brothers were together as they prepared to go overseas a few months later.

On October 30, 1915, Albert and his brothers embarked from Montreal aboard the SS *Corsican* for Plymouth, England, arriving over a week later, on November 9. Albert received the rank of lance corporal and was attached to a machine-gun unit for training during the winter of 1915–16. He remained in England as a machine-gun instructor over the next year. Newspapers reveal, however, that by spring 1917 he had given up his rank in England for an opportunity to go to France in search of his younger brother Henry, who had been reported missing. By this time, both John and Robert Jr. had been killed in France, and so the desire to get into the action was a likely motivator in his decision to go to the front. According to his service record, Albert submitted a request to join the 9th Machine Gun Company in July 1917, landing in France on August 2 with his unit after more than a year and a half in England. The next day, August 3, Albert left immediately with his unit for northern France and the Ypres

Salient, where, according to newspapers, he reunited briefly with his brother Henry prior to the Battle of Passchendaele. A few months later, on October 27, Albert was admitted to hospital suffering from poison gas and gunshot wounds to his right leg received while fighting near Ypres. He was evacuated to England for medical treatment at the Queen Mary's Military Hospital in Lancashire and later the Ontario Military Hospital near London over the winter of 1917–18 before being discharged back to Canada on May 6, 1918. According to Albert's medical records, he sailed home to Saint John aboard the hospital ship HMHS *Llandovery Castle*, which would be sunk by a German submarine a month and a half later during one its many trips across the Atlantic Ocean. After receiving treatment in Saint John for two weeks, Private Morris was transported to the Carleton Street Hospital in Fredericton, where he was be admitted for medical treatment on June 1. He passed away in the middle of the night on June 2. According to Albert's circumstances-of-death report, he died of heart failure. Albert Morris was twenty-four years old, and left behind his parents, friends, and extended family.

Lest We Forget

Private Albert Morris is buried in the Fredericton Rural Cemetery located on Woodstock Road in Fredericton. The cemetery is owned by the Wilmot United Church.

Gravestone of Private Albert Morris, Fredericton Rural Cemetery.
James Rowinski

76. Duffie, David William (June 27, 1918)

Private 536338, 16th Canadian Field Ambulance

Private David William Duffie was born on January 5, 1901, in Fredericton to David Duffie and Ellen Eliza Kaye, who resided at 337 Aberdeen Street. His parents married on April 5, 1893, in Fredericton. Growing up, William was the youngest in the family, having two older sisters, Ellen May, who passed away at the age of twenty-three in 1912, and Mary Louise. David's mother, Ellen Eliza, passed away some time prior to David's service. His records reveal that his father was a widower and remarried a woman named Agnes Tribe on November 3, 1913. According to David's attestation paper, before his enlistment on September 29, 1916, in Saint John, he was working locally as a drug clerk, was unmarried, and belonged to the Presbyterian Church. Duffie was described as being five feet three inches tall, having a scar on his right thigh caused by a burn, and had brown eyes, light brown hair, and a medium complexion. Interestingly, his enlistment record also reveals that, although he claimed to be eighteen years of age, in truth David, or "Billy," as he was known to the community, was only fifteen, as his birth certificate confirms. He would never return home to his family.

After enlisting with the 16th Canadian Field Ambulance (CFA) in Saint John in the fall of 1916, David arrived in Liverpool seven months later on April 7, 1917, aboard the SS *Missanabie*. Another young man from Fredericton, Frank Chandler Williams, was on the same ship, also serving with the 16th CFA. On March 25, prior to leaving Halifax for England, David had written his will in Saint John naming his stepmother, Agnes, as his sole beneficiary. For the next eleven months, David remained in England training with the Canadian Army Medical Corps (CAMC). An interesting note in his medical history sheet highlights his being brought before a medical proceedings board at Witley Camp on July 9, 1917, to determine if his small physical stature was a developmental impairment. The likelihood of questions surrounding his age because of his

Propaganda poster depicting the
German U-boat attack on
HMHS *Llandovery Castle*.

small stature possibly led to his continued training with the CAMC until assigned to HMHS *Llandovery Castle* on March 21, 1918. On June 27, while en route from Halifax to Liverpool after having brought injured soldiers back to Canada, *Llandovery Castle* sent out an emergency signal 70 miles (113 kilometres) off the coast of Ireland. It had been torpedoed by German submarine U-86 even though, as a hospital ship, it was clearly identified as such and was running with full lights. According to international law, an enemy vessel had the right to stop and search a hospital ship, but not to sink it. The ship sunk in minutes. As news of the disaster spread, outrage followed, as reports revealed that while the crew were attempting to escape in lifeboats, U-86 surfaced and began attacking the craft with machine-gun fire in an attempt to destroy evidence. In addition to David and Frank, there was a crew of 164 men, 80 officers and personnel of the CAMC, and 14 nursing sisters. Only twenty-four people survived what became one of the most significant war atrocities and Canadian naval disasters of the Great War.

On Tuesday, July 2, the *Daily Gleaner* reported two Fredericton and three Marysville soldiers on board. In addition to David, Frank Williams, Edward McPherson, Harry Harrison, and Walter Sacre—all Fredericton and Marysville area boys—were lost and presumed to have died at sea. David was only seventeen years old. According to his service record, by 1921 David's family had relocated to 15 Morris Street in Halifax. The names of McPherson, Harrison, and Sacre appear on the Marysville Cenotaph.

Lest We Forget

Private David "Billy" William Duffie is remembered on the Halifax Memorial along with 274 individuals from the First World War and 2,847 from the Second World War. This memorial was built by the Commonwealth War Graves Commission to honour and commemorate the Canadian sailors, merchant seamen, soldiers, and nursing sisters who died at sea during the First and Second World Wars.

The Halifax Memorial at Point Pleasant Park, Halifax, commemorates Canadian military personnel lost at sea during the two world wars, including Privates David Duffie and Frank Williams.

Brent Wilson

77. Williams, Frank Chandler (June 27, 1918)

Private 536236, 16th Canadian Field Ambulance

Frank Chandler Williams was born on September 29, 1898, in Fredericton to Blanche Delong and Charles Williams, who lived at 70 Saunders Street. According to census records, Frank had four siblings: two brothers, Morris and Archie, and two sisters, Violet and Eva. He was the second-youngest in the family. While little is known of his upbringing in Fredericton, his service record suggests that he was educated in Fredericton schools before the war began in 1914. His attestation document reveals that, at the time of his enlistment on July 25, 1916, Frank was a student, unmarried, and belonged to the Baptist Church. He was a slight five feet four inches tall and had a light complexion with blue eyes and light brown hair. Although he claimed to be eighteen years of age at the time of his enlistment with the 16th Canadian Field Ambulance in Saint John, he appears to have been an underage recruit like another Fredericton boy, David William Duffie, who had also enlisted with the 16th Field Ambulance.

HMHS *Llandovery Castle*, sunk by the German submarine U-86 off the coast of Ireland on June 27, 1918. Courtesy of Harold Wright

On March 26, 1917, one year after joining up, Frank was sent overseas with the 16th Field Ambulance aboard the SS *Missanabie*, arriving in England on April 7. After being in England for three months Frank was sent to a military hospital for treatment of an infection before being discharged and then rejoining the 16th Field Ambulance in the fall of 1917. On March 21, 1918, Frank was posted to HMHS *Llandovery Castle*, sunk three months later by U-86.

Frank's service record reported him as missing and presumed to have died because of drowning. In early July newspapers, began reporting on the disaster and notifications were sent to families with relatives on board. On July 2, 1918, the *Daily Gleaner* reported that "two Fredericton and three Marysville boys" were aboard the ship, with notified families "prostrated over the news." Frank was just seventeen years old.

Lest We Forget

Frank Chandler Williams is memorialized and remembered with honour on the Halifax Memorial to those who died at sea in both world wars and have no known grave.

78. Moore, Earle Alexander (August 8, 1918)

Private 742839, 115th Battalion, 26th Battalion

Earle Alexander Moore was born on October 13, 1892, in Fredericton to Christina and Joseph Moore. Census records show that the Moores had five children: George, Ethel, John, Earle, and Helen. Other documents suggest there might have been two additional children named Frank and Nettie. Although Earle grew up in downtown Fredericton at 289 Westmorland Street, by the time he was a young adult he was living on and operating a farm in the Lincoln area. Earle's father worked as a carpenter in Fredericton. Newspapers highlight how well the family was known in the area, describing Earle as a "clean-cut man, held in the highest esteem by all his friends and associates in the city." Although there are few accounts of his early life growing up in Fredericton, documents show that Earle had no military training prior to the war and that he was unmarried. At the time of his enlistment in Saint John on March 1, 1916, with the 115th Battalion, he was twenty-three years old and had blue eyes and a light complexion, and stood five feet nine inches tall. He and his brother, John C., enlisted in Saint John together, along with other young men from the area, and together they trained in Valcartier for a few months in preparation for going overseas. It is unclear if Earle ever saw his family again.

On July 23, 1916, Private Moore and his brother left from Halifax aboard the SS *Olympic* for England. Upon arrival, Earle remained with the 115th Battalion until transferred to the 112th at Bramshott Camp in October. While in England, Earle wrote his will naming his mother, Christina, as sole beneficiary. After more than a year of training, Earle left the 112th for the 26th Battalion, landing in France in the summer of 1917. Although his record offers few details of his movements in late 1917 and early 1918, it is likely he was with the 26th Battalion at Passchendaele in November and later in the area of Vimy during the German offensives in the spring of 1918. By the early summer, the German army had pushed as far as Amiens, and the Canadians were given an opportunity to lead a series of counter assaults to push the Germans back, as they had done elsewhere during the war. At Amiens, the 26th Battalion became part of a combined force with French and Australians on the early morning of August 8 that aimed to break the German army at last. According to the 26th Battalion's war diary, the Battle of Amiens began at 4:20 a.m. under good conditions, and by the afternoon the battaion had reached its objectives just beyond the villages of Wiencourt and Guillaucourt. Private Moore's circumstances-of-death record reveals that, while taking part in the attack from the northeast on the opening day, he was hit by enemy machine-gun fire and died instantly. Private Moore's sacrifice, along with that of many other Canadians, led to what was considered the "black day of the German Army." Shortly after Earle's death, the *Daily Gleaner* reported that the community had lost a "young man of great promise...a hero every inch of him to make the supreme sacrifice so that the world might again be a decent place to live in." Private Moore was twenty-five years old.

Lest We Forget

Private Earle Alexander Moore is buried with honour at the Villers-Bretonneux Military Cemetery, near Amiens, France. According to the Commonwealth War Graves Commission, Earle is one of 1,547 identified casualties from the First and Second World Wars.

79. Brewer, William D. (August 15, 1918)

Sergeant 40138, 71st York Regiment, 1st Battery, Canadian Field Artillery

William Douglas Brewer was born on January 14, 1896, in Fredericton to Sergeant-Major Herbert Thomas Brewer and Hattie Melissa Guthrie. William was one of the eldest brothers in a military family that included LeRoy, Raymond, Ernest, and Cecil, as well as an elder sister named Edith. William's sister later married Harry E. Sutherland and moved to Ottawa, where she resided during the war. William's family had strong ties to the local militia through their father, who had been with The Royal Canadian Regiment and was recruiting with the local militia. As a result, the family resided on Carleton Street in Fredericton close to the local armoury. Sergeant Brewer's service documents and archival records suggest that he had a close relationship with his older sister and that he was without any particular calling before the war. Edith was named his next-of-kin during the war. His attestation paper shows that he was unmarried and without any identified form of work in the fall of 1914. Newspapers illustrate that he was living in Ottawa, and enlisted for active service at Valcartier on September 22, 1914. Given his military upbringing, William had spent two years in Fredericton with the 71st York Regiment and was fit for duty, standing five feet nine inches tall, with a fair complexion, blue eyes, black hair, and a tattoo with the initials W.B. on his left forearm. Brewer was eighteen years old in the fall of 1914; he would never return home.

After being at Camp Valcartier for a month with the 1st Battery, Canadian Field Artillery, his unit left Canada on October 3, 1914. Although his service record reveals little about his training during the winter of 1914–15, documents do show that he had been trained as a signaller and spent time as a driver with his unit. He left England from Avonmouth, near Bristol, on February 8, 1915, with the 1st Brigade, Canadian Field Artillery for northern France and Belgium. The Canadians did not see action until later in March, supporting the British, but they arrived at a turning point in weapons use, as deadly chlorine gas was soon unleashed against the Allies. After surviving the Second Battle of Ypres and other battles that followed, William was granted a week-long leave of absence on November 20, 1915. During 1916, as Canadians were involved in St. Eloi, Mount Sorrel, and the Somme, William was seriously injured in the leg for the second time, according to a letter home informing his sister, apparently not wanting to let his parents know what had happened. He was granted a second leave of absence to England for treatment of the leg wound after receiving a Good Conduct Badge for two years of quality service to the Canadian Army. The next two years of the war, 1917–18, found William promoted to the rank of corporal and then, by January 1918, to sergeant. In the meantime, he was suffering from influenza as well as complications from mustard gas received at Passchendaele. After having served more than four years, Sergeant Brewer found himself an integral part of the August 1918 Battle of Amiens, the opening battle of a series of pounding assaults that had become code-named *Llandovery Castle* out of respect for those lost by the ship's sinking. It is here that documents show William Brewer's battery unit was behind the village of Les Quesnel during heavy enemy shelling, when, at approximately 7:30 p.m. on August 15, he was reported killed instantly when a shell exploded nearby, hitting him in the head and stomach. An official board of inquiry followed a month after his death, as it was initially unclear whether his death was caused by shellfire or shots from a gun. Three witnesses were called to testify, and the court heard Lieutenant H.L. McCulloch, Sergeant C.J. Peppin, and Corporal J.G. Boyd all claim that William's death appeared to be the result of enemy shelling. As he had served for almost three and half years, news of William's death was met with sorrow in Fredericton. Newspapers reported that "his letters to his parents were always the most cheerful nature, and he always looked forward to returning home at the close of the war." In addition to William, his brother Ernest Alfred died a few months later. Sergeant William Douglas Brewer was twenty-two years of age.

Lest We Forget

Sergeant William Brewer is buried in the Cerisy-Gailly Military Cemetery located in Cerisy, France, ten kilometres southwest of Albert. Originally buried at Beaufort British Cemetery, near the area that was captured by 1st Canadian Division in August 1918, Sergeant Brewer's grave was later moved to Cerisy. According to the Commonwealth War Graves Commission, there are 631 identified casualties at the cemetery.

Cerisy-Gailly Military Cemetery, Cerisy, France, where Sergeant William D. Brewer is buried. Commonwealth War Graves Commission

80. Ross, Frederick James (August 27, 1918) Military Medal

Corporal 817530, 140th Battalion, 26th Battalion, 2nd Battalion, Canadian Machine Gun Corps

Frederick James Ross was born on November 9, 1890, in Taymouth, New Brunswick, to Wesley A. Ross and Catherine Elizabeth Young. Wesley and Catherine, both from the Nashwaak area, married in the summer of 1888. According to the 1911 census, the Ross family lived in Fredericton at 336 Queen Street with their three daughters, Nellie, Maggie, and Vera, and their only son, Frederick James. While little is known of Fred's early life growing up in Fredericton, records reveal that the Ross family were Methodists and attended the local Wesleyan Church, while Fred eventually became a student at the Fredericton Business College. Just prior to the war, he worked locally as a bookkeeper. Newspapers indicate that his older sister, Nellie, married a Keswick Ridge man named Arthur Jewett, while Maggie married George Flewelling. Fred never married. Without any prior military training, Fred enlisted for service on September 17, 1915, in Sussex with the 140th Battalion. According to his attestation paper, Ross was taller than most men, standing five feet nine inches with a fair complexion, blue eyes, and light brown hair. He was twenty-three years of age. His service was delayed early on during the winter of 1915–16 after he contracted pneumonia and, while at Camp Valcartier, spent time in hospital with German measles. Once discharged from hospital, he left with his unit to go overseas, never to return.

By the summer of 1916, Private Ross was with the 140th Battalion again and travelled with his unit from Halifax on September 9 aboard the SS *Corsican* for Liverpool. While many soldiers experienced an extended period of time in England training with their units, Fred's time was less than a month before he landed in France in November after joining a draft with the 26th Battalion, likely needed as reinforcements after Canadian involvement during the Somme battles. While remaining with the 26th Battalion over the winter of 1916–17 at

Tanks advancing during the Battle of Amiens in August 1918. Among the local
soldiers who died during the battle was Corporal Frederick J. Ross.
Canada, Department of National Defence/LAC (Mikan no. 3395384)

various fronts in northern France and southern Belgium, by the spring
of 1917 he was involved in operations by the Canadians at Vimy. The
"Fighting 26th" was part of 2nd Division's 5th Infantry Brigade, which
saw action near the centre of the Canadian attack on the morning of April
9. It was here that Private Ross received his Military Medal for "conspicuous gallantry and devotion to duty." According to his military citation:
"When attached to a carrying party [Fred] showed exceptional courage
and bravery in following up the infantry to establish ammunition and
water dumps under heavy shell fire, and at great personal risk. His fine
example, and perseverance, was a great incentive to the remainder of his
party in accomplishing a most trying and dangerous task."

After the success of Vimy and battles that followed, Ross joined the
5th Battalion, Canadian Machine Gun Corps (CMGC), in June and
later spent a week in hospital for treatment of an undocumented illness.
Between November 22 and December 6, 1917, Fred was granted time away
in England, likely in recognition of his award and efforts in the field until
that point in the war. A few months later, in early 1918, Fred earned the
rank of corporal and was absorbed into the 2nd Battalion, CMGC, in

preparation for expected German attacks in the spring and the Canadian response that would follow. By August, Ross and his unit were preparing for what many hoped would be the breakthrough needed to end the war over the next few months. According to Corporal Ross's circumstances-of-death record dated August 27, during the final operations around Amiens, Fred was commanding a machine-gun section when his team was attacked by heavy enemy gunfire at 12:30 p.m., and Fred was severely wounded. His wounds were quickly attended to and he was carried to a dressing station, but he died before he could receive emergency medical assistance. Fred was twenty-seven years old.

Lest We Forget

Corporal Frederick James Ross, Military Medal, is buried at the Wancourt British Cemetery, in the village of Wancourt, France, eight kilometres southeast of Arras. The village was recaptured by the Canadian Corps on August 26, 1918. According to the Commonwealth War Graves Commission, the cemetery has 1,107 identified casualties.

81. Machum, Ronald Sutherland (August 28, 1918)

Lieutenant, 62nd Regiment, St. John Fusiliers, 55th Battalion, 104th Battalion, 52nd Battalion (New Ontario)

Ronald Sutherland Machum was born on September 15, 1892, in Saint John to Edward R. Machum and Leila R. Harrison. According to census records, Ronald had three sisters named Elva, Marion, and Elizabeth, and together the Machum family resided in Westfield, near Saint John, prior to the war. After attending school and later graduating from Mount Allison University, Ronald became a broker in his father's life insurance business in Saint John, the Manufacturers Life Insurance Company. Little is known of how they met, but Ronald became engaged to Mildred Meredith

Walker of Fredericton before the war. Ronald, twenty-two years of age, and Mildred married on August 19, 1914, in Fredericton, witnessed by his sister Elva. As Ronald's work was in Saint John, they lived in the Port City before occupying a family residence at 230 York Street in Fredericton during the war. According to records, Ronald stood approximately five feet four inches tall and weighed a slight 140 pounds at the time of his enlistment for service. While he did not have extensive military experience, Ronald was commissioned as a lieutenant in February 1915 prior to enlisting at Sussex in November of that same year. Later, he was attached to the 55th Battalion at Camp Valcartier and then the 104th, the unit he signed his officer's declaration papers with in spring 1916 in Fredericton. According to his official service record, just prior to leaving for England with the 104th, Lieutenant R.S. Machum was twenty-three years old, married, and had approximately one year of military service in Canada with the 62nd Regiment, St. John Fusiliers, and the 55th Battalion. It is unclear if he was aware that Mildred was pregnant with their first child. While Ronald was overseas, Mildred Marion Machum was born on May 31, 1917, at the Maternity Hospital on 260 Princess Street in Saint John. Documents reveal that, after her daughter's birth, Mildred moved back to Fredericton, where she found support with her family while her husband was away.

On June 28, 1916, Ronald embarked with the 104th Battalion from Halifax aboard the SS *Olympic*. After arriving in England on July 5, Lieutenant Machum remained training over the next year with 5th Canadian Division. In the fall and winter of 1917, he was admitted to a military hospital at Bramshott for a short period suffering from a skin infection. By early April 1918, Ronald had arrived in France with a Manitoba reserve regiment and then was attached to the 52nd Battalion from Ontario. According to his active service record, Machum was with the 52nd as it prepared for the Amiens offensive, a significant period of the war for the Canadians. Lieutenant Machum was with the 52nd in the early morning on August 27 near Lens when shrapnel caught him in the right leg, wounding him severely. He was brought back from the front line to receive medical treatment at No. 1 Casualty Clearing Station and to have his leg amputated. He bled too quickly, however. According to his circumstances-of-death record, Ronald passed away August 28 as a result of his wounds. (his date of death is incorrectly listed as August 18 by the CWGC).

News of his death spread quickly throughout New Brunswick and was reported in the *Daily Gleaner* on Wednesday, October 9, revealing that his wife had received a letter indicating Ronald had passed away on the "firing line" and that condolences were being received from the King and Queen, the Governor-General, and Prime Minister Robert Borden. "Praised by everyone who knew him," Lieutenant R.S. Machum was twenty-six years of age when he died, less than three months before the Armistice. He left behind his wife and young daughter, his widowed father, and three sisters.

Lest We Forget

Lieutenant Ronald Sutherland Machum is buried at Ligny-St. Flochel British Cemetery, located in Averdoingt, France, approximately 24 kilometers from Arras. According to the Commonwealth War Graves Commission, Ronald is one of approximately 630 burials honoured here.

82. Rutter, Arthur Murray (August 28, 1918)

Private 709786, 104th Battalion, 26th Battalion

Arthur Murray Rutter was born on February 26, 1894, in Fredericton to Mary Annie Aitkens and Murray C. Rutter. According to records, Murray and Annie married in October 1878. Early in their marriage, the couple dealt with the loss of three young children. On Christmas eve 1880, their one-year-old daughter, Janet A., passed away; six years later, Henry Charles, two, and Bessie Frances, four, both died from illnesses. Their fourth child, Thomas, was born in 1886. Arthur was the youngest and last child. Arthur's father was well known in Fredericton as the city's fire department chief prior to the war, and both Thomas and Arthur also volunteered with the fire department. Although there are few details of Arthur's upbringing, the family attended St. Paul's Church and the children were pupils in local schools. By 1911, Arthur was working as a clerk in the city and later as a telegraph operator. During this time, he met a young woman from Marysville named Eva C. Fitton, and they were married on July 31, 1913. When war broke out in 1914, Arthur and Eva were living at 119 St. John Street. According to his attestation paper, on November 17, 1915, he enlisted at Sussex with the 104th Battalion a year after his brother Thomas. He was described as having hazel eyes, dark brown hair, a fair complexion, and standing five feet nine inches tall. Over the next few months, Arthur remained in Canada training with the 104th preparing to go overseas. While it is unclear if he saw Eva again before he left, he might have had the opportunity. At the time of his enlistment, Arthur was twenty-one years old and without any previous military training.

On June 28, 1916, Private Rutter embarked from Halifax aboard the SS *Olympic* for Liverpool, along with other young men from the area. After arriving, Arthur was attached to a signalling brigade, given his work experience at home in Canada. For the next year and a half, he remained in England involved in training while others headed to the Western Front. After eighteen months in England, Arthur joined a draft in February 1918 and was attached to the 26th Battalion. He arrived in France on February 24 and joined the 26th near Arras. It proved to be a hard introduction to the realities of fighting in the final year of the war. In the early spring of 1918, the German army began a series of devastating attacks along a wide area of the Western Front that erased territory gained by the Allies in December 1917. By July 1918, the Germans had advanced as far as Amiens, an impressive blow to the British and French armies. However, they had avoided the territory around Arras controlled by the Canadian Corps. Despite the losses, the Allies had regrouped by August and had shifted more than a hundred thousand Canadian "shock troops," as they became known, to Amiens in secret. On August 8, Canadian, Australian, British, and French units overran the German army. A few weeks later, on August 27, Arthur was advancing west of Cherisy with signallers of the Headquarters Company near the Drocourt-Quéant Line when, according to his circumstances-of-death record, he received gunshot wounds to his legs and shoulders. He was immediately attended to and evacuated to No. 1 Casualty Clearing Station, where he succumbed to the effects of his wounds the following day. Although newspapers reported the return of his brother Thomas to Fredericton after the war, little mention appears to have been made of Arthur's death. On November 8, 1923, the *Daily Gleaner* shared information about the unveiling of bronze tablets at St. Paul's United Church in memory of those killed from the congregation. Arthur Murray Rutter was honoured alongside twenty-five others who had given up their lives. At the time of his death in the summer of 1918, Arthur was twenty-four years old and left behind his wife, Eva, and his family.

Lest We Forget

Private Arthur Murray Rutter is buried at the Ligny-St. Flochel British Cemetery, in Averdoingst, France. Arthur is also honoured on the plaque located outside the old Fredericton Fire Station, dedicated to firefighters in the city who served during the First World War.

Among the local soldiers named on the St. Paul's United Church Honour Roll is Private Arthur M. Rutter. James Rowinski

83. Vradenburg, William (September 3, 1918)

Gunner 1257852, 9th Siege Battery

William H. Vradenburg was born on August 11, 1898, in Fredericton to William Henry Vradenburg and Alice Louise Gough. William's father worked in Fredericton as a carpenter and, according to records, the family lived at 531 Brunswick Street before moving to 230 Carleton Street. He had two brothers, Corporal Percy Vradenburg, who would also serve during the war, and John C., who worked for the Royal Bank of Canada in Saint John. His two sisters were Francis, a schoolteacher in Saint John, and Josephine, known in the Fredericton community as "Jessie." According to newspapers, William grew up in Fredericton with his family while attending school and was described as an "exceptionally bright young man." After his schooling, he worked for the Canadian Bank of Commerce in Fredericton before transferring to the bank's branch in Sherbrooke, Quebec. A hard-working young man, William was advancing in his career as a banker when war broke out in the late summer of 1914. With a brother who had already enlisted, by October 1916 William was living in North Hatley, Quebec, when he chose to give up a promising career to fight for his country. According to his attestation papers, Vradenburg had no prior military experience when he enlisted in Sherbrooke on October 16, 1916, in the 9th Overseas Siege Battery. He was not married. A slight five feet seven inches tall, William had a fair complexion, blue eyes, and brown hair. A month later he returned to New Brunswick, where he joined other Fredericton boys in Saint John who had signed up with the 9th Siege Battery. Only eighteen years old, Gunner Vradenburg would never return home, although newspapers indicate he wrote home often to tell of his experiences.

After joining the 9th Siege Battery in Saint John, Gunner Vradenburg trained with his unit at Partridge Island over the winter of 1916–17 until his battery left for England from Halifax on March 4, 1917. The New Brunswick boys arrived in Liverpool on March 15. William was with his unit training in England for five months until the 9th Siege Battery joined the 1st Brigade, Canadian Field Artillery in the summer of 1917. William left with the 1st Brigade in late August for France. Newspapers reveal that, over his two years of service, the young gunner always wrote letters of optimism and encouragement about the progress of the war. After serving with the 1st Brigade for almost a year throughout southern Belgium and northern France, by September 1918 William and the 9th Siege Battery were near Vimy. According to the official war diary of the 1st Brigade, the 9th was providing fire support for "opportunity targets," including aeroplanes and harassing fire to neutralize German positions on the Drocourt-Quéant Line. In what the *Daily Gleaner* described as "brilliant work of Canadian troops," Gunner Vradenburg was part of one of the most successful periods of fighting by Canadians during the First World War. By September 3, newspapers were reporting "ten thousand Germans were captured and many more killed" during fighting that saw rapid German retreating throughout Flanders and northern France. On September 3, during a time when Canadians were having tremendous success in helping to bring an end to the war, William lost his life. He was only nineteen years old. Little is known about exactly what happened to William because his circumstances-of-death record did not survive. Newspapers reveal, however, that news of his death, when it reached Fredericton on September 12, was "fearfully sudden" and met with "sincere regret."

Lest We Forget

William H. Vradenburg is buried at Upton Wood Cemetery, Hendecourt-lès-Cagnicourt, France, near Arras. According to the Commonwealth War Graves Commission, the cemetery has 218 identified casualties and eight burials of soldiers who are unidentified.

84. Winslow, Rainsford Hannay (September 9, 1918)

Major, 71st York Regiment, 48th Battalion, 1st Tramways Company,
Canadian Engineers

Rainsford Hannay Winslow was born on October 19, 1887, in Fredericton, the youngest of eight children born to Byron E. Winslow and Emma Barbara Winslow. Rainsford had five brothers, Wentworth B., Jasper Andrew, John James Fraser, Francis Edward, and Robert Napier, as well as two sisters, Elizabeth Caroline (Mrs. G.D. Ireland) and Marguerite (Mrs. E.L. du Domaine). His service record reveals that, when he enlisted at the age of twenty-seven, he had blue eyes, dark hair, and a fresh complexion, and stood five feet nine inches tall. Like other members of his family, he belonged to the Church of England and had close ties to the congregation of Christ Church Cathedral. He had two years service with the 71st York Regiment, serving as an orderly room sergeant. Newspapers and records show that Rainsford attended the University of New Brunswick in the fall of 1904 and later McGill University, graduating from there in 1909 with a Bachelor of Science in mining engineering. Prior to enlisting, he had been working in British Columbia as a land surveyor and was a member of the Canadian Society of Civil Engineers. At the time of his enlistment, Rainsford was single. In December 1914, Rainsford was commissioned as a lieutenant in the 48th Battalion and would accompany them to England.

Rainsford arrived at Shorncliffe, England on August 19, 1915. According to his service record, in March 1916, eight months after arriving, Rainsford went to France with the 3rd Pioneer Battalion and was promoted to temporary captain in July 1916. In September, Rainsford's medical history reveals, he was wounded by shrapnel, treated, and released only to be readmitted the following day after again being wounded by shrapnel. Soon after that, he was admitted to hospital with laryngitis. In November 1916, Rainsford was attached to the Canadian Corps Training School and was later part of 2nd Canadian Infantry Brigade. Newspapers reported his marriage in December 1916 to Doris McLaggan, whom he had met in British Columbia and who came overseas to see him. By 1918 Rainsford had been given command of the 1st Tramways Company, Canadian Engineers, which built and maintained light railways behind the lines. He was soon promoted to major and in August granted a special thirty-day leave of absence to England to visit his wife.

Upon his return to the field, Rainsford was dangerously wounded on September 5 by a bomb, which caused serious injury to his arm and hip. According to the company's war diary: "Whilst Major Winslow and the Adjutant were up forward on the way to visit the 10th Batt'n, C.E.... the Cambrai Road was shelled at the Crossroad ... Major Winslow was wounded and sent to the Dressing Station at Haucourt by ambulance, and later evacuated to C.C.S. at Arras." On September 10, the war diary further reported that "Word was received on the evening of the 9th that Major Winslow had died of wounds at No. 7 C.C.S. Ligny St. Flochel. The funeral took place at Ligny at 2 P.M. on the 10th." Rainsford was thirty-one years old. General Sir Arthur Currie described Major Winslow as "a most valued officer in our Tramways Department and, while knowing him well, all engineers and infantry with whom he served spoke of him in the highest possible terms of praise."

Lest We Forget

Major Rainsford Winslow is buried at the Ligny-St. Flochel Cemetery in France. He was the second in his family to die during the war, as his elder brother Jasper was killed on March 22, 1917.

85. Foster, Howard Addington (September 29, 1918)

Private 709464, 104th Battalion, 5th Canadian Mounted Rifles

Howard Addington Foster was born on April 22, 1876, in Fredericton to Charlotte Farris and Charles Foster. According to records, Howard had four siblings named Fletcher, Judson, Charles, and Sheldon. By all accounts, the family appears to have remained in the Fredericton area up to and during the Great War; Howard's mother, Charlotte, eventually lived in Gagetown after the war. Documents suggest Charles was a labourer in the area, while Charlotte raised the boys and worked at their home. Although few records show details about his early life in Fredericton, Howard eventually met and married a young woman named Mary Gray and started a family living at 217 Brunswick Street. Newspapers and census documents show that they had nine children: Sheldon, Thurston, Shirley, Addison, Charles, Sarah, Margaret, Marian, and Lily. Howard's attestation form reveals that he had no prior military experience, although his work as a labourer likely appealed to the Canadian Expeditionary Force. On September 7, 1915, he enlisted in Sussex with the 64th Battalion and later transferred to the 104th. At the time of his formal enlistment, Howard was described as standing five feet ten inches, with a fair complexion, blue eyes, and brown hair. Along with his brothers Fletcher, Judson, Charles, and Sheldon, who had also enlisted, as well as other Fredericton area boys, Howard soon began training to prepare to go overseas. Newspapers do not disclose his name, but one of Howard's sons also enlisted and served alongside his father and uncles. It is unclear if Howard ever saw Mary and his children again. A few months after he left, Mary gave birth to their last child, a girl named Marian.

On June 28, 1916, Private Foster left Halifax aboard the SS *Olympic* for Liverpool, and arrived on July 5. Howard remained with the 104th in England over the summer and fall before joining the 5th Canadian Mounted Rifles (CMR) on November 29, landing in France a day later. Perhaps expecting hard times ahead, prior to leaving England Howard wrote his formal will leaving everything to Mary. Perhaps somewhat fortunately for Private Foster, he arrived at the end of the Battle of Somme during a lull in the fighting throughout the winter of 1916–17. Over the next year and a half, he remained with the 5th CMR at Vimy, Hill 70, and Passchendaele, as well as during the German Spring Offensive of 1918, described in the *Daily Gleaner* as "the greatest battle in the history of world." Howard was with the 5th CMR near Boisleux-Saint-Marc, south of Arras, in late September 1918 when he received gunshot wounds to his legs and face. Immediately evacuated to No. 38 Casualty Clearing Station, Private Foster's wounds were too severe for medical assistance. According to his circumstances-of-death record, Private Foster passed away two days later, on September 29, leaving behind nine children, brothers, and his wife, Mary. Less than a week after his death, newspapers reported information on his passing indicating that he had been in hospital for two days of treatment before his untimely death. Howard was forty-two years old at the time of his death.

Lest We Forget

Private Howard A. Foster is buried at the Sunken Road Cemetery, Boisleux-Saint-Marc, France. According to the Commonwealth War Graves Commission, Howard is one of 444 casualties at this cemetery.

86. Jukes, Clifford Wilfred (September 29, 1918)

Private 1030308, 236th Battalion (The New Brunswick Kilties),
42nd Battalion (Royal Highlanders of Canada)

Clifford Wilfred Jukes was born on April 8, 1894, in Birmingham, England, to Alfred and Annie Jukes. While few details describe his early life in England, census records reveal that he had eight siblings.

Documents also show that in 1902 Clifford and his brother, Leonard, moved to Canada as part of the Middlemore Children's Emigration Homes program. Records reveal that they were very young, with Clifford just eight years old, when the boys moved to New Brunswick. Eventually they were placed in a home in the Stanley area. As a young adult, Clifford found work as a lumberman before meeting a young woman, Edna Green, who came from Plaster Rock. Edna and Clifford were married on April 30, 1913. At the time of his formal enlistment for service, however, Clifford named his mother, Annie, as his next-of-kin, perhaps because something had happened to their relationship. Records show that he eventually found work in Fredericton as a cook and also that he was in a relationship with a young woman named Elizabeth Briggs of Fredericton. Upon his enlistment on November 3, 1916, Clifford identified himself as single, but in April 1917 he married. Their daughter, Doris, was born on March 5, 1918, so it is likely that Clifford and Elizabeth had time together before he left to go overseas. Along with other Fredericton boys, he began preparations for training shortly after enlisting with the 236th New Brunswick Kilties and eventually left in the fall of 1917. Clifford was described as having dark eyes, black hair, a dark complexion, and standing five feet eight inches. He was twenty years old.

On October 30, 1917, Private Jukes embarked from Montreal aboard the SS *Canada*, landing in Halifax a few days later. According to records, on November 11 the *Canada* left Halifax for England, arriving on November 17. Granted the rank of lance corporal, Jukes remained in England for the next four months until arriving in France with the 42nd Battalion on March 7, just before the German Spring Offensive began. Over the next six months, Clifford stayed with the 42nd as the Canadians held ground near Vimy and Arras, and as they began preparations for attacks in the summer of 1918. By September, the 42nd Battalion and Clifford were near Cambrai as part of the battle for the city. Letters written home and published in the *Daily Gleaner* reveal what happened to Jukes:

Dear Mrs. Jukes, it is with a heavy heart that I write these few lines about your husband, No. 1030308, Pte. Clifford Jukes, who was killed in action on September 29, 1918, during the battle of Cambrai. I was his platoon officer, and it is no exaggeration to say that he was one of the finest men in my platoon, both personally and as a soldier. He was in charge of a Lewis machine gun during the battle and did splendid work until hit by a piece of shell and mortally wounded. He died shortly after on the battlefield before he could even be moved. Although we all miss him greatly in the platoon it seems almost wrong to grieve for one who died so gallant a death for so great a cause. Such a death can only be a stepping-stone to immortality. Please, let me know if there is anything else that I can tell you or do for you out here. I would be happy to try to find out anything else you would like to know about him. With kind regards, I am, yours sincerely, A.E. Andrews.

Confirmed by this letter and by his circumstances-of-death record, Clifford was reportedly wounded and killed from the same shell that led to the death a day later of fellow Fredericton resident, Private Robert McArthur. Clifford would never meet his daughter, born earlier that year. He was twenty-three years old.

Lest We Forget

Private Clifford Wilfred Jukes is buried at the Mill Switch British Cemetery, near Cambrai, France. According to the Commonwealth War Graves Commission, Clifford is one of 107 burials at this location.

87. Robinson, Ronald Campbell (September 29, 1918)

Private 1030024, 236th Battalion (The New Brunswick Kilties),
42nd Battalion (Royal Highlanders of Canada)

Ronald Campbell Robinson was born on August 14, 1899, in Marysville to Alexander Robinson and Celia Robinson. According to records obtained from the Provincial Archives of New Brunswick, his parents married on May 23, 1863, and together they had a large family of nine children named Roy, Helen, Mary, Florence, John, Ron, Dorothy, Frank, and Moreland. Records reveal that the family lived in Marysville on Canada Street; however, Ron's medal card also points to a residence at 225 Brunswick Street in Fredericton's downtown. Ron's service record shows that he attended Fredericton High School and that, when war broke out, his brothers Roy and John enlisted, but he was not allowed to because of his age — he was only fifteen. According to family stories, Ron had left school wanting to do his part in the war, but when he was rejected he left for Amherst, Nova Scotia, where he served as a guard at a German internment camp. Although not legally allowed to serve, at some point Ron was given a white feather as a sign of cowardice. Not surprisingly, family stories suggest that "Ron's youthful pride was crushed." After this experience, Ron again attempted to enlist on July 15, 1916, with the 236th Battalion in Fredericton, and this time he was accepted. When news of his enlistment reached his family, Ron's father rushed to speak with the commanding officer for an explanation. The family was assured that no harm would come to Ron and that he would be given a desk job because of his skills as a writer. His record actually reveals his birthday was scratched out and corrected so that he would be allowed into service. Still only fifteen, Ron's attestation paper described him as having blue eyes, fair hair, a fresh complexion, and standing five feet four-and-a-half inches tall. Along with other Fredericton area boys who joined the Kilties, he soon began training in Quebec in preparation for going overseas. In May 1917, Ron wrote his

If you possess the fighting spirit of your forefathers
JOIN THE
236ᵀᴴ KILTIES BATTALION
All the officers have already been in the trenches- and are going back-
THEY KNOW THE BOYS NEED THEM - AYE - AND NEED YOU, TOO
Don the MACLEAN TARTAN and do your bit -
THE KILTIES WILL GO QUICKLY - AND AS A UNIT -
God Save the King
Lt.Col. PERCY A.GUTHRIE O. C.
(Formerly 10ᵗʰ Battalion White Ghurkas)
Go to the nearest recruiting office and insist on joining the Kilties.
THE 236 MACLEAN KILTIES BATTALION.

Recruiting poster for the 236th Battalion (The New Brunswick Kilties). Many local soldiers joined the Kilties, including Private Ronald Robinson. Courtesy of Brent Wilson

formal will leaving everything he had to his sister, Helen M. Robinson, likely reflecting a close bond they shared as siblings.

On October 30, 1917, Private Robinson embarked from Montreal aboard the SS *Canada* for England. Upon arrival at Seaford, in Sussex, Ron remained with the 236th Battalion until the summer of 1918. He received word that his brother Jack was being discharged and sent home to Canada due to his injuries. As the need for more men at the front increased, Ron eventually was sent to France in August as a volunteer stretcher-bearer just as Canada and its allies were beginning the final campaign of the war. According to his active service record, on August 11 Ron joined the 42nd Battalion, arriving just three days after the opening of the Battle of Amiens. As part of this effort, Ron's skills as a stretcher-bearer would be important, as the vicious fighting on both sides resulted in thousands of casualties. Over the next few months, Canadian, French, and British forces pushed the German line back beyond their original trenches and punched a hole through the German army at the Canal du

Nord. Throughout this period, Ron was active with the 42nd Battalion as it pressed toward Cambrai. The 42nd, along with the PPCLI, and 49th Battalion entered the small town of Tilloy, northwest of Cambrai. It was here, on September 29, that Ron was hit by a German sniper while helping those wounded and needing assistance. According to family accounts, when the head of the Western Union telegram company came to their door to deliver the news of Ron's death, Ron's mother Celia knew exactly which of her sons she had lost. The family was devasted, experiencing a painful feeling of senselessness with the news that their "Ronny" had been killed. Ron was seventeen years old. His elder brother Jack would pass away from injuries in 1921.

Lest We Forget

Ronald Campbell Robinson is buried with honour at Mill Switch British Cemetery, near Cambrai. His name also appears on the Marysville Cenotaph.

88. McArthur, Robert R. (September 30, 1918)

Private 1030059, 236th Battalion (The New Brunswick Kilties), 42nd Battalion (Royal Highlanders of Canada)

Robert McArthur was born on October 4, 1887, in Richibucto, New Brunswick, to Gilbert McArthur and Olive Rebecca Boyce. According to records, both Gilbert and Olive were from the Richibucto area. After marrying, they moved to Prince Edward Island for work, but eventually moved back to New Brunswick, settling in Victoria Mills, with Gilbert finding work as a mill labourer in Marysville. Together, the McArthurs had a large family of six boys named William, John, George, Alex, Gilbert Jr., and Robert. The third youngest in the family, Robert, grew up in a family of young men who all worked at local mills and attended local churches. Then, in December 1893, tragedy struck the family when Robert's father, Gilbert, who was working in the woods, had a tree accidentally fall on him. He spent the next twenty-one days receiving care until succumbing to his injuries on January 1, 1894. Robert was eight years old at the time of the accident. The death of her husband and the reality of having to raise six children on her own was likely hard for Olive. It is not surprising that the boys all had to find work in the mills to support the family in Gilbert's absence. Robert's mother eventually met Harry Allen from Marysville, who had also lost a spouse. They married on October 5, 1904. Records suggest, however, that, by 1911, Harry was no longer living with the family; there are few details explaining what happened. Census records reveal Olive and her children, including Robert, had changed their family name to Allen, but newspapers and other documents suggest she kept using her previously married name of McArthur.

By the time war broke out in 1914, Robert had worked for a long time as a labourer at the Marysville mill, was unmarried, and had no previous military experience. A twenty-eight-year-old single male with extensive experience as a labourer was the ideal candidate for enlistment. His service record shows that he enlisted in Fredericton on August 4, 1916, along with other local boys in the 236th Battalion, The New Brunswick Kilties. Robert was described as standing five feet seven inches tall and having a swarthy complexion, grey eyes, and dark brown hair. For the next year, Private McArthur remained at Valcartier Camp training in preparation for going overseas. It is unclear if his family saw him again before he left.

Private McArthur left Canada with the Kilties aboard the SS *Canada* on October 30, 1917, arriving in England on November 19. Robert's service was affected early on by infections that were common among soldiers. According to medical records, Robert sought early treatment in Montreal, and he received continuous treatment for the duration of his service in Europe. After nine months of training in England with the 20th Reserve Battalion, Private McArthur left for France on August 19, 1918, joining the 42nd Battalion. By late September, the 42nd had smashed through German lines and moved beyond the Canal du Nord toward Cambrai. A month later, according to his circumstances-of-death record, during the early morning hours of September 30, Robert's unit was in a village called Neuville-Saint-Rémy, outside of Cambrai. While organizing in an enemy gun pit, Robert was reportedly killed instantly by enemy machine-gun fire, along with other members of his company. A few weeks after his death, newspapers revealed that Robert and another soldier from Victoria Mills, Clifford Jukes, had been killed together while assembling a Lewis machine gun. Newspapers highlighted that Clifford "had been killed by the same exploding shell that had killed Robert McArthur" on the morning of September 29. The confusion regarding whether Robert had been killed by a shell or machine-gun fire was worsened by reports in late October in the *Daily Gleaner* that suggested Olive McArthur had not received a proper notification of death. Although there are few records available to reveal the full effect of Robert's death on family and community, the news likely was met with profound sadness. Private McArthur was thirty years old at the time of his death.

Lest We Forget

Like Privates Clifford Jukes and Ronald Robinson, Private Robert McArthur is buried and honoured at the Mill Switch British Cemetery, west of Cambrai.

89. Bidlake, Walter Geoffrey (October 2, 1918)

Gunner 303457, 4th Canadian Siege Battery

Walter Geoffrey Bidlake was born on February 20, 1893, in Wellington, Shropshire, England, to George Bidlake and Margaret Cottell Kynoch. According to information obtained from interviews with family, Geoff grew up in England and studied in private schools as a young boy until moving to Canada in 1905. He had six siblings: Frank, Jude, Kit, Rod, Gwen, and Marge. At the time, Geoff was only about ten years old and had grown accustomed to private schools. Arriving with his family at Fredericton, he made the choice to work instead of going to public school. As a young teenager growing up in Fredericton, he found work at the Queen Hotel, where he became very popular with the local community. According to George Bidlake, Walter's great-nephew, it was during this time that Geoff met a girl named Greta Gertrude Gaskin, a young normal school student from Albert County. In 1908, Geoff was only fifteen years old, two years younger than Greta. Over the next few years, their relationship blossomed, and by 1915 Geoff and Greta had become serious enough that he was invited to meet her parents and family at their home in Cloverdale, New Brunswick. Interviews suggest that it was likely the warmth of family that drew Geoff close to Greta's family, especially her brothers Cyrus and Ewart, who were about the same age as he was. On October 15, 1915, Geoff and Greta married, just two days after he had volunteered for service with the 4th Canadian Siege Battery. His choice to do so was likely motivated by the fact that Cyrus and Ewart had also enlisted around the same time, creating friendships that lasted throughout the war as they all left Canada for Europe. Geoff formally enlisted in Saint John on October 25, 1915. According to his attestation paper, he had three years of training with the local Canadian Garrison Artillery and was twenty-one years of age. Gunner Bidlake was five feet six inches tall, had a fair complexion, with blue eyes and light brown hair. Although Geoff would write many letters home and send postcards to family and friends while in Europe, especially to his sister Marge, he would never return home to Greta.

Private Bidlake trained over the fall and winter of 1915–16 with the 4th Siege Battery on Partridge Island, near Saint John. It was a good training location that could simulate the often cold, wet, and windy weather of England and France. According to his service record, Geoff left Canada for England aboard the SS *Olympic* on April 1, 1916, arriving in England on April 11. By late July, the 4th Siege Battery had landed in France at Le Havre. Over the next year, Geoff served throughout northern France and Belgium with his unit as a gunner alongside Greta's brothers Cyrus and Ewart. Sadly, only a month after the Vimy Ridge assault, Cyrus was killed by an enemy shell that hit the hut in which he was working. A few days later, Geoff wrote a letter home to Greta's mother offering his sincerest condolence for their loss, a loss he also felt:

It is with the deepest sympathy for you and all at home, in this dark hour, that I sit down to do what I feel is my duty of writing and giving you, what perceptions I can and am allowed, of poor Cy's sudden death, which happened yesterday at noon. I could not believe it at first, but I found out in a very short time that... a shell had hit right in the centre of the hut where "Cy" and three more boys were sitting in, killing them all instantly. When I heard the news, I was struck speechless for a few minutes and couldn't believe it. When they asked me if I care to see "Cy" I said I would rather not so that I could remember him as I saw him last (which was when I passed him going out on duty and he was coming in). I went up to Headquarters at 5:30 to find Ewart, and we went for a little walk up the road where I told the boy as easily as I could what had happened. He took the news well, poor boy. It has cast an awful cloud over the Battery as it is such a heavy blow. We had just begun to get over the shock of losing two more of the boys the other day and then this came. It all happened in less than fifteen seconds. Death to all was instant and thank God they were spared any pain or suffering. Please accept and tender to Mr. Gaskin, Carmen and Audrey my deepest heartfelt sympathy... in "Cy" I have lost my greatest friend. He was a good one and more like a brother to me. Yours, Sincerely, Geoffrey.

Geoff, now truly changed by the effects of war, was granted a short leave of absence in October 1917, one that saw him leave for England and return by the beginning of November. By late May 1918, Gunner Bidlake had returned to England again to train as a motorcycle despatch rider, a job that many saw as one of the most hazardous but important roles along the front to ensure lines of communication. After only a month of training, he was back in France, where he played a crucial role in allowing messages to be shared between and within units. According to his circumstances-of-death record, on October 2, as he was sitting in a shallow but covered depression in the ground near the village of Haynecourt, northwest of Cambrai, waiting for his despatches to arrive, a shell burst nearby, wounding him severely in the face and in the back of the head. First aid was administered and he was rushed to a field ambulance, but Geoff died before reaching medical attention. According to interviews with family, it is believed that Geoff was writing a letter home at the time of his death. Bidlake was twenty-four years old, leaving his wife, Greta Gertrude Gaskin, a widow. On October 17, two weeks after his death, New Brunswick papers began reporting the sad news of his passing through information received by Greta and the Bidlake family. By 1921, Greta had moved away from Fredericton and was living in Moncton, later marrying a gentleman from British Columbia, while becoming a well-respected educator and writer. Geoffrey's parents both passed away by 1936 and are buried at the Forest Hill Cemetery in Fredericton.

Lest We Forget

Gunner Walter Geoffrey Bidlake is buried at Haynecourt British Cemetery, near the small village of Haynecourt, northwest of Cambrai, France. According to the Commonwealth War Graves Commission, the cemetery contains 281 identified casualties.

90. Adams, Walter Jackson (October 3, 1918)

Gunner 2100320, 9th Canadian Siege Battery, 12th Canadian Siege Battery

Walter Jackson Adams was born on December 7, 1896, in Fredericton to Sarah Haines Macfarlane and Robert Brooke Adams. His parents married on September 19, 1894, in the parish of St. Mary's. Walter had two sisters named Jean L. and Roberta and two brothers named James and Bert.

Records reveal that the family lived in Fredericton, residing at 607 Queen Street. Walter's father worked as an undertaker and later was the sexton at St. Andrew's Presbyterian Church. Although few records account for Walter's early life, newspapers indicate that he was incredibly well liked by the Fredericton community and grew to be active with the city band and the Presbyterian Church choir. His service record reveals that he became an employee of the government as a mail carrier in the community and, according to newspapers, would always have a "cheery word and pleasant smile for everyone whom he met." Perhaps most important about his character was his willingness to help others. Wilfred Allen recalled in an interview given on June 12, 1994: "Walter Adams saved my life during the winter of 1913–14... We used to slide out onto the river's ice. One time I miscalculated and slid right into the open water. I went under and the other kids all started hollering... Walter Adams was a mailman and was walking by on his route when he heard the noise and rushed down and pulled me to safety."

At the time of his enlistment in the 9th Canadian Siege Battery at Partridge Island, on September 6, 1917, Walter was twenty years old and unmarried. Just two months short of his birthday, he was described as having hazel eyes, dark brown hair, a fresh complexion, and five feet eight inches in height. Along with many other Fredericton boys, Walter joined the 9th Siege Battery and soon began preparing to go overseas that winter with a draft in what had been described as one of the finest trained batteries in Canada. On October 6, 1917, Walter wrote his formal will while at Partridge Island, naming his mother Sarah as his beneficiary.

On December 18, 1917, Walter embarked from Saint John on the SS *Grampian* for Halifax before heading to Glasgow, Scotland. Temple Sutherland's memoir recounts how the devastation of the Halifax Explosion kept men on their ships before a thirteen-day journey overseas, arriving on December 31. Walter transferred to the 12th Canadian Siege Battery on January 22, 1918, before landing in France on June 2, after more than five months of training in England. While on leave before going to France, Walter and Gordon Boyd biked to the town of Rye, Sussex, visiting relatives of the Smith family from Fredericton. Walter attended church on

Sundays when given the opportunity. After arriving in France, the 12th Siege Battery was active during the German Spring Offensive of 1918, when it was responsible for defending the area around Lens and Vimy and reinforcing the 3rd Brigade, Canadian Garrison Artillery. Four months later, at 1:30 in the afternoon of October 3, while along the Amiens front near Haynecourt, Walter's battery position was heavily shelled, killing him instantly. In a letter written home the next day, Walter's friend Albert McElveney spoke highly of the young man:

> Well, mother, this has been a sad two days for me. Walter Adams was killed yesterday, and we buried him today. I was talking and joking with him not five minutes before. Saw him get his cup and plate and go for dinner about twenty yards away. But poor Walter did not return, for a shell landed in the cook house and twenty-two casualties was the result. He was the only one killed instantly. He and I have been such great friends since coming to France and have had such good times together. I know this...that a better living boy could not be. I certainly feel it keenly myself, as I have lost one of the best friends I ever had, and it sure has cast a gloom over the whole battery. But we must go on regardless of what happens, and things like this only give us greater determination. I will write to Walter's mother tomorrow. It sure will be an awful blow to her. You and Bess had better go down and see her.

According to documents, a shell burst thirty feet (nine metres) away from Walter and a large piece hit him near the heart. Walter was only twenty-one years old, a much loved and highly respected young man. The signing of the Armistice occurred a little more than a month later, on November 11, ending the fighting on the Western Front.

Lest We Forget

Walter Jackson Adams is buried at Sains-lès-Marquion British Cemetery, located in the village of Sains-lès-Marquion, between Cambrai and Arras, France. According to the Commonwealth War Graves Commission, he is one of 227 identified casualties in the cemetery, 177 of whom are

Canadian, along with 49 British and 1 Australian soldier. This cemetery was designed by noted British architect Wilfred C. Von Berg.

91. Edgecombe, Charles Hedley (October 6, 1918)

2nd Lieutenant, Royal Flying Corps, Royal Air Force

Charles Hedley Edgecombe was born July 16, 1888, in Fredericton to Helen Lydia Eaton and Fred B. Edgecombe. According to records obtained from the Provincial Archives of New Brunswick, his parents married in Saint John on October 28, 1887. Census records show that Charles was the eldest of four children, the other siblings being named Emerson, Louis, and Helen. The Edgecombe family was well known in the Fredericton business community, as Charles's grandfather manufactured horse carriages before passing the business on to Charles's father, Frederick. He then entered dry goods and railway businesses, operating a store downtown. The family resided at 736 King Street. Although there are limited detailed accounts of his early life in Fredericton, newspaper records show that Charles attended school at the Wesleyan Academy, a private boys' school, and Mount Allison University, where he studied and played for the university's hockey team. Described as one of the most prominent young businessmen in Fredericton at the time, Charles was expected eventually to take over his father's business. He appeared to have the kind of disposition that allowed him to make friends and acquaintances easily. When war broke out in the summer of 1914, Charles left for Camp Borden, north of Toronto, to become an aviation instructor. He also spent time in Texas, where Canadian students joined and trained alongside American students. He eventually returned to Canada and formally enlisted at Toronto in the winter of 1917 with the Royal Flying Corps, completing the remainder of his training by July 1918 and graduating with honours. According to his attestation record, Charles was twenty-nine years old, had brown hair, and stood about five feet three inches tall. The *Daily Gleaner* reports that by July 1918, Edgecombe was unhappy with being assigned as an aviation instructor and requested to go overseas, "anxious to get in the thickest of the work among airmen." During the summer of 1918, Charles spent a brief period with family as he prepared to go overseas. Newspaper accounts note that, "before leaving here he knew full well the uncertainties that were facing him. He had no fear but went courageously forth determined to do his bit, and, if must be, face death in his country's cause."

Overseeing a company of twenty-five aviators, Edgecombe left Canada from Quebec, arriving in England on September 25. Upon arrival, Charles was sent to Salisbury Plain's aviation headquarters for ten days of training before being assigned to a Royal Air Force squadron. He was to complete two trial training missions before going to France. During the second of these training missions, Charles lost his life. While news of an accident had been received by family on October 8, details of his death were not disclosed until a month after the Armistice had been signed. According to a letter received by the *Daily Gleaner* in late 1918, the details of what happened to Charles are made clear:

> Dear Sir, the late Lieutenant Edgecombe went as a passenger with 2nd Lieutenant Forster on a cross country flight on the 6th of October flying in the observer seat of a DH9. Second Lt. Forster was qualified to carry a passenger. He had a forced landing nothing serious was wrong. About 3 o'clock the following day the machine was ready to start again. The machine took off alright and climbed to 300 or 400 feet [90 to 120 metres] when 2nd Lt. Forster made a steep left turn. The wind was gusty and appeared to get under the machine and turn it over and it spun into the ground. It burst into flames and by the time assistance arrived Lt. Edgecombe was beyond help and 2nd Lt. Forster was badly injured and died the same evening. Lt. Edgecombe's body was buried with full air force honors at Salisbury... he had been full

of enthusiasm over the work ahead and expressed his great pleasure [upon] being assigned to the bombing section.

According to Charles's casualty card, he died on October 6 at 3:26 p.m., the result of injuries sustained in the accident. He was thirty years old.

Lest We Forget

Charles Hedley Edgecombe is buried at the Salisbury (London) Road Cemetery, in Salisbury, Wiltshire. According to the Commonwealth War Graves Commission, 103 casualties from the First and Second World Wars are buried here. (No LAC record available.)

92. Brewer, Ernest Alfred (October 8, 1918)

Private 710058, 104th Battalion, 25th Battalion, 26th Battalion

Ernest Alfred Brewer was born on February 5, 1898, in Fredericton to Sergeant-Major Herbert T. Brewer and Hattie M. Guthrie. His parents married during the summer of 1889 in Fredericton. According to the 1901 census, Ernest was the second youngest of six siblings, the others being four brothers, LeRoy, Raymond, William, and Cecil, and an elder sister, Edith. Given the family's strong ties to the local militia through their father, who served with The Royal Canadian Regiment and was in charge of recruiting with the local militia, the family resided on Carleton Street in Fredericton near the local armoury. Newspapers reveal that all five brothers enlisted for service with their father when war broke out in 1914. Just prior to the war, Ernest worked locally as a clerk and served for five months with the Halifax Composite Battalion before enlisting in Sussex with the 104th Battalion on February 17, 1916. According to his attestation paper, Ernest had a fair complexion, blue eyes, brown hair, weighed 148 pounds, and stood five feet five and a half inches tall. Records reveal that his family identified as free Baptists and highlight how the Brewer boys were all held in high esteem by the community, with Ernest described as an exceptional young man. William enlisted in Ottawa with the 1st Battery, LeRoy with the Canadian Engineers, Raymond with the 26th Battalion and received a commission with the 236th Battalion, and Cecil enlisted as a piper, also with the 236th. William and Ernest never returned home to their families.

Documents reveal that Ernest enlisted just prior to meeting the required military age for service. After spending a few months with the 104th Battalion in Sussex and then shifting to Nova Scotia, his unit left Halifax on June 28, 1916, for England on the SS *Olympic*, arriving in Liverpool on July 6. Over the next twenty-four months, Ernest was in and out of military hospitals in England for a variety of illnesses and ailments while being assigned to the 13th Reserve Battalion. After the winter of 1916, the spring found Ernest in isolation for approximately one month while recovering from a case of the mumps. After a full recovery, he was once again admitted to hospital a few months later — medical records reveal that he fractured both bones in his left leg during a football game in November 1917. He needed nearly four months to recover fully and was eventually discharged in February 1918 only to be immediately readmitted due to ligament complications and swelling in his knees. It was not until August 1918, nearly two years after arriving, that Ernest saw action for the first time when he joined the 26th Battalion to France. It is likely that this sudden thrust into action might have been caused by the sudden news of his brother's death. Sergeant William Douglas Brewer died on August 15 near the village of Le Quesnoy, just three days before Ernest stepped foot in France. Private Brewer was active in late August and nearly all of September with both the 25th Nova Scotia Rifles and the "Fighting 26th" in engagements at Amiens and then near Cambrai, areas where his brother would have been as well. His own circumstances-of-death document indicates that, on October 8, while in an area west of Cambrai, he was killed instantly when a piece of shrapnel struck him in the head. Ernest was nineteen years old.

93. Young, Stanley George (November 4, 1918)

Private 709659, 104th Battalion, 26th Battalion

Stanley George Young was born on April 23, 1897, in the small community of Taymouth, New Brunswick, to Annie Gertrude Richardson and Charles Duncan Young, both Methodists. According to his attestation documents, Stanley had hazel eyes and brown hair and was five feet seven inches tall. Census records reveal that he had two older sisters named Layla and Alice Louise. Alice, who would have been twenty-one years of age when Stanley enlisted, later became a teacher in the area and married Henry G. Beacom in the summer of 1925. When he was still young, Stanley's family moved to Fredericton and occupied a residence at 338 Westmorland Street. Newspapers reveal that Stanley attended Fredericton High School, graduated, and then became a clerk. At the time he enlisted in Sussex on November 8, 1915, he was eighteen years old and unmarried. Although his motives for joining the Canadian Expeditionary Force are difficult to know, it was probably that, like most young men at the time, he felt the war would offer adventure and glory and be short lived. Over time, this perception of the war would be challenged. It is likely that he was both excited and nervous about the experience ahead.

Private Young embarked from Halifax for England with the 104th Battalion in the summer of 1916 on the SS *Olympic*. Upon arrival in Liverpool, he was sent to Witley Camp and promoted to lance corporal.

He spent most of his time while in England training. Almost a year and a half later, Stanley was transferred to the 13th Reserve Battalion in Seaford, Sussex, before proceeding to France with the 26th Battalion. In the early part of 1918, the 26th was preparing for the expected German spring offensive. On August 14, Stanley was shot in the hand and sent to the 4th Canadian Field Ambulance, was hospitalized, and then sent back to his unit nineteen days later. On October 10, during the Allied push on Cambrai, Private Young's service record reveals that he received multiple gunshot wounds in his left arm and shoulder and was subsequently taken to No. 22 Casualty Clearing Station before being struck off strength and sent to the Pavilion General Hospital in Brighton, England. Nearly three weeks later, as the Canadians and their Allies continued to push the Germans out of France and Belgium, Stanley became dangerously ill, and passed away at 11:55 p.m. on the evening of November 4, just seven days before the Armistice. Stanley was twenty-one years of age. News of his death was reported in New Brunswick papers by November 8.

Lest We Forget

Stanley George Young is buried in Brighton City Cemetery, in Brighton, Sussex, alongside the graves of 275 other Commonwealth servicemen of the First World War. Stanley also has a headstone in his hometown of Fredericton in the Fredericton Rural Cemetery.

94. Fullarton, Frederick White (November 8, 1918)

Private 817868, 71st York Regiment, 140th Battalion, Princess Patricia's Canadian Light Infantry

Frederick (Fred) White Fullarton was born on January 27, 1899, in Williamsburg, New Brunswick, to John Alexander Fullarton and Joanna Gilmore. Newspaper records indicate that he came from a very strong

Scottish heritage known for its loyalty to King and country: Fred's great-grandfather, Donald Fullarton, was a mate in the "Mary of King George III," and the family received lands in the days of Robert Bruce as a reward for service in an area of Scotland that became known as Fullarton's Glen. The family later moved to New Brunswick, settling in Williamsburg, near Stanley. According to the 1911 census, Fred had five siblings and a few half-siblings. His eldest brother, Charles Gilmore, was born April 2, 1895, while another elder brother, William Ingles, was born on January 7, 1897. Fred's younger siblings were Winifred Ines, born on June 4, 1901, who passed away on August 2, 1910, at the age of nine; Ian Reginald, born on May 6, 1907; and Mary Abigail, born on November 22, 1911. According to death records, on July 12, 1912, Fred's father, John Alexander, passed away at the age of fifty-five when Fred was approximately thirteen years old. Fred's mother Joanna eventually remarried William Henry Sewell in 1915 and then Albert B. Neill in 1919, both from South Devon. When war broke out in 1914, all three brothers, Charles, William, and Fred, enlisted. According to his attestation paper, Fred served one year in Fredericton with the 71st York Regiment. At the time of his enlistment with the 140th Battalion, Fred was working as a woodsman and claimed to be eighteen years of age when he was in fact younger. Documents reveal that cables received clarifying his actual age had little impact on his service. At the time of his enlistment on January 22, 1916, in Saint John, Fred was five feet nine and a half inches tall, weighed 175 pounds, had blue eyes, brown hair, and a fair complexion. He and his brother, William, would never return home, while his eldest brother, Charles, later returned after five months of service.

After spending time at Camp Valcartier with his unit, where he was treated for measles for two weeks in July, Private Fullarton sailed on the SS *Corsican* from Halifax with his unit for England on September 25. He arrived a week-and-a-half later, on October 6. Fred continued to train with The Royal Canadian Regiment and then the PPCLI at Seaford until going overseas in December. Prior to leaving for the front, Fred wrote his formal will leaving everything to his half-sister, Margaret, who had been living on St. John Street in Fredericton and who was the daughter of Fred's father from his previous marriage. Given that Fred's brother, William, also listed Margaret as his next-of-kin, it is possible that there might have been some rift with their mother. On December 17, 1916, Fred left with his unit for France, where he saw active duty during an important time for the Canadian military. Records reveal that he served twenty-two months of active service with only one leave-of-absence during that time. During a crucial period of seven months in 1918, the Canadian Corps engaged in increasingly successful attacks on German lines to push the enemy out of northern France and Belgium. Fred was killed on November 8, just a few kilometres from Mons, Belgium, three days before the war ended. According to his certificate of death, Fred was "at an advanced post near Boussu, Belgium and while taking his Lewis gun into a house, he was killed instantly by enemy machine gun fire." Fred was only nineteen years of age. His brother William had been killed at the age of twenty during the Battle of Hill 70, in August 1917. William's body was never be found; he is honoured on the Vimy Memorial.

Lest We Forget

Private Frederick White Fullarton is buried at Boussu Communal Cemetery, Belgium. According to the Commonwealth War Graves Commission, Fred is the only Canadian buried here along with only four other Commonwealth burials of the First World War. The cemetery is 10.5 kilometres west of Mons, Belgium.

95. Clark, Frederick Leroy (December 13, 1918)

Gunner 1257947, 9th Siege Battery

Frederick Leroy Clark was born on July 6, 1891, in Maugerville to Henry Finch Clark, of Clarks Corner (Maquapit Lake), and Ada Blanche Chase, of French Lake. The 1901 census reveals that Frederick, born into a farming family, was the youngest of four siblings: a sister named Mary and three brothers named William, James, and Harry. Records suggest that the Clark family was hard working and very involved with their church community. According to the 1911 census, Fred lived most of his early life at home with his parents helping with the farm until he was in his early twenties. While few records exist detailing the family's life in rural Maugerville, by the time war came to the community Frederick's sister had married and was living in Fredericton. His elder brothers were working the farm, as their father was aging. Frederick enlisted in Fredericton on April 2, 1917, and arrived a few days later at Partridge Island for training with the 9th Siege Battery. His attestation paper indicates that he was twenty-five years old, stood five feet six and a half inches tall, weighed 125 pounds, and had a dark complexion, hazel-coloured eyes, and dark brown hair. His attestation also states that he was unmarried, had never been vaccinated, and had limited military training and experience. Slightly older than many other young men enlisting from the area, upon arrival Fred was quickly exposed to a variety of viruses and almost immediately became ill as a result.

The specific details of Gunner Clark's military experiences were difficult to research because there is limited information in his service record or in newspapers. Records that do exist suggest that, after beginning his training with the 9th Siege Battery in April 1917, one month after the 9th Battery left for England, Fred was diagnosed in Halifax and admitted to a military hospital in June with mumps. He was treated and discharged two weeks later, on June 14, and transferred back to Partridge Island. Between June 1917 and December 1918, very little is known regarding Fred's service because there are so few records. What does appear in the documented record seems to be contradictory. Clark's service record shows that he was never formally transferred to any other unit, even as the 9th Siege Battery sent more men overseas in 1918. Fred, however, appears not to have served overseas at all, and pay sheets have no record of his ever being paid for his service. It seems that he was later with the 7th Canadian Artillery Depot, suggesting he had transferred from the Canadian Expeditionary Force to the militia, which would explain the absence of details in his service file.

While the war continued into the fall of 1918, ending with the signing of the Armistice on November 11, the only entry for his record of service was made on December 12, when Fred was admitted to the St. James Street Military Hospital in Saint John, complaining of "severe pains in left side of chest." His medical history sheet reveals that Fred had been sick for a week with severe pain in his chest and, upon closer observation by doctors, had an increased but weak pulse, with fast and shallow breathing. Military doctors found fluid in his lungs and that he had been suffering from pneumonia and was already in a "dying condition." Although it is not often discussed as a cause of death of soldiers during the First World War, many became casualties due to illness and disease. At the time of his death, the Influenza Pandemic of 1918, also known as the Spanish Influenza, was affecting thousands in the province. On December 13, only a day after being admitted, Fred Clark passed away due to complications related to pneumonia. According to newspapers, his remains were brought to Fredericton before being moved to Maugerville, where his father was also buried during the winter of 1918. At the time, Fred's mother was

Grave of Gunner Frederick L. Clark, Christ Church Cemetery, Maugerville, New Brunswick.
James Rowinski

living in Fredericton with her son on Woodstock Road; given the family's connection to Maugerville, however, Christ Church Cemetery was chosen as his place of burial. Fred was twenty-seven years of age.

Lest We Forget

Fred is buried behind Christ Church in Maugerville, in the north part of the cemetery alongside his father. His mother passed away in the winter of 1929 and is buried alongside her son and husband.

Soldiers convalescing in the New Brunswick Military Hospital, Old Government House, Fredericton. Courtesy of the Clarence Gillies Collection

Chapter Five

1919–1923

Although the Armistice was signed on November 11, 1918, the lengthy and often complex process of demobilizing soldiers had just begun. Some remained overseas as part of occupying forces immediately following the war's end. Many soldiers had already returned to Canada due to injuries and sickness sustained during their service, but many others waited for months to get home, including some who remained in hospitals overseas, unable to be moved because of health issues. As a result, while Canada was celebrating the end of the war, it was only the beginning of a difficult road for many soldiers requiring support for a host of complex health issues and programs, such as job training, needed to help them reintegrate back into society and their pre-war lives. Ultimately, it was decided to include on the Fredericton War Memorial the names of ten soldiers who had succumbed to their wartime afflictions after the Armistice (as well as one soldier who was presumed killed in action but had returned to a different city).

96. Leadbetter, John (March 3, 1919)

Sergeant 477526, The Royal Canadian Regiment

John H. Leadbetter was born on May 8, 1883, in London, England, to John Sr. and Julia Leadbetter. Although little is known of John's early experiences growing up in England prior to the war, at some point he met a young woman named Jennie May Edwards. The two married and eventually made their way to Canada, where they began raising a family. John's records reveal that he had extensive military experience, having served in the Boer War at a young age with The Royal Canadian Regiment (RCR) and Canadian Mounted Rifles, and later with the 71st York Regiment beginning on June 10, 1908. According to the *Daily Gleaner*, Leadbetter was one of the most "prominent non-commissioned officers of the RCR in Fredericton before the war." He and his wife had four children before John left Canada with the RCR in August 1914 for Bermuda. While there, he served on garrison duty after war was declared. John eventually returned from Bermuda to New Brunswick and enlisted for overseas service with the RCR in Fredericton on August 22, 1915. Records suggest that he spent a brief period at the Wellington Barracks in Halifax in 1915, just before leaving for overseas. At the time of his enlistment, he was thirty-two years old and was described as having brown eyes, brown hair, a medium complexion, and standing five feet eight inches tall. In late summer 1915, Sergeant Leadbetter left his wife and four children to go overseas with his battalion. His family would not see him for two years.

After arriving to England with the RCR, already with extensive military training and experience, Leadbetter immediately left for Boulogne, France, on November 2, 1915. Over the next few months, local newspapers reported his fighting in various engagements over the winter of 1915–16. On March 13, 1916, John received important news from Canada: the birth of his son, Arthur Wilfred. Unfortunately, this happy news was short-lived. Three months after the birth of his son, John was with the RCR in Belgium when he received serious gunshot wounds to his face, arms, and chest, and was buried alive for several hours as a result of an exploding shell. Documents suggest that this was a trying time for both John and Jennie: after giving birth, Jennie had undergone treatment and surgery in a Saint John hospital for an undisclosed ailment. Meanwhile, at the same time as his wife was undergoing surgery in Canada, John had been admitted to hospital and began treatment to address the pulmonary tuberculosis he had developed in his right lung. According to medical reports, it is likely that this condition worsened as a result of having his chest "severely crushed" and by being in close proximity to poisonous gas that had been used in the Ypres Salient. Nearly a year would go by before Sergeant Leadbetter could be discharged and sent home to New Brunswick. Although he received treatment at various hospitals in England during this time, little could be done to reverse the development of the tuberculosis that spread as a result of the exposure of his injured chest. On July 21, 1917, John embarked from Liverpool for Halifax aboard the hospital ship HMHS *Letitia*. After arriving, he was transported to his family home at 324 Campbell Street, on the northside of Fredericton. While seeing his family for the first time in years would be welcomed, John's condition worsened less than a year later. Medical reports reveal that, by August 1918, his health had weakened, he had lost weight, was suffering from shortness of breath, and was becoming malnourished because of his illness. While receiving treatment at the Park Barracks Hospital over the winter of 1918–19, John's tuberculosis got progressively worse. On March 3, 1919, he passed away, leaving behind his wife and five children. According to the *Daily Gleaner*, his funeral took place the following afternoon at his home, conducted by Reverend Dean Neales, and interment took place at the Fredericton Rural Cemetery with full military honours. Sergeant John H. Leadbetter was thirty-five years old.

Lest We Forget

Sergeant John H. Leadbetter is buried in the Fredericton Rural Cemetery Extension, located in Fredericton on the Woodstock Road.

97. Edgecombe, Frederick Allison (May 10, 1919)

Private 427621, 46th Battalion, 58th Battalion

Frederick Allison Edgecombe was born on February 3, 1893, in Saint John to Arthur C. Edgecombe and Mabel Estey. Arthur and Mabel, both from Fredericton, married on September 16, 1891, and went on to have another son named Arthur Clarence, born in the fall of 1896. According to records, the Edgecombe family lived in Saint John, where Arthur worked as a mail clerk. Then, only a few months after their second son was born, tragedy struck: in January 1897 Arthur died at the age of thirty-two. Frederick's mother was forced to return to Fredericton with her boys. She spent time living with her parents, Richard and Catherine, getting help as she raised her two boys, as the 1901 census shows that she and the boys were living at the home of her parents in Fredericton, along with her younger brother, Fred. Over this period, she met Robert Bedford H. Phillips, also of Fredericton, whom she eventually married in June 1901. By 1911, Robert and Mabel had two children together, J.R. Darrell and Grace Ireland, and, according to the 1911 census, Frederick and Arthur Clarence were still living at home at 582 George Street. Also living on the property was a domestic house servant named Amelia McConaghy. A few years later, as a teenager, Frederick Allison moved out west for work and found a job as an electrician. He enlisted in Regina, Saskatchewan, on September 15, 1915. According to his attestation paper, Frederick joined the 46th Battalion, from south Saskatchewan, and was reportedly unmarried and without any prior military training or experience. He was described as having a ruddy complexion, hazel eyes, and black hair, and standing five feet six inches tall. Frederick was twenty-one years of age. His brother, Arthur Charles, also enlisted and served with the 58th Howitzer Battery from New Brunswick.

Private Edgecombe only had a month of training with his western unit before he left for England from Halifax on October 21, 1915, aboard the SS *Lapland*. By October 30, the 46th Battalion had arrived at Devonport,

England. Frederick trained with his unit over the winter of 1915–16 until transferring to the 58th Battalion, from central Ontario, arriving in France on June 17, 1916. The 58th had just been involved in the Battle of Mount Sorrel and were in need of reinforcements, although it continued operations in Belgium, where constant enemy fire and the use of gas made conditions difficult. After being in the field for only two months, Frederick illustrated in letters written home some of the harsh conditions he faced. In September, the *Daily Gleaner* shared Frederick's experience of being buried alive. While assisting in dressing the wounds of another soldier, Frederick was completely buried by an exploding shell that would cause shrapnel to be embedded in his left eye and legs. Luckily, he was able to dig himself out and then was removed to No. 1 Casualty Clearing Station for treatment. Around this same time, he was also diagnosed with shell shock. The trauma of his experiences was made clear by words later written home explaining that the men beside him in the trenches always happened to be the ones killed. Private Edgecombe was sent to England for medical treatment relating to his eye injury. While there, he would receive further treatment over the winter of 1916–17 for other illnesses. By March 1917, his records show, he was on command with the Canadian School of Stenography at St. Leonards, Sussex, until being admitted two months later to a Canadian Military Hospital because of a suspected case of tuberculosis. Medical records show that, on May 4, 1917, Frederick was diagnosed with tuberculosis and was invalided home to Canada, leaving on the hospital ship HMHS *Araguaya* from Liverpool on June 11, 1917. After arriving home, Private Edgecombe spent time being treated at the Jordan Memorial Sanitorium in River Glade, New Brunswick, before being formally discharged from service on May 31, 1918, because he was no longer fit for duty. On May 10, 1919, a year after being discharged, Private Frederick Allison Edgecombe passed away due to complications from his illness. He was twenty-six years old.

Lest We Forget

Private Frederick A. Edgecombe is buried in the Fredericton Rural Cemetery in Fredericton. Frederick's grave and headstone are located close to the St. John River.

98. Tennant, Walter Anderson (June 30, 1919) Military Medal and Bar, Italian Bronze Medal

Company Sergeant Major 430262, 107th East Kootenay Regiment, 48th Battalion, 29th Battalion, Canadian Forestry Corps

Walter Anderson Tennant was born on October 9, 1885, in Fredericton to James Tennant Sr. and Margaret Telford Anderson Tennant. According to records, Walter grew up in a large family and lived on Government House Avenue, now a heritage home located beside the Fredericton Rural Cemetery. Besides Walter, there were three brothers, Norman, James, and Archibald, and three sisters, one of whom, Margaret, was named after her mother. Records reveal that his mother passed away in 1898 when Walter was thirteen years old. His father died in 1910, leaving the children in the family to fend for themselves as young adults.

According to newspapers, three of the boys served during the war. In addition to Walter, Norman, who was serving with the Northwest Mounted Police in Calgary, and James, who lived in Fredericton, both joined up. Walter's attestation paper show that he was raised a Presbyterian and when he was nineteen years old, he moved to Cranbook, British Columbia, and took a job as a lumberman. At the time of his enlistment, Walter was twenty-nine years old, unmarried, stood five feet nine inches tall, and weighed 170 pounds. He had brown eyes, brown hair, and a distinctive scar on his right shoulder received from an accident early in his life. Before the war, he served in the militia's 107th East Kootenay Regiment. On March 3, 1915, Walter enlisted in the 48th Canadian Infantry Battalion in Victoria, British Columbia, which was preparing to leave for England two months later. Walter's official service record indicates that his sister, Margaret Atherman, who lived at 388 Woodstock Road in Fredericton, was his next-of-kin. Walter never returned home.

Walter left for England aboard the RMS *Grampian* on July 1, 1915, and arrived at Shorncliffe the early summer 1915. He transferred to the 29th Battalion, and in late September he left with his unit for France.

Walter was in the field for most of his eighteen months of service, being promoted to lance corporal and then sergeant in the same year. In less than seven months of service, Tennant was awarded the Military Medal twice for bravery in the field and the Italian Bronze Medal for military valour in the spring of 1917. During this time, he was wounded multiple times from shrapnel fire in the arm and chest and was admitted to a military hospital from October 15 to December 3, 1916, for treatment, and then again in the summer of 1917 with a bullet and shrapnel embedded in his left forearm. When Walter's injuries led to his being declared unfit for duty in the field, he joined the Canadian Forestry Corps in Skibo, Scotland, putting his skills as a lumberman back home to good use. On November 13, 1918, only two days after the Armistice was signed ending the war, Company Sergeant Major Tennant contracted double pneumonia and had to be hospitalized. He stayed at Orpington Hospital, in London, for about six months waiting to return home, when his condition suddenly worsened. On June 30, 1919, medical records report, Walter passed away in Liverpool after succumbing to a case of empyema, which caused the collapse of his right lung. A highly decorated soldier, Tennant was thirty-three years of age.

Lest We Forget

Walter Anderson Tennant is buried at the Liverpool (Kirkdale) Cemetery in Liverpool, England. According to the Commonwealth War Grave Commission, the cemetery was established when No. 5 Canadian General Hospital opened at Kirkdale in July 1917. Of the 386 First World War burials, more than 100 are Canadian.

99. Lifford, David (January 6, 1921)

Private 4651/307026, 3rd Kings Liverpool Battalion, British Army

David James Lifford was born in 1877 in Cork, Ireland, to Ellen Mary Hurley and David Lifford Sr. Although Ellen and David married in Fredericton on January 28, 1869, the family spent time in Ireland and England because of David Sr.'s work and his service with the British Army. Few records detail his work life other than showing that he was a butler at the Government House residence and that all of his children were born in either Ireland or England. The Liffords were a large family of eight children: William, Mary, Harry, Elizabeth, Louisa, Joseph, John, and David, and they occupied a residence at 272 Regent Street. Once old enough, the younger David eventually left Canada and found work in the United States, settling in Cambridge, Massachusetts. While working as a teamster in the local coal industry, he met a young woman named Elizabeth Kenney, and they married on October 3, 1911. Newspapers indicate that he had a child with Elizabeth, but she contracted pneumonia prior to the war and succumbed to the illness in 1915. A few months after the start of the war, David began making his way from Boston to England, arriving by the early summer of 1915. Records appear to show that David had previously served with American units in Havana, Cuba, before 1914, and that he had experience through his father's connections and service with the British Army. This might account for his wanting to go directly to England rather than enlist with a Canadian unit in New Brunswick. A more likely reason is that his brothers, John, Joseph, and Harry, had all joined up and were already heading overseas. In 1915, David was thirty-eight years old.

Private Lifford left Boston on July 15, 1915, aboard the SS *Bohemia* en route to Liverpool. Documents suggest that his work as a teamster made him an important asset to the military because he knew how to handle and work with horses. It is not surprising to find in documents that the US government had asked him to help deliver horses to the Allies from the United States. After arriving, David spent three months in

England training with the British Army's 3rd Battalion, King's Regiment (Liverpool) before arriving in France on November 19, 1915. Newspapers painted a vivid image of his time once in the field. David spent the winter of 1915–16 in the trenches, then took part in the Battle of the Somme between July and November 1916. He and his brothers had a rough introduction. John was killed on June 9, 1916, while fighting with the 26th Battalion in Belgium and was never found, while Joseph was forced to return home after suffering injuries in the field. To make matters worse for the family, on September 13, the *Daily Gleaner* reported that David had gone missing during action on August 8. A year went by before family received word that he had been taken prisoner and was being held in a German prison camp. As the war continued and little new information of his whereabouts was known, the family began fearing the worse had happened and started to mourn his death. Their father, David Sr., passed away on June 9, 1918. As late as August 1918, two and a half years after being taken prisoner, documents suggest that many had given up hope of finding young David Jr. alive. With the end of the war in sight, however, the Red Cross reported to his family that it finally had been able to make contact with him in Germany. A few months later, a letter from King George V confirmed David's release and repatriation to England:

> The Queen joins me in welcoming you on your release from the miseries and hardships, which you have endured with so much patience and courage. During these many months of trial, the early rescue of our gallant officers and men from the cruelties of their captivity has been uppermost in our thoughts. We are thankful that this longed-for day has arrived and that back in the old country you will be able once more to enjoy the happiness of a home and to see good days among those who anxiously look for your return.

Private Lifford was formally discharged in April 1919 and returned home to Fredericton to be reunited with family. Now almost forty-three years old, David had experienced much during the war, including the loss of his wife and a brother, two other brothers wounded, and having to deal with his own scars. Newspapers report that he eventually moved to Saint John with his child and found work with the Christie Woodworking factory. There, he met a young woman named Madelaine Lavina Birch, and they married on September 20, 1920. On January 6, 1921, while working his shift as a nightwatchman at the factory, David suffered a heart attack. Around nine o'clock that evening, newspapers reveal, two police officers found him alive in the boiler room and had gone to get an ambulance and a doctor. When they returned, he was dead. As the coroner stated, there were no signs of struggle or violence, and it appeared to be a case of heart disease. David's brother, Joseph, made funeral arrangements days later and returned his body to Fredericton. David Lifford was forty-five years of age at the time of his death, leaving behind his wife and child.

Lest We Forget
Private David Lifford is buried at the Fredericton Hermitage Cemetery in Fredericton, located along the St. John River off the Woodstock Road. (No LAC record available.)

100. McLeod, Harry Fulton (January 7, 1921)

Colonel, 71st Carleton Regiment, 12 Battalion

Harry Fulton McLeod was born on September 14, 1871, in Fredericton to Jane F. Squires and Joseph McLeod. According to the 1891 census, Harry had four siblings named Ida, Norman, Jennie, and Myrna. The family was well known in the area and resided in a home near Carleton and Charlotte Streets, as their father, Dr. Reverend Joseph McLeod, was the pastor of the George Street Free Baptist Church (later the Grace Memorial United Baptist Church) for twenty-six years. Specific details of Harry's early childhood are difficult to find, but records show that he was well educated and attended the Old Fredericton Grammar School. According to newspaper accounts, he was known as a very athletic young man involved in many sports, including rugby, baseball, boxing, and curling. After finishing school, Harry attended the University of New Brunswick and graduated with a Bachelor of Arts and recipient of the Stanley Gold Medal. He later joined Judge George Gregory's office to study law. Prior to the outbreak of war in 1914, Harry worked tirelessly as a politician, lawyer, and military leader. Although not elected as a Member of Parliament until 1913, Harry had been active politically early in his career, becoming a political candidate for the first time in 1903, and later mayor of Fredericton. He was promoted to provincial secretary for New Brunswick in 1911. His military experience was just as impressive, and he became the youngest to reach the rank of lieutenant-colonel with the local militia's 71st York Regiment. Although leading a busy life, Harry met a young woman named Ina Florence Mersereau, originally from Bathurst, and they married on December 30, 1908. They had three children named Jean, Norman, and Mary, and lived at 488 Charlotte Street.

As commanding officer of the 71st York, he was invited overseas several times by Sam Hughes, Minister of Militia, on behalf of the government. On September 22, 1914, Harry received command by King George V of the Canadian Expeditionary Force's 12th Battalion. At the time he signed his formal attestation paper at Surrey Camp in England, on December 23, 1914, Lieutenant-Colonel McLeod was described as standing six feet one inches tall and having a dark complexion, brown hair, and brown eyes. He was forty-three years old.

Given his position as an officer in the Canadian military, Lieutenant-Colonel McLeod's service record does not contain all the details of his military experience as was the case for other ranks. As a result, while we know that he was in England by December 1914 with the 12th Battalion, details of how he arrived are not known. Letters he wrote home suggest, however, that he had gone overseas aboard the SS *Scotian* in early October after having been at Valcartier Camp as part of the First Contingent after war broke out. By November 1914, McLeod was at Pond Farm Camp, on Salisbury Plain, England, where he took up important diplomatic, administrative, and training duties over the winter of 1914–15. Like many soldiers dealing with the harsh conditions of England that first year, although a high-ranking officer, Harry's overseas experience would centre largely around a variety of illnesses and ailments due to the environment, his age, and a combination of limited supplies and medicines. He arrived in France on June 6, 1915, but his time in the field was limited to six months. By December 14, while still in the field, Harry developed pneumonia and returned to Folkestone, England, where he received treatment over the early months of 1916. News of his condition as "dangerously ill" was reported in local papers, where his sickness caused "tremendous anxiety among his large circle of friends." His condition would leave him so debilitated that, by April 1916, the medical board debated if he was fit for duty. They discharged him a month later for duty in England, but Harry was readmitted with pneumonia in the late fall of 1916. Realizing that his condition was not going to improve, doctors discharged him to Canada in July 1917 after he failed to respond to treatment.

Although he had survived this part of the war and was returning home to family, his battle with continuous illness as a result of his service was just beginning. In 1918, his mother, Jane, passed away. Newspapers at the time reported that, in his final years of continuously battling pneumonia, Harry's health greatly interfered with his public activities. Some accounts describe him feeling trapped as a person. Two and a half years after the war was over, in January 1921, his condition rapidly worsened, and this time he was unable to recover. He passed away on January 7, 1921, at the age of fifty. As news of his death spread across the province and country, condolences poured in for the family. When thousands flocked to his funeral, the municipal government put forth a resolution in council to make its sincere sympathies a matter of public record as reflected in the minutes:

Whereas, we have learned with great regret of the death last night of Colonel Harry F. McLeod . . . be it resolved that this council place on record an expression of its regret at the great loss sustained by the county of York and extend to the family its sincere sympathy in their bereavement. The Council also desires to record its appreciation of the valuable public services rendered by Colonel McLeod as a patriotic and public-spirited citizen. For many years he held a prominent place in the military and political life of the province and his death will be a distinct loss to the whole community.

Lieutenant-Colonel McLeod's funeral was reported in local newspapers as one of the largest military funerals ever held in the city. The significance of his contributions as a leader and builder in Fredericton during a very trying time in New Brunswick's history warrants Harry McLeod's legacy a more prominent place in the community.

Lest We Forget

Lieutenant-Colonel Harry McLeod was buried with honour at the Forest Hill Cemetery in Fredericton.

Grave of Lieutenant-Colonel Harry F. McLeod, Forest Hill Cemetery, Fredericton. Brent Wilson

101. Coffyn, William Vernon (January 11, 1921)

Captain, Royal Army Medical Corps

William Vernon Coffyn was born on November 12, 1884, in Bristol, Prince Edward Island, to Francis Joseph and Mary A. Coffyn. In addition to William, the youngest in the family, there were three brothers named James Russell, Ernest, and Wesley, and two sisters, Bessie and Estella. According to records, it appears that his father was a farmer. William's childhood was spent in Prince Edward Island, and when old enough he studied to become a schoolteacher. After teaching for some time, he moved to Halifax and enrolled at Dalhousie University to study medicine. Upon graduation in 1910, William moved to Bathurst, New Brunswick, to practice medicine with his brother Wesley, who was a physician as well. During this time, he met a young woman from Pokiok named Sadie Saunders Burden, whom he married on September 6, 1911, in Canterbury, New Brunswick. Sadie's father was a well-known politician, George Burden. It appears that, over the next few years, William and Sadie continued living in Canterbury while also spending time near Sadie's family home in Dumfries. When war broke out in 1914, Dr. Coffyn enlisted with Royal Army Medical Corps (RAMC) and in 1916 agreed to go to England and then to the Middle East under Major-General Sir Frederick Maude. Because he chose to enlist with the British Army, there are limited government records of his military service. From information found in provincial newspapers, however, at the time of his enlistment Dr. Coffyn was approximately thirty years of age.

In early 1916, William left Canada for England on a military supply ship. Once in England, he went to London for a post-medical graduate training course before being promoted to the rank of captain. Here, he trained in operations requiring spinal anesthetic. From England, William left with the RAMC to support Imperial troops in the Middle East. After serving in Malta, Mesopotamia, and then Egypt, William contracted malaria and was sick for a short time. Physicians such as Dr. Coffyn were essential in all areas of the four-year conflict because of the high number of casualties inflicted on both sides. They also put themselves at risk of infection through their repeated contact with those who were sick and suffering from wounds. From accounts in newspapers, Dr. Coffyn appears to have done exceptional work while overseas and was believed to be one of the few Canadian officers in Baghdad when it fell to the Allies. By late 1917, the *Daily Times* reported that William was discharged to Canada after lengthy service with the British Army.

On October 2, 1917, he arrived home in Fredericton, where he was greeted by his wife, Sadie, and his father-in-law, George. Immediately after arriving home, he was offered a position at the local military hospital in the city to become the chief surgeon. Two years later, the *Daily Gleaner* reports that William had a thriving medical practice in the city and had been hired by the Board of Health to be the chief medical inspector of Fredericton schools. His background in teaching, as well as his experiences overseas, likely helped him in his work. In July 1920, Dr. Coffyn performed the very first appendectomy with a patient fully awake under a spinal anesthetic. According to the *Daily Telegraph* report: "The operation was performed by Dr. W. Vernon Coffyn of this city, assisted by Dr. Allan Sterling, and was unique in one respect as the patient was not rendered unconscious. As a matter of fact, he smoked a cigarette while the operation was being performed and coolly watched the surgeons at their work...he suffered no pain at all."

Records suggest that, at this time, his wife had just given birth to their first child. In December, Dr. Coffyn suddenly fell ill with pneumonia and experienced difficulty recovering because of his service overseas during the war. Two weeks later, on the evening of January 11, 1921, at 9:35 p.m., William passed away. He was thirty-six years old, leaving behind his wife and infant son, William Vernon Jr., just nine months of age. On the afternoon of January 13, 1921, surrounded by family, friends, members of the public, and returned soldiers, a funeral was held in his home on Brunswick Street, conducted by Reverends Sutherland and Warren, and singers from the Devon Quartette. The procession followed with William being taken from his home to the Fredericton Rural Cemetery on the Woodstock Road. The pallbearers for the funeral were Lieutenant-Colonel Mersereau, Lieutenant-Colonel Osborne, Major Pincombe, Major Rowe, Major Clements, and Captain Scott. A decade after her husband's death, Sadie remarried Alexander Gibson from Moncton, whose records show had also lost a spouse.

Lest We Forget
Captain Dr. William Vernon Coffyn is buried at the Fredericton Rural Cemetery, on the Woodstock Road in Fredericton. (No LAC record available.)

102. Robinson, John Alexander (January 26, 1921)

Private 444251, 71st York Regiment, 55th Battalion, 14th Battalion, 23rd Battalion

John Alexander Robinson was born on December 29, 1894, in Marysville, to John G. Robinson Sr. and Celia Fisher. Records suggest that he grew up in the Marysville area with six siblings named Roy, Ronald, Moreland, Mary, Helen, and Florence, although the family later moved to 225 Brunswick Street in Fredericton. Although few records detail his parents' work, John himself worked as a labourer and mill hand in the Marysville area as soon as he was of age. Later, he gained military experience with the 71st Regiment stationed in Fredericton. A few years before the war, John met a young woman from the Nashwaak area named Beatrice Dunbar and they married on November 22, 1913. Like John, Beatrice was Methodist and young at the time of their wedding. Their marriage certificate suggests they were twenty years old, but newspapers reveal that John and Beatrice were only sixteen. As well, records suggest that Beatrice was pregnant at the time, as their only son, Edward

Morley, was born on February 26, 1914. At the time of his enlistment on May 17, 1915, in Sussex, Private Robinson stood five feet four inches tall, weighed 127 pounds, and had light brown hair, blue eyes, and a medium complexion. According to his service record, John was eighteen years old, with just under a year of training with the local militia. Along with other Fredericton boys, Private Robinson joined the 55th Battalion at Camp Sussex and left for Quebec for additional training before going overseas. It is unclear if he saw Beatrice and Edward again prior to leaving for England in the spring of 1915.

On June 19, 1915, Private Robinson embarked from Lévis, Quebec, aboard the SS *Corsican* for England, reaching Shorncliffe ten days later. Upon arrival, John immediately transferred to the 12th Battalion before joining the 14th in a draft heading for France on August 28. Over the fall and winter of 1915–16, John sustained a series of injuries and illnesses that caused him to be in and out of hospital until he contracted German measles in June 1916 and was sent to England, where he was put in isolation. Newspapers indicate that he was badly gassed in attacks near Sanctuary Wood around this same time, although his service record does not mention it. Details of his movements over the course of 1917 are unknown, but Private Robinson's series of illnesses, such as trench fever, migraines, and general fatigue, as well as various injuries, appears to have limited him to England for much of this time, until returning to France with the 23rd Battalion in 1918. By July, John was formally discharged from service as a result of continued medical complications, and stayed in hospitals in England until the signing of the Armistice in November. In December, he returned home to Fredericton, arriving on January 23, 1919. Although John had not seen Beatrice and Edward for over four years, time and distance must have taken its toll on their relationship. Records indicate that Beatrice had remarried a man named Hilbert Anderson, also a soldier from the area, and John quickly moved out west, where he found work as a surveyor in British Columbia and Alaska. In September 1920, John began having heart trouble as result of injuries sustained during the war. He admitted himself for treatment at Shaughnessy Hospital in Vancouver for six months, but on January 26, 1921, John passed away from heart failure without any family around him. The *Daily Gleaner* reported his death on January 27, indicating that his remains were being brought home to Marysville. John was twenty-four years old.

Lest We Forget

Private John Alexander Robinson is buried in the Marysville Methodist Cemetery, in Marysville. According to the Commonwealth War Graves Commission, John is the only burial from the First World War here.

103. Allen, Royden Arthur (April 24, 1921)

Private 223384, The Royal Canadian Regiment, 85th Battalion (Nova Scotia Highlanders), 10th Battalion, Canadian Railway Troops

Royden Arthur Allen was born on October 1, 1899, in Fredericton to Elsie Deleta Thomas and Charles Henry Allen. Charles originally came from Grand Lake and Elsie from Prince William. They married on March 22, 1890, in Fredericton and went on to have four children. Royden grew up with two brothers, Harry and Sydney, and a sister Lillian, who married Stanley Corey in 1910. The Allen family lived in Fredericton at 208 Brunswick Street before moving during the war to Halifax, where his father was stationed with his unit for four years. Royden's parents lived at the Windsor House in Halifax. Before the war, Royden joined The Royal Canadian Regiment at age fourteen and served in Bermuda for eight months. Royden formally enlisted in Halifax on December 7, 1915, with the 85th Battalion (Nova Scotia Highlanders) as an underage soldier. At just sixteen, Royden stood five feet six inches tall, weighed 134 pounds, and had a dark complexion, with brown eyes, and black hair. Documents suggest he had numerous scars and tattoos on both forearms, which might have made his claim to being eighteen on his attestation paper plausible.

Grave of Private Royden A. Allen, Fredericton Rural Cemetery.
Brent Wilson

He was unmarried, although he would later return home to marry his sweetheart, Clare.

After spending a year in training with the 85th Battalion in Halifax, Private Allen left with his unit on October 12, 1916, aboard the SS *Olympic*, arriving in Liverpool on October 18. Service documents reveal that Royden held the important role of company bugler, a distinguished position for any soldier of the Canadian Expeditionary Force. Royden remained at Witley Camp and then Bramshott for seven months before being attached to the 10th Battalion, Canadian Railway Troops as a sapper. Sappers played a critical role in building and repairing roadways and bridges. As well, they were responsible for clearing areas of deadly explosive materials. He left with his unit for France on June 17, 1917, arriving two days later in Le Havre, two months after the success of Vimy Ridge. According to family records, during the Battle of Hill 70, near Lens, Royden and many others of his battalion were wounded by enemy mustard gas shells, forcing him out of the line before rejoining on September 19. After Passchendaele, his medical history sheets reveal a winter in which Royden suffered severely from the effects of his injuries, noting that Royden "had a cold all winter long which slowly grew worse...likely a result of having sensitive lungs from typhoid fever as a child." Medical records highlight as well how doctors learned that Royden stated he had two sisters who died from tuberculosis when they were young. By May 1918, Private Allen had been admitted to No. 10 Casualty Clearing Station suffering from a severe cold that was later diagnosed as tuberculosis of the lungs. After being in England for treatment related to his illness, Royden was deemed medically unfit and discharged from service, arriving in Halifax aboard the hospital ship HMHS *Neuralia* on October 1, 1918. After arriving home, he lived at 128 King Street and married his sweetheart, Clare. Together they had a son named Sydney, who was born after the war in 1919. Family records reveal that Sydney enlisted during the Second World War as a young man himself. The *Daily Gleaner* reported in April 1921 that, for ten months, Royden's condition had been worsening and that he had been "confined to his bed and was patient and cheerful, endearing himself to all." However, Royden passed away on April 24 due to complications from his prolonged illness. The funeral took place two days after his death in his home on King Street. He was twenty-three years old.

Lest We Forget

Private Royden Arthur Allen is buried along with twenty other servicemen in the Fredericton Rural Cemetery.

104. Clark, John Thurston (October 17, 1921)

Gunner 1257781, 3rd New Brunswick Regiment, Royal Canadian Artillery, 9th Siege Battery, 53rd Siege Battery

John Thurston Clark was born on March 13, 1899, in Fredericton to William G. and Harriet Clark. John grew up at 82 Waterloo Row with his brother, Alden, and sister, Esther. Documents reveal that his father and mother were married in Jersey City, New Jersey, on April 25, 1894, and that John was the middle-born child. His father later became mayor of Fredericton for ten years, a Member of Parliament, and lieutenant governor of New Brunswick from 1940 to 1945. According to records, John was a student at Fredericton High School and then took university courses while also belonging to the provincial artillery's 3rd New Brunswick Regiment. Having some prior military experience, John enlisted in Saint John on July 26, 1916, with the 9th Canadian Siege Battery. He was nineteen years of age. His attestation paper shows that he stood five feet ten inches tall, weighed approximately 158 pounds, and had a fair complexion, with blue eyes and light brown hair.

According to his service record, John trained with his unit for about a year before leaving Halifax on March 4, 1917, arriving in Liverpool on March 15 along with other local members of the 9th Siege Battery, including Walter McAdam and Alan Wetmore. After training in England for three weeks, John was transferred to the 53rd Canadian Siege Battery and went to France as a reinforcement, arriving on April 19 just after the Canadian victory at Vimy Ridge. A month later, a report in John's service record on accidental or self-inflicted injuries reveals he had broken his wrist as a result of falling down a set of stairs at his billets on the morning of May 19, at approximately 7:30. The report indicates that "his foot slipped and he fell headlong to the ground... he then started to faint when Corporal Murnaghan came along and laid him down pouring water on his face... until he was taken to hospital." Gunner Shuttuck, one of the witnesses, saw John coming down the stairs and within three feet of the ground his foot slipped, and he fell to the ground. According to Shuttuck, John tried to get himself up, brushing off dirt, before he started to faint because of the fall. The report indicated no blame or disciplinary action occurred. By May 24, he was in a military hospital in Glasgow, Scotland, before being sent south to Camp Witley, where he was discharged in July and sent to an artillery reserve battalion. According to the *Daily Gleaner*, "after he recovered from the accident, he went back to France with a mortar battery and was involved in all engagements until the signing of the armistice in November of 1918." Afterwards, John was also part of the Army of Occupation in Germany before returning to England, and then to Canada on June 18, 1919, arriving on June 25. He was discharged from service on July 10, 1919, and arrived home in Fredericton the same month. Newspapers indicate that he was never able to recover from the

The John Thurston Clark Memorial Building, Queen St., Fredericton, named in honour of Gunner John T. Clark. Brent Wilson

effects of being gassed during his war service, and went to the Battle Creek Sanitorium in Colorado Springs, Colorado, for a few months. He returned home but would be confined to his bed until his death two years later, on October 17, 1921. John was only twenty-two years of age.

Lest We Forget

John Thurston Clark is buried in the Fredericton Rural Cemetery. The funeral service took place at 82 Waterloo Row and was presided over by Reverends G.C. Warren and J.H. MacDonald. His funeral notice states that he "held a high place in the esteem of his schoolmates, with his comrades in the army and the public in general, and throughout the city there was great regret of his passing." He was remembered by the commemoration of the John Thurston Clark Memorial Building at 503 Queen Street, Fredericton, formerly the city's post office and library, and presently occupied by the New Brunswick Sports Hall of Fame.

105. King, Robert (April 13, 1922)

Private 22669, 71st York Regiment, 12th Battalion, 2nd Battalion

Robert King was born on December 25, 1885, in Summerside, Prince Edward Island, to Robert Albert John King and Susanna Doyle. According to census records, Robert was an only child. At some point in his childhood, the family relocated to New Brunswick and lived at 145 Regent Street in Fredericton. Although very little is known about his birth father, his mother remarried a man named Patrick McClay. Few details are known of his early childhood, but records show that Robert eventually found work as a porter at the Waverly Hotel in Fredericton and by all accounts was well known and liked by many in the community. In addition to working at the hotel, he apparently worked odd jobs as a labourer. According to his attestation paper, Robert had previous military experience, spending four years with the 71st Regiment before his enlistment on

August 23, 1914, in Fredericton with Lieutenant-Colonel Harry McLeod's 12th Battalion. Robert was thirty-five years old, single, and was described as having grey eyes, black hair, and a dark complexion, and standing five feet seven inches tall. Along with other Fredericton enlistees, he arrived at Valcartier Camp in Quebec in early September. Newspapers suggest he initially was employed as a cook with his unit before requesting training for frontline service to get to the Western Front.

On October 3, 1914, Private King embarked from Quebec aboard the SS *Scotian* for England. Upon arrival Robert remained with the 12th Battalion, employed as a cook at Shorncliffe during the winter of 1914–15. In late June 1915, Private King gave up his position as a cook and went to France with the 2nd Battalion just before the Battle of Festubert. This early battle was a grim fight that saw many Canadians involved in frontal assaults against powerful German defences, resulting in few gains and many casualties. Few, if any, recognized at the time that this period marked the start of a long and bloody war of attrition. In their contribution to the Allied efforts here, the Canadians sustained thousands of casualties. According to Robert's active service record, over the next few months he received a series of debilitating injuries to his knees, back, ribs, and lungs, as well as numerous health problems, that limited his time in the field. By early November 1915, Robert was in hospital suffering from a rifle grenade wound and other injuries after being buried alive by an enemy shell. The spring of 1916 again saw King back in hospital after receiving a contusion to his back and ribs during fighting. In June 1916, the *Daily Gleaner* reported these injuries under the heading "Pte. Robt. King, of Fredericton, is among wounded," suggesting that he had been admitted to the 3rd Western General Hospital in Manchester, England. His medical history sheet highlights a soldier unwilling to leave the front, indicating that he had "no complaints and feels fit," while continuing in the trenches for fourteen months. Yet his series of injuries and ailments became so difficult that medical staff eventually declared him unfit for service and discharged him home to Canada in September 1917. On September 13, Robert sailed from Liverpool under special authority from the Canadian Army. After spending the next two years in military hospitals in Saint

John and Fredericton, medical staff eventually recommended that he be discharged altogether from treatment because, in their opinion, "he will always have this disability as a result of his service." By 1920, Robert had met Jennie Scott Burton, who had previously lost her husband to pneumonia, and they married on October 2, 1920, in Saint John. While his mother, Susanna, remained in Fredericton, Robert and Jennie lived in Saint John, and he became the adoptive father to her two sons, Vernon and Burton. By the winter of 1921, both Robert and his mother became increasingly ill from lung infections. Susanna passed away in Fredericton on November 28, 1921, while Robert eventually was admitted to the Lancaster Military Hospital in Saint John, where his conditioned worsened. He died on April 13, 1922, due to tuberculosis. News of his death was reported in local Saint John and Fredericton papers on April 15, indicating that his funeral took place at the Church of the Assumption in Fairville. Robert was thirty-nine years of age.

Lest We Forget

Private Robert King is buried at the Holy Cross Catholic Cemetery in Saint John.

106. Johnstone, Archibald (April 23, 1948)

Trumpeter/Gunner 147, The Royal Canadian Regiment, 2nd Divisional Ammunition Column, 3rd Canadian Field Ambulance

Archibald Johnstone was born on December 20, 1888, in Glasgow, Scotland, to Alexander and Margaret Johnstone. According to newspapers, Archibald was orphaned as a young boy and came to Canada in 1908 when he was twenty years old. Eventually, he met Ada Fraser in northern New Brunswick, and they were married on September 20, 1911, in Dalhousie. Their marriage record shows that Archibald had been living in the Dalhousie area for work and that Ada was living there as well but was from Quebec. Records also suggest that he had moved to Fredericton before their marriage, joined The Royal Canadian Regiment (RCR), and also found work as fireman and labourer in the area. According to the St. Paul's Church Yearbook, Archibald was also a member of the congregation, and his name is listed as living in the Queen Street Soldiers' Barracks. His attestation paper reveals that the couple kept a residence in Gibson, York County, on the northside of present-day Fredericton. On April 17, 1912, Ada gave birth to twins, named Archibald Harry and Euphoria Ada. Two years later, the couple had another daughter, Louisa Pearl. During this time, they attended Sunday services at St. Paul's Church with their children. Archibald continued his work as a labourer and member of the RCR.

Archibald enlisted for overseas service on March 11, 1915, in Fredericton for service with the artillery's 2nd Divisional Ammunition Column. These divisional columns provided essential supplies to artillery batteries while overseas. According to his attestation form, he was five feet tall with a dark complexion, brown eyes, and dark brown hair, and weighed 120 pounds. His smaller size perhaps explains why he was given the important rank of trumpeter. After enlisting, Archibald remained in Canada over the next two months for training and preparations before going to England. It is unclear if he saw his family again. Archibald was twenty-six at the time.

On June 13, 1915, Archibald and his unit embarked from Saint John aboard the SS *Caledonia* and arrived in England on June 24. He stayed in England during the summer of 1915 before landing in France on September 9 with 2nd Divisional Ammunition Column. Shortly after his arrival, he was attached to the 3rd Canadian Field Ambulance while in the field. Archibald's active service forms suggest that he spent the entire duration of the war on the Western Front with this unit. When not in the field, however, he spent a great deal of time in hospitals suffering from a variety of illness that developed during his service, including colitis, influenza, scabies, and orchitis. All of these conditions reveal the difficult environment that soldiers were living and working in during their time in the field. His service record also reveals that, sometime between January

Headquarters and No. 1 Section of 2nd Divisional Ammunition Column parading at Officers' Square, Fredericton, prior to departure for England in June 1915. Among the unit's personnel was Private Archibald Johnstone.
PANB P651/4

and June 1917, he contracted a disease that was common to many men who were away from family and friends for long periods of time. Despite his numerous ailments, Archibald's service appears to have been well received: on September 1, 1917, he was presented with a good conduct badge.

Over the course of the war, the field ambulance units played a critical role in treating the ailments and wounds of all service people, and lived in every condition faced during the four years of the war. Given that he was often surrounded by those suffering from illness, disease, and wounds, it is not surprising that Archibald was often sick himself. His absence from Ada for four years appears to have been difficult for her as well, because records show that she relocated to Montreal with the children. According to his service record, after the war ended on November 11, 1918, Archibald stayed in England until the spring of 1919 waiting for a transport home. On April 16, 1919, he embarked from Liverpool for Halifax aboard the SS *Belgic*, arriving on April 23. It appears that because Ada and the family had already moved, Archibald went directly from Halifax to Montreal, bypassing Fredericton altogether. It is unclear why the 1917 St. Paul's Church yearbook noted that Archibald had been "supposed killed in action." Despite having been in and out of hospitals for treatment during the war and a newspaper report from Ontario indicating that he had received a shrapnel head wound at one point, after the war Archibald

lived out the rest of his life in Port Arthur, Ontario (now Thunder Bay). In his later years, he became quite sick and was admitted to Deer Lodge Hospital in Winnipeg, a facility run by Veterans Affairs. Archibald passed away there on the evening of April 23, 1948. He was fifty-nine years old, and left behind a large family of eight children.

When the Fredericton community began making plaques and memorials in 1923 for those killed overseas, his name was added to the St. Paul's Church plaque and later the Fredericton War Memorial because it was presumed that he had died while overseas. As the family had already left and Archibald never returned, this would have been an easy mistake to make. Today his name is still on those memorials — a mistake, perhaps, but one that likely should remain given how it reflects the context of the Fredericton community at the time.

Lest We Forget

Archibald Johnstone is buried with honour in the Riverside Cemetery in Thunder Bay, Ontario.

George Street Middle School students Dora, Luke, and Brayden,
who wrote the entry for Lieutenant Charles Blair. James Rowinski

Chapter Six

Fredericton War Memorial Omissions

The following soldiers, while publicly honoured on local commemorative church plaques as being among the Fredericton community's official war dead, were never included on the Fredericton War Memorial when it was unveiled on November 11, 1923. Three individuals, Charles E. Blair, William MacDonald, and Albert Walker, appear on the St. Paul's United Church plaque honouring its First World War dead, but these three do not appear on the Fredericton War Memorial. Two individuals, John Carten and William MacDonald, also appeared on the early list published in the *Daily Gleaner* on Tuesday, November 13, 1923, highlighting "Fredericton's 109 Soldier Dead." Nevertheless, they were never included on the War Memorial, which bears only 106 names. Students came across these discrepancies early in their research, particularly the possible reason for Charles E. Blair's exclusion. It is a serious omission whose correction is long overdue, one that we hope will be rectified now that we are honouring the Fredericton War Memorial's centenary.

107. Carten, John Francis (June 2, 1916)

Private 111082, 6th and 4th Canadian Mounted Rifles

John Francis Carten was born on July 21, 1893, in Chicago, Illinois, to John F. Carten Sr. and Mary A. Burke. According to records, John and Mary were married in Fredericton in 1887. At some point later on, they moved to Chicago, where John Francis Carten Jr. was born soon after their arrival. John Jr. spent his early childhood between Chicago and Fredericton. He had five siblings named Mary, Violet, Martin, Walter, and Albert. Although there are few details of John Jr.'s early life in Fredericton, records show that, upon returning to Fredericton in 1895 his father was admitted to the insane asylum in Fairville, Saint John County, on August 23, suffering from what was described as intemperance and mania. He was released a month later. Newspapers report that John's mother passed away suddenly around this time, and that might have been a reason for their return to Fredericton and for his father's illness. According to death records, John Sr.'s mother passed away a few years later from consumption, known also at the time as tuberculosis. Like many families in the area, the Cartens attended their local church, St. Dunstan's Roman Catholic Church. Once he was old enough, John Jr. worked as a drug clerk in downtown Fredericton for C. Fred Chestnut. His uncle also worked as a druggist in the area and, according to the *Daily Gleaner*, John's father had been working in the same business as well.

Prior to the war, John was living with extended family at 260 Brunswick Street before enlisting. Newspapers suggest that his father was preparing to move the family to Boston around this time. John enlisted on May 27, 1915, in Fredericton, and arrived three days later in Amherst, Nova Scotia, as a recruit with the 6th Canadian Mounted Rifles (CMR) along with other young men from Fredericton. He was described as standing five feet eight inches tall, with blue eyes, light brown hair, and a fair complexion. He was single, had no formal military training, and was twenty-one years of age. From Nova Scotia, John left with the 6th CMR for Valcartier. Little did he know at the time, but he was never to see his family again.

After spending a month in Quebec training, on July 18, 1915, Private Carten embarked for England, aboard the SS *Hershel*. After more than a week on the Atlantic Ocean, John arrived with his unit on July 26 at Devonport, Plymouth, and then on to Folkstone, in Kent. There are few details of his exact whereabouts in his service record, but it appears he arrived the same time as his friend, Private John F. Dolan. Both had attended St. Dunstan's Church in Fredericton. Privates Carten and Dolan, along with other local area soldiers, left Folkstone for France three months later. On November 8, Carten was given two days without pay for insolence during a parade march, likely illustrating a young man adjusting to new routines at the front. By January 1916, Carten, Dolan, and other members of the 6th CMR were transferred to the 4th CMR heading north to the Ypres Salient. By June 2, John was in forward trenches close to Armagh Wood when a four-hour "tornado of fire" came down on Canadian positions. According to a German eyewitness, "the whole enemy position was a cloud of dust and dirt where timber, tree trunks, weapons, equipment and occasionally human bodies were flung into the air." According to Nicholson's *Official History*, the 4th CMR suffered 89 percent casualties, including 702 officers and men; only 76 came through unscathed that day. John was not one of them. On June 29, 1916, three weeks later, the *Daily Gleaner* reported, "five young men from Fredericton who were members of the 4th CMR were reported missing on the 2nd of June 1916. The five members were Corporal Alleyne Y. Clements of Clairmont, Private Fred W. Boyd, John F. Dolan and John F. Carten and John Saunders of St. Mary's."

Given the intensity of the battle, John's body was never recovered. He was twenty-two years of age at the time of his death. Six years later, John's name was included on an official list of 109 Fredericton soldiers published in the *Daily Gleaner* who had given their lives for Canada during the First World War. However, John's name was never added to the First World War plaque.

John Francis Carten is remembered with honour on the Ypres (Menin Gate) Memorial, located in Ypres, Belgium.

108. MacDonald, William (April 27, 1917)

Gunner 5998, Royal Canadian Horse Artillery, 4th and 6th Howitzer Brigade

William MacDonald was born on July 29, 1893, in Inverness, Scotland, to David G. and Ellen MacDonald. According to records, William had three brothers, John, David, and George, and spent the first nine years of his childhood living in Inverness. Newspapers reveal that William's father was very involved with the British Army's Seaforth Highlanders Regiment, having served in India and Afghanistan in the late 1880s and then in South Africa during the Boer War in 1899. In 1902, the MacDonald family moved to Canada, first living on and working a farm in Victoria County, New Brunswick, before coming to Fredericton and settling in a home at 264 Woodstock Road. Prior to the war, David Sr. moved to British Columbia for work, while William left for Lajord, Saskatchewan, southeast of Regina. Although researching the details of William's early life was difficult because the family moved often, it is clear from newspapers that the MacDonald family held close ties to the congregation of St. Paul's Presbyterian Church in Fredericton. After graduating, William worked for a short time as a farmer in Woodstock before moving to Saskatchewan with his brother, David, where he found work as a rancher. According to his attestation paper, he served three years as a volunteer with the Carleton Light Infantry Regiment. It appears that he and his brothers were highly influenced by their father's military career because all would enlist when the time came to serve, as would their father, who joined the 26th New Brunswick Battalion. At the outbreak of war in the summer of 1914,

William joined up in Regina in late August before formally enlisting on September 20, 1914, in Valcartier with the Royal Canadian Horse Artillery (RCHA). William's service record indicates that he stood five feet seven inches tall, and had a fair completion, blue eyes, and fair hair. He was twenty-one years of age and unmarried. Prior to going overseas with his unit, records suggest that he spent a limited amount of time at Valcartier. It is unclear if he ever saw his mother and extended family again.

On October 3, 1914, Gunner MacDonald left Canada for England with the First Contingent. Arriving at Shorncliffe in late October, William stayed in England for the next six months training with the RCHA and the Canadian Field Artillery's 1st and 3rd Brigades. During the fall and winter months, his service record shows that there were points during his time in England when he was absent for training and, in some instances, appeared intoxicated when reporting for duty. Although this earned him many days of detention and loss of pay, because the first year was often difficult for Canadian soldiers this kind of behaviour was common. After being transferred to 2nd Divisional Ammunition Column in late August 1915, Gunner MacDonald landed in France on September 16. Less than a month after arriving in the field, William again lost pay after causing a disturbance in his billets, failing to comply with orders, and for poor military conduct. This was the last time these issues would arise during his service. By late December 1915, William was attached to the 4th Canadian Field Artillery in northern France and southern Belgium. Although diagnosed and treated briefly with tonsillitis, his service continued until June 1916, when he was admitted to a hospital in Zillebeke, Belgium, suffering from gunshot wounds. He was transferred back to England for recovery before rejoining his unit in northern France in the later months of the Battle of the Somme. Like many gunners at the time, William eventually made his way to the area of Vimy and Arras in early 1917. Gunners were critical to success at Vimy because they were able to knock out enemy guns, clear barbed wire, and give infantry opportunities to advance. According to his circumstances-of-death record, after the German army retreated from Vimy in mid-April 1917, William was positioned with his battery unit near Thélus on April 27 when he was hit by a German artillery shell and died instantly. Shortly after his death, the *Daily Gleaner* reported first on May 17 and then on May 22 that William had been killed and that his mother had received the sad news. Speaking of William's death, Chaplain Garbot shared that "he was a brave man, a good soldier, and his companions speak the highest terms of him. We reverently laid him to rest, and his battery unit is erecting a suitable cross to his memory." William was twenty-two years old.

Lest We Forget

Private William Macdonald is buried with honour at Bois-Carré British Cemetery, located in Thélus, France. According to the Commonwealth War Graves Commission, the cemetery holds 449 identified casualties from the First and Second World Wars. Although William's name appeared in a 1923 *Daily Gleaner* article indicating that he had been added to the St. Paul's United Church War Memorial plaque, like those of Charles E. Blair and Albert E. Walker, his name does not appear on the Fredericton War Memorial.

109. Walker, Albert E. (September 27, 1918)

Private 1030026, 236th Battalion (The New Brunswick Kilties), 72nd Battalion (Seaforth Highlanders of Canada)

Albert E. Walker was born on March 12, 1900, in Woodlands, New Brunswick, to Victor Walker and Hannah Williams. According to New Brunswick marriage records, Victor and Hannah married in Upper Keswick shortly after the birth of Albert. Originally from Cardigan, Wales, Victor had come to New Brunswick for work and met Hannah, who was from the Stanley area. At the time of their marriage, Victor was twenty and Hannah was sixteen. The 1901 census shows that at a young age Albert came to live with his maternal grandparents, George and Eliza Williams, on their farm, along with three other children,

George Jr., James, and Minnie. Their life during this time involved growing crops for income and food. Few records exist to show where Victor and Hannah were living, although documents do reveal that they had close connections to both St. Paul's Presbyterian Church and Christ Church Cathedral. In August 1909, while working as a domestic in Nashwaaksis, Albert's mother, Hannah, contracted tuberculosis and passed away. Her death record confirms her ties to St. Paul's Church. A year after her death, Victor, now living in Fredericton, married Agnes Blake and together they had a daughter born the next year named Agnes Victoria. Throughout this time, Albert continued to work and live with his mother's family while also attending school. By 1911, he was living with his uncle and aunt, William and Alice Craig, and his mother's brother, George. What appears clear from the records is that Hannah's parents and siblings came together very early on to ensure that Albert had a nurturing upbringing surrounded by family. When war broke out in 1914, Albert was just a teenager, but he enlisted in Fredericton with the 236th Battalion, The New Brunswick Kilties, two years later, on July 17, 1916. At the time of his enlistment, Albert was described as standing five feet two inches tall, and having a fresh complexion, with brown eyes and brown hair. According to his attestation paper, he had no prior military experience and was unmarried. Barely seventeen years of age, Albert named his uncle, William Craig, as his next-of-kin, illustrating how he had become close with Hannah's sister and brother-in-law. He spent the next year in Canada training and preparing for overseas duty. In August 1917, he was hospitalized at Valcartier for two weeks suffering from a case of tonsillitis. It is unclear if he ever saw his family again.

On October 30, 1917, Private Walker embarked from Montreal aboard the SS *Canada*, arriving in England on November 19. He remained in England in reserve over the winter of 1917–18 until being transferred to the 72nd Battalion from Vancouver at Seaford Camp in March 1918. On March 8, he landed in France and proceeded to the Canadian Corps Reinforcement Camp with the 72nd. By July, Albert and his battalion were near Lens in the town of Auchel. According to the battalion war diaries, on July 23 his unit was in the trenches when the Germans unleashed a terrible gas attack. The diaries described the day as "a quiet day until 10 p.m. when the hun filled the valley occupied by battalion HQ with gas... casualties were very heavy totaling 85 of all ranks." Albert's service record reveals that he was injured on that day and evacuated to Boulogne for treatment. A few weeks later, Albert rejoined the 72nd as they moved into positions near Anzin-Saint-Aubin, a village near Vimy, where, according to the war diaries, "it was the first occasion in which Canadians had visited the village and the welcome was sincere." By August 6 Albert had arrived south of Amiens just as the Battle of Amiens was about to begin. More than a hundred thousand Canadian "shock troops" had secretly shifted to Amiens, where, on August 8, along with Australian, British, and French units, they overran the German army. Although being injured again from mustard gas, Albert continued with his unit into late September. On the 27th, he was killed by shellfire during operations just north of Cambrai. According to a letter written home to Mr. and Mrs. Craig, Major James Hamilton, commanding officer of the 72nd, reveals Albert's final moments describing, "at the time of your nephew's death... he was employed as a battalion runner and was proceeding to one of the companies with an important message when a high explosive shell exploded close to him, killing him instantly. It may be of some small consolation to you to know that he suffered no pain." Devasted by the loss, the Craigs took great care to ensure the inscription where Albert was laid to rest read as follows: "Our only boy is sleeping in Flanders' Fields where poppies blow, Uncle and Aunt." Albert was eighteen years old at the time of his death.

Lest We Forget

Private Albert E. Walker is buried and remembered with honour at Quarry Wood Cemetery, located in Sains-lès-Marquion, twelve kilometres northwest of Cambrai, France. Although Albert's name appeared in a 1923 *Daily Gleaner* article indicating that he had been added to the St. Paul's United Church War Memorial plaque, his name does not appear on the Fredericton War Memorial.

110. Blair, Charles E. (September 27, 1920)

Lieutenant, 71st York Regiment, 12th Battalion, 13th Battalion (Royal Highlanders of Canada), 236th Battalion (The New Brunswick Kilties)

Charles Edward Blair was born on January 9, 1885, in St. Mary's, York County, New Brunswick, to Reid Blair and Ann Tomlinson. While little is known about his upbringing, at the age of four, Charles's mother passed away; she was thirty-six years old. According to marriage records, Reid remarried a woman from Prince William named Jane Hamilton later that summer. In total, Charles had nine siblings: James, Harry, Isabelle, William, Thomas, Frederick, Ralph, John, and Margarette. Margarette, Ralph, and John died at young ages. For Charles and the family, it must have been tragic to experience this additional loss. From all accounts, it appears that the family was well known in the St. Mary's community and in Fredericton, although the details of Charles's childhood are difficult to find. On May 10, 1907, his father passed away. Charles began attending St. Paul's United Church and eventually met Ida Kennedy, who came from Maxwell, New Brunswick. They married on July 6, 1910, in Carleton County. According to the 1911 census, Charles and Ida lived in North Devon, and it appears they never had any children. In addition to working as a carpenter and general labourer, Charles was quite active with the local militia, serving a total of eight and half years with the 71st York Regiment. When war broke out in the summer of 1914, Charles was one of the first to leave Fredericton for Valcartier, enlisting on August 29 with the 12th Battalion. He was described as standing five feet eleven inches tall, with blue eyes, a fair complexion, and dark brown hair. His attestation paper notes numerous scars on his hands, suggesting the hazards of the carpentry work he did in the community. Despite records showing he was married, he stated that he was single at the time. This might reveal that he and Ida were having difficulties in their marriage. Very little is known about where Ida was during this period, but Charles's service record suggests that she left Fredericton to live in Boston. His brother, William, was listed as his next-of-kin. He spent the next two months in Quebec training with his unit while preparing for overseas duty. He was twenty-nine years old at the time.

On October 3, 1914, Sergeant Blair left Canada with the First Contingent from Quebec aboard the SS *Scotian*, arriving a little more than a week later in southern England. Because he arrived so early in the war, detailed records of his service during the winter of 1914–15 are limited. On February 11, 1915, however, he was assigned as regimental quarter-master sergeant with the 13th Battalion (Royal Highlanders of Canada). According to accounts from the *Daily Gleaner*, in the early spring of 1915 Charles volunteered to go to France with a draft so that he could get in on the action. Although there are limited details of his exact whereabouts, it is likely that he witnessed the impact of the first gas attacks during the Second Battle of Ypres before then serving as sergeant through the Battles of Givenchy, Festubert, St. Eloi, and Mount Sorrel. These actions saw some of the harshest fighting early in the war. It was around this time that Charles wrote home to his sister:

> Just a few lines to let you know the Germans have not got me yet and that I am still hale and hearty. This is, certainly, an awful war and people at home do not realize how bad it is. I never realized it until I came over to France where there is not a second that passes without the sound of cannon...one sees men by the score fall on all sides and we have passed through cities that are in ruins. It is then that one thinks about the horrors of this war...It is sad to hear them call the roll after battle, hearing the names of the missing called out and no one answers.

By 1916, Charles was promoted to lieutenant with the 236th Battalion and returned to Canada in October to receive his commission. Newspaper accounts indicate that he arrived back in France with another unit in the winter of 1917–18. By then, however, his health had begun to worsen. Medical records show that, in addition to other ailments, he was suffering from severe abdominal pains due to appendicitis. He was never able to get

Grave of Lieutenant Charles Blair, Sunny Bank Cemetery, Fredericton North. James Rowinski

back into action due to his increasingly poor health. Charles remained in England until the spring of 1919, months after the Armistice had been signed. Newspaper reports later indicated that he was also suffering from severe shell shock and war fatigue at the time, something his records never revealed.

Charles was discharged to Canada as part of a general demobilization from Southampton, England, arriving in Halifax on July 8, 1919, aboard the SS *Olympic*. A week and a half later, Charles was admitted to the Fredericton Military Hospital, where he underwent an appendectomy. He spent the next year and half trying to return to his life prior to the war, despite his wife no longer residing in Fredericton. Newspapers suggest that, while living with family on the city's northside, he had become "increasingly despondent over the condition of his health, which resulted in him being in hospital much of the time." On September 27, 1920, papers described Charles's coming to the city from Devon to purchase five shells at Lawlor and Cain's hardware store. That same morning, just before noon, he returned to his stepmother's home and shot himself in the heart. Charles was thirty-six years old at the time of his death.

Lest We Forget

On September 29, 1920, two days after his death, Charles's funeral took place at the home of his stepmother in North Devon. Interment took place at Sunny Bank Cemetery in Devon shortly afterwards. Documents show that many from the community attended his funeral, including members of the Great War's Veteran Association and the Masonic order. Newspapers described it as an impressive service with numerous beautiful floral tributes that reflected how the community saw him. Although Charles's name would later be added to the First World War commemorative plaque at St. Paul's United Church, it is not on any community memorial, he was never given a veteran's headstone, and it appears that he was buried without having his name added to the family's memorial. In the winter of 2019, community members as well as senior commanders and an honour guard from The Royal New Brunswick Regiment gathered for a rededication service after students worked to install a military headstone donated by the Last Post Fund. We believe that because of how he died, a decision was made not to have his war service publicly memorialized on the Fredericton War Memorial.

Acknowledgements

This book is about involving students in critical historical investigation that contributes to what we know about the First World War, its impact on New Brunswick communities, and post-war commemoration practices. Thanks should go first to the principals and teachers who played a pivotal role in sharing their classrooms and providing time for students to engage in all aspects of the project. Sarah Brooks, Christina Kelly, Sonya Lee Lacelle, Pierre Plourde, and Stephen Stone, you deserve much credit for seeing the potential of your students. Without you this would not have been possible. Thank you as well to the many families with close ties to individuals in this book who reached out to us from across Canada, the United States, and Europe with messages of support and encouragement. Your kind words often gave students the confidence to trust their research and motivation to work harder to piece together their stories. Thank you to the Beaverbrook Art Gallery for your collaboration on many events designed to give students an opportunity to share their work with the public and for the public to pose important questions to students. These public engagements proved to be well attended and served as opportunities to connect with families of soldiers being researched. Many thanks as well to Ron Tremblay and Walter Paul, who drew important attention during these events to the contributions and experiences of Indigenous soldiers, many of whom are underrepresented on public memorials and in histories taught in school. Thank you to the *Telegraph Journal* and *Daily Gleaner* for your support publishing drafts of student work each week to a broader audience. This was important to help students fill in the gaps in their work and for affirming their interpretation of available evidence with which they were working. A huge thank you to the Provincial Archives of New Brunswick (PANB) for your tireless support of student research throughout the project. In particular, the support of Fred Farrell, Robert Gilmore, Josh Green, Joanna Aiton Kerr, and Heather Lyons, as well as many other archivists with the PANB, was critical for student research each year and for them to learn your craft. I am particularly thankful to the Government of Canada, Veterans Affairs Canada, and the Government of New Brunswick, Tourism, Heritage, and Culture. Without your financial support, this project would never have come to fruition and might have only been partially realized. Thank you to Brent Wilson, editor-in-chief of the New Brunswick Military Heritage Project, for working diligently to make this book a reality. Thanks as well to freelance copy editor Barry Norris, and the team from Goose Lane Editions, Julie Scriver and Alan Sheppard, who guided things seamlessly behind the scenes. To the hundreds of students who worked tirelessly during the four years of this project, you never cease to amaze. Your dedication to your research and writing demonstrates clearly that young people can participate in the complexities of critical historical research and that you can do it well when properly supported and resourced. You should be incredibly proud of your accomplishment. You have provided an invaluable addition to what we know about these individuals' lives, and have applied that learning to important public debates about what it means for us today. Thank you to my three children, Olivia, Isaiah, and Rhys, for your patience, love, and support throughout this project. The three of you continue to inspire me in my work. Lastly, Sarah, my partner and inspiration in life, thank you for being a shoulder I have leaned on often when the stories of loss have proved too much for me to comprehend or make sense of.

Appendix

Student Participants in the Project

The following students contributed biographies to *In Perpetuity*.
The original biographies have since been edited for publication.

Chapter 1: 1914–1915
1. Cody McMillan and Ryley Lofstrom
2. Lily Keays
3. Nick Dang, Connor MacIntosh, and David Redman
4. Niloufar Niazzadeh, Dakota Mowry, and Colbie Campbell
5. Keegan Kelly and Murray Ferris
6. Precious Fatoki and Alivia Carmichael

Chapter 2: 1916
7. Amir Mohammadian, Jeremy Green, and Jeremy Brewer
8. Nicole Vedin and Hayvin Sacobie-Solomon
9. Mohammed Khan and Mahdi Habibi
10. Aurora Brown, Mishel Goudzendo, and Aiden Garnett
11. Luka Rikanovic
12. Kylie Solomon, Jasper Green, and Rileigh Arbeau
13. Mohamed Alsaleh, Miguel Pinto, Tony Jeong, and Rukeme Akalusi
14. Khamen Macpherson and Sam Marquis
15. Hannah Hartley and Brett Cormier
16. Brayden Brewer-Dunnett and Sebastian Falkenberg
17. Abdelrahman Granem
18. Caitlyn Hetherington and Cameron Whitlock
19. Serena Chase
20. Jake Reid, Omar Al Kreiz, and Jenna Scott

21. Aiden Foster and Yuly Goudzenko
22. Prince McCoy, Gavin Ryan, and Nick Coughlan
23. Jennifer Earle and Nick Polchies
24. Jacob Morrell and Michelle B.
25. Jasper Wyers, Logan Guenther-Squires, and Caylen Hunt
26. David Emery, Kuenga Penjor, and Olivia King
27. Tianna Smith and Aiden Lawrence
28. Robert Christie, Joseph Porter, and Jacob Fullarton
29. Samuel Harris, Josh Johnson, and Hayley Polchies
30. Madelaine Green, Jordan Sisson, and Russell Yerxa
31. Kayla Gracie and Samara Wagenaar
32. Felix Gerasimov, Victoria Stachov, Alex McBrine, and Nick Pope
33. Vincent Trowbridge-Starr and Ariane Herpers
34. Jayden Resmer
35. Tessa Warren and Frank Yu
36. Meg Johnston and Arya Pai

Chapter 3: 1917
37. Kiera Pugh
38. Russell Preston and Meghan McKay
39. Keegan McMullin
40. Vyktoria Woodcock
41. Michael Leblanc and Ryan Innes
42. Kyle Gilbraith, Hailey Heslop, and David Nguyen
43. Mohammed Shawesh, Lexie Boyle, and Shirley Andow
44. Olivia Rowinski
45. Tyler Porter and Zack Breau
46. Emma Rongen
47. Majestic MacMillan and Diana Kopp
48. Ricardo Bautista Garcia
49. Sadie Warren and Sam Lam
50. Ruby Whamond and Gregory Phillips
51. Bryson Maher and Ayden Hawkes
52. Cameron Taylor and Mona Wong
53. Isabella Mehlitz
54. Swati Jayachandran, Rahaf Rashid, Rachel MacDonald, and Emma He
55. Sunaa Hansen, Javen de Jong, and Mohammed Shawesh

56. James Davis and Alyssa Orchard
57. Scott Mitchell and Connor Urquhart
58. Ryan Landry and Jack Quesnel
59. Grace Doherty
60. Belle Schriver and Aidan Aubin
61. Austin Allen and Jiun Chung
62. Eden Jones, Brittany O'Neil, and Sheldon Parker
63. Shaleen Dixon and Mwape Benaya
64. Cody Graham and Jacob Hogan
65. Cole Dakiv and Corey McDonough
66. Alex Strong-Saad
67. Victoria Matthews
68. Lucas Glenn
69. Danielle Brideau

Chapter 4: 1918

70. Dante B. and Ivey Cowland
71. Reann Fournier
72. Sarah Tapley, Michael Hawkins, and Jacob Oborn
73. Christian Fraser, Matthew Leduc, and Erika Rawlines
74. Dekchaya Adhikari, Alysha Newton, and Jack Fletcher
75. Sydney Smith
76. Rachel Boucher and Rodney Maillet-Robichaud
77. Lucas Wilson
78. Sean Clark and Andie Cain
79. Brandon Hanson, Isel Perez-Lopez, and Emma Whitlock
80. Orion Solomon and Roan Solomon
81. Rachel Boucher and Brianna Coburn
82. Philip Truong and Eleanor Caulfield
83. Brooklyn Power, Grace Murdoch, and Isaac Seale
84. Patricia Forestell
85. Matthew Quinn, Daniel Wielemaker, and Julien Blanchard
86. Corrie MacDonald, Tayah Ross, and Eli Pierce
87. Daniel Millership and Mauricio Sanchez
88. Edvard Matevosyan and Hannah Maillet-Robichaud
89. Tasha Appleby and Mehrsa Khoshpasand
90. Quinn Gorman and Chris Cano
91. Alexander Groom, Sam Gorman, and Liam Coughlan

Selected Bibliography and Source Notes

Primary Sources

Library and Archives Canada. *Personnel Records of the First World War Collection*.

Note: Specific reference to records obtained for use relative to individuals contained in this collection can be accessed directly via individual QR codes that have been positioned prominently in the body of the text for ease of access and transparency.

Additional Primary Sources

Personal interviews, email correspondence, and family documents shared with student researchers in coordination with family members related to individuals in this collection.

Secondary Sources

Clark, A. *History's Children: History Wars in the Classroom*. Sydney, Australia: University of New South Wales Press, 2008.

Clark, P., S. Lévesque, and R. Sandwell. "Dialogue across Chasms: History and History Education in Canada." In *History Teacher Education: Global Interrelations*, ed. E. Erdmann and W. Hasberg, 191–211. Frankfurt-am-Main: Wochenschau Verlag, 2015.

Clark, P., and A. Sears. *The Arts and the Teaching of History: Historical F(r)ictions.* Gewerbestrasse, Switzerland: Palgrave Macmillan, 2020.

Cook, T. *At the Sharp End: Canadians Fighting the Great War 1914–1916 Volume One.* Toronto: Penguin, 2007.

———. *Shock Troops: Canadians Fighting the Great War 1917-1918 Volume Two.* Toronto: Penguin, 2008.

Nicholson, G.W.L. *Canadian Expeditionary Force 1914–1919: Official History of the Canadian Army in the First World War.* Monreal; Kingston, ON: McGill-Queen's University Press, 2015.

Osbourne, K. "A History Teacher Looks Back." *Canadian Historical Review* 93, no. 1 (2012): 108–37.

Seixas, P., and T. Morton. *The Big Six Historical Thinking Concepts.* Toronto: Nelson Education, 2013.

Vance, J. *Death So Noble: Memory, Meaning, and the First World War.* Vancouver: UBC Press, 1997.

Newspapers and Periodicals

Provincial Archives of New Brunswick, *Daily Gleaner, Saint John Globe,* and the *St. John Standard.*

Note: Specific reference to newspaper records obtained from the Provincial Archives of New Brunswick throughout student research in this collection and the introduction can be found on microfilm (F-2934 to F-2963) as it pertains to the *Daily Gleaner,* (F13876 to F13894) as it pertains to *Saint John Globe,* and (F-3784 to F-3802) as it pertains to the *St. John Standard.*

Websites

Automated Genealogy: http://automatedgenealogy.com/index.html

Note: Automated Genealogy was used throughout student research as an important accessible and user-friendly tool to access census data from the late 1800s to early the 1900s. This resource supported the development of background information on individuals in this collection that was often unclear and/or unavailable in individual attestation and service records.

Commonwealth War Graves Commission (CWGC): https://www.cwgc.org

Note: The Commonwealth War Graves Commission database was used throughout student research to confirm details contained in an individual's soldier attestation and service records, information relative to an individual's final resting place, as well as general information about CWGC cemeteries and memorials, and its general mission and mandate.

Library and Archives Canada: https://www.bac-lac.gc.ca/eng/discover /military-heritage/first-world-war/personnel-records/Pages/search.aspx

Note: Library and Archives Canada was used throughout student research to obtain essential information about an individual's First World War service, as documented by the Government of Canada and the Canadian Expeditionary Force (CEF). The Personnel Records of the First World War collection were important both for attempting to detail an individual's movements during war service, and also to confirm personal details about an individual's life at the time.

The National Archives: https://www.nationalarchives.gov.uk

Note: The National Archives of the United Kingdom were used throughout student research to access individual war service records of individuals who served with British units during the First World War. For example, as Canada did not have its own air force, records of Canadians who served with the Royal Flying Corps (RFC), Royal Naval Air Service (RNAS), or the Royal Air Force (RAF) could be found in these collections, as they would not be held at Library and Archives Canada.

Provincial Archives of New Brunswick (PANB): https://archives.gnb.ca /Archives/?culture=en-CA

Note: The Provincial Archives of New Brunswick Federated Database was used throughout student research to access family and individual death, marriage, burial, and birth records, as well as other important source documents to support biographical details on individuals in this collection.

Index

The New Brunswick Military Heritage Project

The New Brunswick Military Heritage Project, a non-profit organization devoted to public awareness of the remarkable military heritage of the province, is an initiative of the Brigadier Milton F. Gregg, VC, Centre for the Study of War and Society of the University of New Brunswick. The organization consists of museum professionals, teachers, university professors, graduate students, active and retired members of the Canadian Forces, and other historians. We welcome public involvement. People who have ideas for books or information for our database can contact us through our website: www.unb.ca/nbmhp.

One of the main activities of the New Brunswick Military Heritage Project is the publication of the New Brunswick Military Heritage Series with Goose Lane Editions. This series of books is under the direction of J. Brent Wilson, Director of the New Brunswick Military Heritage Project at the University of New Brunswick. Publication of the series is supported by a grant from the Province of New Brunswick and the Canadian War Museum.

The New Brunswick Military Heritage Series

In Perpetuity is volume 30 in the New Brunswick Military Heritage Series.
For a full list of books in the series, see:
https://gooselane.com/collections/new-brunswick-military-heritage-series